In Praise of
The Inspiring Journeys o Entrepreneurs and Jane Noble Knight

G000127383

If we are the Pilgrim Mothers then Jane Noble Knight is the 'Mothership' in which we sail to a brave new world of loving-kindness, oneness, faith, hope and integrity – values which the Feminine has always represented throughout time.

RACHEL ELNAUGH
Founder of Red Letter Days, star of BBC TV's Dragons' Den series 1 and 2
www.rachelelnaugh.com

At this time of personal and planetary transformation, women like Jane Noble Knight are unearthing stories, myths and women leading legendary lives to inspire and encourage us all on our pilgrimage to our own Truth. By reading this book you will voyage on a journey and find yourself inspired, uplifted and encouraged to make your life your greatest adventure!

KATHARINE DEVER
Intuitive Business Coach
www.katharinedever.com

Jane Noble Knight is a special knight with a noble cause. Every knight in history fought for revolutionary change. In this inaugural book, Jane presents a blueprint for global change. Her personal journey is a call for each one of us to embark on our own transformation. This book provides the guiding light along the journey for each one of us to embrace a new pathway for human evolution. The time is now. The way is clear. The wisdom contained here is eminently practical. All it needs is for you to say: Here I am – use me. Women hold the answer to bring about this much needed change! Their united power is waiting to be gathered and unleashed. Heed the call or ignore this book at your peril!

DR. DAVID PAUL
Specialist in Large-Scale, Complex Change & Eupsyhian Leadership
Best-selling Author of *Life and Work: Challenging Economic Man*
dpaul@attwise.com

It is our time…

I have felt for many years that our time was coming, and now it is here. And so Jane has 'timed' the publication of this book to perfection. It is time for us women to step into our power, which we know is within each of us. It is time for us to believe in ourselves again and help move the world to a better place. It is time not only for us to dream, but to live our dreams.

The female pioneers blazing the trail, some of whom Jane has written about in this book, have shown us that we can all do this. But it is up to us to believe in ourselves when others don't and to know that there is a better way when others say there isn't. We all can turn our dreams into reality and be the amazing woman we were born to be. And our time is now!

SUSAN HARPER TODD
Only British woman to sail the Atlantic *and* climb Everest. First British female leader of an Everest expedition and only the fifth British woman to have reached the summit of Everest.
www.susanharpertodd.com

Jane Noble Knight's books offer the opportunity to study and immerse oneself in the lives of other women: extraordinary women who somehow still manage to be every woman. We are all on a quest. Some of us have grown weary, some have been misled. Some have strayed from the path of freedom, creativity and love. And some of us are looking for angelic messenger voices that will guide us into the light. Jane's books offer a gathering of loving, inspirational, gentle yet strong she-voices. You can read and relax, and let the truth of the testimonies of these women sink in, like an enriching moisturiser into dry skin.

JAN TCHAMANI
Prize-winning Author, Communications Director of The Red Tent (Heart of England)
burjan@blueyonder.co.uk

Once I read 'one of the secrets of success was the unconditional support of your opposite sex parent'. For me it's been just so true. The love and 'alwaysthereness' of my mother was the underlying force in all my early success. As time goes by, more and more mother figures appear in one's life, each with an appropriate and invariably timely lesson to be shared.

What better, then, for men (and I suppose for women too!) than a collection of female wisdom, inspiration and a dose of pioneering spirit to lift our hearts and set us again to the path.

Jane Noble Knight is described so aptly by her name. Working closely with her for over a year showed me her true character, her outward-focused-ness and her love of her fellow traveller on this spinning blue.

Read on, smile, think and act on the lessons she's extracted so carefully for our use – will you?

PETER THOMSON
'The UK's Most Prolific Information Product Creator'
www.peterthomson.com

Rarely in life do you meet someone who really walks the talk and embodies their message and life's work. Jane Noble Knight is one such inspirational woman. Selfless in her devotion to empowering others, she positively breathes her passion and absolutely is 'The Pilgrim Mother'. Read Jane's stories and prepare to be changed.

SHELLEY BRIDGMAN
Keynote Speaker, Psychotherapist, Stand-Up Comic
TV and Radio Commentator, Author of *Stand-Up For Your Self*
www.stand-upforyourself.com

I think what you're creating is so beautiful. You're an inspiration to women. I read a couple of years back, and it was a great validation to my instincts, that people really need role models in order to move forward in life. Concepts or insights alone are not enough. What people really need, in order to embody change, are role models – people who have done it. That is what you're doing – providing role models.

KATHERINE WOODWARD THOMAS
Best-selling Author of *Calling In "The One"*, Co-Creator of *Feminine Power*
www.katherinewoodwardthomas.com

Jane Noble Knight has done what many women only dream about. She's followed her passion and let her heart lead her to her truth, and in turn empowering women, just like you, to freely unleash the quietened mother, healer, nurturer and lover, and discover a life filled with possibility and passion.

Eliciting stories that move the reader to explore her uniqueness is what Jane does best. Simply inspiring – can't wait to read the next book.

VANESSA MCLEAN
Co-Author of *Fight For Your Dreams: The Power of Never Giving up*
www.vanessamclean.com

When I first met Jane, I was taken by her gentleness and warmth, together with her desire to understand more about herself and the role of women in business and the wider world. And when she spoke about her 'pilgrimage', it was clear that she was going to create something unique and special – which she has. The world needs to wake up to the power of authenticity, of living our own truths and being brave enough to step out of the mainstream views when they don't fit with our own life purpose. This is precisely what Jane has done and her mission and book is inspiring to both women AND men, who equally need to hear her message.

PAUL HARRIS
Writer, Speaker, Coach and Founder of The Real Academy
www.real-success.co.uk

It's still tough for us ladies in the business arena, but Jane's informative and inspirational take on it really motivates and guides you! Having had the pleasure of filming with Jane a few years ago, I knew instantly that this very calming, kind but dynamic lady had something a little bit special about her. We all knew she would go on to do something a tad out of the ordinary but interesting. Hence, I wanted to stay in contact and see where her journey took her! This book is a fabulous vehicle for her, and exploring the greatness of her fellow females is completely apt. Jane herself is such a generous-spirited lady with an abundance of knowledge and warmth that she radiates. It's no surprise that this is her path...... What next, Jane? .... Bravo Jane, we love what you're doing!

SUNITA SHROFF
Presenter, Actress, Property Expert and Red Carpet Reporter
www.sunitashroff.com

Tucked up in bed, one night, I thought I would just read a few pages ... Within seconds I was gripped and couldn't put the book down.

I've read several personal growth books. This particular one is written so beautifully and authentically, I really wanted to keep reading to find out more about the author's journey and what we could learn from these inspirational and pioneering women.

Jane has hand-picked some very wise women from our industry whose insights and honesty are both profound and refreshing. They installed a feeling of excitement and possibility within me as I read on.

Jane has a gift of pulling all this wisdom together in a way that makes you feel that it's not only possible for these women but possible for women everywhere!

With this compilation Jane has brought a much-needed gift to the world.

Thank you.

LUCIE BRADBURY
CEO of Damsels in Success - the Transformational Network for Female Entrepreneurs
www.damselsinsuccess.co.uk

THE INSPIRING JOURNEYS
OF WOMEN ENTREPRENEURS

THE
INSPIRING
JOURNEYS
OF WOMEN
ENTREPRENEURS

*Exploring New Ways of Business
That Answer Your Calling*

JANE NOBLE KNIGHT

Noble Knight Publishing UK

The Inspiring Journeys of Women Entrepreneurs: Exploring New Ways of Business That Answer Your Calling

Copyright © Jane Noble Knight

www.thepilgrimmother.com and www.theinspiringjourneys.com

The moral rights of Jane Noble Knight to be identified as the author of this work have been asserted in accordance with the Copyright, Designs and Patents Act 1988.

Editor: Wendy Millgate (www.wendyandwords.com)

Design and typesetting: Tanya Back (www.tanyabackdesigns.com)

Printer: Lightning Source

All rights reserved. No part of this publication may be reproduced, stored in a retrieval system, or transmitted in any form or by any means, electronic, mechanical, photocopying, recording or otherwise, without the prior written permission of the copyright owner.

First published 2013 in UK by Noble Knight Publishing, 1 Broadbent Court, Newport, TF10 7FE. www.thepilgrimmother.com

ISBN: 978-0-9575262-0-4

All the information, concepts, skills, techniques and advice contained within this publication are of general comment only and are not intended in any way for any individual. The intent is to offer a variety of information and circumstances to provide a wider range of choices now and in the future, recognising that we all have widely diverse circumstances and viewpoints. Should any reader choose to make use of the information contained herein, this is their decision, and the interviewees (and their companies), the author and publisher do not assume any responsibility whatsoever under any conditions or circumstances. It is recommended that the reader obtain their own independent advice.

Cover Art "As I Think, So I Become" courtesy of Marie Laywine, The Old Chapel, Back Street, Abbotsbury, Dorset, DT3 4JP. www.marielaywine.com

To my lovely daughters, Siân and Rebecca.

Thank you for always supporting your 'non-conventional' mum.

And, of course, to the original Pilgrim Mothers – your pioneering spirit lives on.

Foreword

In my work as an entrepreneur and business mentor I have the privilege of meeting many driven and interesting people – many of whom are running highly successful businesses. These are people who live life bravely, and who set out to achieve the goals they set for themselves.

Jane Noble Knight is one such person. We first met when she attended one of my events at The Entrepreneurs' Business Academy (EBA). A successful businesswoman, wife and mother, Jane had nothing to prove to anyone, but knew she was not being fulfilled by work and parenthood alone.

Jane found the courage to recognise that she needed to step away from the life she was familiar with, in order to discover her passion and to follow her path. A woman on a mission, she set out on a personal quest to rediscover the meaning in her life – in a camper van, with only her two dogs for company.

The result is this inspiring and uplifting book that tells Jane's story and contains remarkable insights from nine of the UK's foremost female entrepreneurs: Carry Somers, Dawn Gibbins, Gill Fielding, Gina Lazenby, Katharine Dever, Marie-Claire Carlyle, Penny Power, Rachel Elnaugh and Stephanie Hale. Brave, bold trailblazers, Jane views them as the 'Pilgrim Mothers' of the business world, who were unafraid to discover a new way of doing something. Their fascinating stories reveal not only their talent for business, but also their road to personal authenticity and an inner belief that their mission was to 'give something back' to others, along the way.

Jane's philosophy is that 'what sparks our passion is what brings us joy', and she knows all too well that money alone does not deliver happiness. Personal fulfilment comes from within – rather than from material rewards. It is a belief that I hold too, and it is a great pleasure to have been asked to write the Foreword to this timely book.

Bev James, best-selling author of Do it! or Ditch it.

CEO, The Academy Group, Incorporating The Entrepreneurs'
Business Academy (EBA) and The Coaching Academy
www.bevjames.com

Contents

"Look for what makes you come alive …
and do more of it. Therein lies your gift to
the world – and the key to your happiness."

JANE NOBLE KNIGHT
THE PILGRIM MOTHER

Introduction

Jane Noble Knight

Hello, I'm Jane Noble Knight. Yes, that *really* is my name. I was born a Noble and married a Knight. For ages a voice in my head kept asking me time and time again, "When are you going to step into your name?" And each time I would brush it aside with "Go away. I'm too busy," or "How on earth do I become a noble knight?"

I mean, it's not as if I haven't been successful. My career has spanned forty years – the last thirty of them have been in the field of people development. I love people. I've been a teacher, trainer, coach, mentor ... I've headed up national training teams for the likes of Barclays Life, The Law Society and Newton Investment Management in the City of London. But it seemed empty somehow. I felt as if there was something missing.

At the beginning of 1999 I went freelance as a training consultant at a time when my husband was suffering a long period of ME (myalgic encephalomyelitis – also known as chronic fatigue syndrome). Any partner of someone with ME will understand the ensuing stress that drove me to the verge of a nervous breakdown. One major factor was the physical exhaustion of travelling 153 miles each way to work four days a week and taking care of the family's needs. Then there was the emotional exhaustion from my guilt at leaving my younger daughter to cope with his illness while I was away and from seeing my husband suffer like this and feeling powerless to effect a permanent change despite our best endeavours. My life was solely focussed on his recovery and our family's survival.

When, thankfully, he eventually recovered in September 1999, I decided it was my turn to heal. I needed to discover who I was ... because I had absolutely no idea. I knew I was a wife, a mother, a daughter, a colleague, a friend ... but these were merely roles. Who was I? Who was Jane Noble Knight? I hadn't a clue. I felt as if I were an empty shell with nothing inside. If someone had flicked their finger on my skin, I'd have immediately dissolved into a small pile of dust on the floor.

I had always been a lover of learning. After all, that had been my profession for thirty years. So I decided to cast my net more widely and study everything I could lay my hands on ... all the self–help books I could find, the ancient wisdom teachings ... I studied various complementary therapies, qualifying as a hypnotherapist, a past life regression therapist, a Colour Mirrors practitioner and teacher, a Usui Reiki Master and an Angelic Reiki Master ... and all the while I was healing myself ... I was starting to feel whole.

I explored areas that had always held a fascination for me but so far had never indulged in. I went on two Native American holidays, staying on reservations where I attended the world famous Crow Fair, one of the largest powwows, and was invited to an overnight sweat lodge, learning about their tribal traditions. I fell in love with Egypt and travelled back there six times to immerse myself in ancient metaphysical teachings and walk in wonder around the temples and pyramids. I studied

The Way of the Shuvani – the Romany wise women – and learned more about shamanic rituals and practices.

I discovered the magic of crystals and how each stone has its own character and properties. I experienced the deep primal stirrings of sound healing and gong baths. I had always loved trees, but now I appreciated their strength and presence ever more deeply. I had always felt a strong affinity to my Celtic roots, having spent my formative years in North Wales. Now I researched and travelled to ancient Celtic sites from my base in the Shropshire Marches area, which for many centuries had been a region of huge unrest and conflict as battles were fought over boundaries – hard to imagine nowadays in this peaceful, stunning landscape.

I had no idea where all this was leading me … and indeed on many occasions it all felt like total indulgence … and indeed it was. I did whatever I was drawn to, all the while trusting … trusting that this path was guiding me somewhere but who knew where. It just felt as if I was being led … and I followed.

In 2008 my husband and I divorced after our amicable separation two years earlier to continue on our individual journeys. Then in 2009 I started getting an even stronger feeling that I was meant to be doing something. But what? I could almost touch it, but I couldn't quite grasp it. Eventually I asked the Universe for help. "Look, I'm being a bit thick here. I know I'm meant to be doing something, but I'm just not getting it. You need to help me. I need something more *in my face.*"

The Universe sent me Katharine Dever, an intuitive business mentor whose story is told in the first chapter. After a nine–month gestation period, with Katharine as midwife, on 14 January 2010 I finally gave birth to 'The Pilgrim Mother'. Neither of us knew the full significance of the phrase, but we both knew I needed to find out more.

That evening I decided to do what every modern woman does when she starts exploring … I 'Googled'. I typed in 'Pilgrim Mothers', fully expecting for Google to come up with a long list of Pilgrim Mothers. Instead, Google, in its wisdom, asked me, *Did you mean Pilgrim Fathers?* Rather huffily I responded, *No, I did* not *mean Pilgrim Fathers.* I had heard of the Pilgrim Fathers, of course, who in 1620 had crossed the Atlantic from Europe on the Mayflower in search of the 'New World'. But I wanted to know about the women in their life.

I tried again.

This time, listed at the top of the page, was an article from the New York Times written on 24 December 1892 entitled *In Honor of Pilgrim Mothers.* It described how, on the previous day, a group of pioneering women from the New York Woman Suffrage Movement, many of whom were descended from Pilgrim families, had met for a *'Foremother's [sic] Feast' to celebrate 'the achievements of the women, the sufferings and patient endurance of the Pilgrim Mothers … [which] were unsaid and unsung at the masculine tables.'*

… 'unsaid and unsung' … As I read the article and these words popped out, I shivered and experienced one of those moments as if time had stood still. Who were these *unsung* women?

Intrigued, I researched further and discovered in a publication by Edward Arber [1897] that out of eighteen wives, fourteen had died in their first year after landing, yet only three out of twenty children died, and these from families that were totally wiped out. Edward Arber asked the question, 'Did the women sacrifice themselves for the children?' which led *me* to ask myself, *Do women* still *sacrifice themselves … not just for children, but for husbands, partners, parents, colleagues …? Or could women be 'playing small' as Marianne Williamson [1996] so eloquently puts it? Are we sometimes guilty of standing in the shadows?*

Shortly afterwards I read how in September 2009 the Dalai Lama had said at the Peace Conference in Vancouver, "The world will be saved by the Western woman." On reading this I metaphorically rolled up my sleeves and decided *We'd better get on with it then.*

I reflected on how many other amazing women there might be whose stories were lost in history and how many incredible women today whose lives we may know nothing about and yet could be of huge inspiration to us. What a tragedy if as women we don't take this enormous opportunity we have to share our stories and sing each other's praises. What a spectacular legacy we could leave for future generations.

And so I embarked upon my Noble Knight's quest – I was to take up the mantle of the Pilgrim Mothers. I bought myself a motorhome, put the dogs in it and set off on a journey … a pilgrimage … travelling to wherever and to whomsoever I was drawn. As I wandered from place to place, I recorded stories and conversations, asking questions, feeling personally inspired and seeing the uniqueness and yet also the similarities between all the women I met … I had no set plan as to what I was going to do with the information but was, again, just trusting that all would become clear.

In 2011 my inner guidance was that it was time for me to settle for a while. So in October I bought myself a little cottage near my older daughter in Newport, Shropshire, from where I could continue to travel when I felt the urge.

Then on 19 December 2011, just before the winter solstice, I awoke at three in the morning. It was that voice again telling me that I needed to write a book. This was a surprise to me. I know people would often say that everyone has a book inside them, but I would always think, *Not me.*

I wonder how many of us have these limiting beliefs we need to overcome? Quite a few I would imagine.

And so I sat quietly and meditated as the format of the book and its subject matter took shape. I drew up my wish list of the modern Pilgrim Mothers I wanted to interview and immediately began to approach them with my project. Each one responded positively, a confirmation that this was indeed my path. From January till August 2012 I had conversations either face-to-face or via Skype or phone calls with twenty-four women who will be featured in my first three books. When I was not having these conversations or intuiting which women would be amongst my sisterhood of Pilgrim Mothers, I was a hermit, working away constantly at my labour of love.

This is my first book about nine wonderful female entrepreneurs who are pioneering new ways – ways that embrace their womanhood, not deny it – of running successful businesses. The former paradigms are falling apart all around us. These women demonstrate exciting possibilities for the world of work and business for right now and the future … ways that have already proven their worth and have changed the lives of countless others.

Each woman radiated a similar message – one of fulfilment, self–empowerment and service. Whatever they achieve in their world, you can experience in yours.

It is our time. There is a great shift happening in the world. We are all part of it. We can grab the opportunity to be all we can be … or we can hide away and live lesser, more contained lives. There is no right or wrong. It is *our* choice. I believe the time has come for every one of us to step up, to stand out and to shine … by doing what we love, what sparks our passion and what brings us joy.

On my personal pilgrimage I have discovered it is not selfish to do what you love. It is the very opposite. It is self–ful. As each one of us lives a life true to who we are, we allow, support and encourage others to do the same.

What I have also discovered is that it's okay just to be me. We are each important aspects of the jigsaw puzzle of life. We each have our place in the overall big picture. Only we can fit the place we are destined for. All of us make a difference in the lives of others … for some of us it will be in our families or in our local communities, even on a national and international level – and some will impact all areas. We are all unique and each contribution is equally valuable. As we work to change our own lives for the better, so too do we create benefits for others, as every one of us is connected.

Each woman I have met on my Pilgrim Mother journey has her own deeply personal and inspiring story. It has been my great honour to connect with the trailblazing women featured in this book and to discover and share their amazing stories. These women have stepped out of the shadows and are shining their light by being who they are, doing what makes them happy and travelling where they are guided.

They inspire me.

May you too be equally inspired, and more, on your own journey…

KATHARINE DEVER

"…everybody does have genius … when you're working in your gifts … things start to flow and the doors start to open and you're doing what you're here to do."

Personal transformation expert and intuitive business mentor, Katharine is the author of *Bettermorphosis: A Transformation Handbook for Awakening Women* and is featured in *The Indigo Children 10 Years Later* (Hay House, 2009) and *The Atonement Project*, with Revd Michael Beckwith (Jossey-Bass, 2011). Katharine is an Arts degree graduate of London's Royal Holloway University and a lifelong student of metaphysics, human psychology, healing and energy. She is the founder and director of Bettermorphosis Ltd and the creator of mindset and entrepreneurial trainings 'Find Your Money Spot' and 'Get Your Gift Out'. Katharine has a strong philanthropic drive and is passionate about the preservation of the world's remaining virgin rainforests. She lives with her delightful son, Ludo, near Bath, UK.

www.katharinedever.com

A Conversation with
Katharine Dever

Gift Unwrapper

When Rachel Elnaugh, one of my Pilgrim Mother Entrepreneurs and founder of Red Letter Days, called Katharine a 'Transformational Leader', I took note. Katharine was obviously someone for me to check out. Little did I know then what a significant role she would play in the transformation of my own life.

I signed up to Katharine's emails and in December 2009 I noticed that Katharine's contact address had changed from London to Shropshire – less than 20 miles away from me. *Interesting.* I got in touch right away to see if she would like to meet up. For months I had had the feeling there was something I was meant to be doing. When I met Katharine just after Christmas at a traditional 'olde worlde' café in nearby Shrewsbury, I sensed that the Universe had presented me with a source of help.

Shortly afterwards, Katharine visited me at home to help me find my 'gift'. I offered suggestions of what I might do in the future and each time Katharine would say, "No, that's not it," or "That's not *big* enough." (… *that sounded scary ….not big enough?!*)

Eventually, when I felt as if I had exhausted every possibility, I said, "There is the Pilgrim Mother" …

Katharine responded keenly with "What's that?"

I explained my participation in a BBC1 House Swap programme, the final stage of which was to negotiate a house exchange deal – or not in our case. At its conclusion, the presenter asked me, "What next?" And out of my mouth popped, "Oh, I'll probably get a camper van, put the dogs in it and travel round ancient sites." *Whoa … Where did that come from?*

I told Katherine how, over time, I had begun to 'see' in my mind's eye a white camper van … and then the phrase 'The Pilgrim Mother' came to me.

"I've heard of The Pilgrim Fathers who crossed the Atlantic in the Mayflower, Katharine, but I'm not aware of any women."

Undeterred Katharine looked me straight in the eye and said with finality, "That's it."

I immediately felt this huge swell of emotion. I burst into tears. In fact I sobbed. It was clear to both of us that 'it' was significant and I needed to find out more.

From there I went on to discover the story of the original Pilgrim Mothers, which then set me off in search of present-day women pioneers – modern Pilgrim Mothers.

And the rest, as they say, is history.

Since Katharine is now a mum, we are having an evening Skype call while Ludo is asleep. Her voice is soft and gentle; I would even say slightly husky. Definitely not a voice to wake a baby up! And sure enough, he is a good baby just as Katharine had assured me he would be. So we begin what will be a completely uninterrupted call. Lucky for you… Meet my first Pilgrim Mother Entrepreneur …

I'm so thrilled that you're one of my Pilgrim Mothers, Katharine.

I'm very honoured, Jane. I love what you're doing. It's so important because I think as women we have lost our medicine, especially in the West, and it's about really reclaiming our power and our wisdom.

Let me start right at the beginning, Katharine. At what age were you first aware of your intuitive gifts?

I probably wasn't fully aware until my late twenties. For my whole life I had a sense of being slightly different. I was having spiritual experiences but no channel or reference for them. So I ended up feeling disillusioned and perhaps scared, instead of being empowered by them.

It would have been easier if it had all been *normal*. I've had good job offers and marriage proposals, which I refused, and my mum was saying, "What's wrong with you?" So it wasn't like *that* life path wasn't available to me at a young age – to have security and normality or whatever we think we want when we're growing up. But there was always this deeper itch that I had to scratch. It became too painful *not* to follow the path that I was meant to take and get on purpose with my life. I felt so determined to find my place in the world, even if it wasn't the *normal* path, whatever normal is. It became my mission to identify my own gifts and then allow myself to bring them into my life and come out of the closet.

You were featured in a book on indigo children, Katharine, as an indigo child.[1] What was happening to you as you were growing up that was maybe different to others around you?

Certainly a sense of knowing things before they happened and sometimes knowing people in quite unusual ways. I remember being very young and my father had a friend who I never liked. That was unusual for me because I pretty much like everyone. But with this particular man, I always used to say, "I don't like him, Daddy," and just never wanted to go to his house and things like that. Anyway, many years later, my dad told me that they were on quite a big expedition together, like an

---

1   Children believed to have special and sometimes supernatural abilities. The idea is based on concepts developed by Nancy Ann Tappe in the 1970s.

overnight walk, and this guy had left him on his own when he wasn't doing very well. My dad had blisters and had to stop and this guy abandoned him.

You could maybe call it 'extra-sensory perception'. I knew things but didn't know how I knew. I could definitely *feel* other people. I was very empathetic. I still am. And I had quite a strong intuition about when things weren't right – not that I could see the future – but I could *feel* the truth and *see* the way for people from a young age. In terms of spiritual experiences, I used to have very strong dreams, flying dreams, visions. I certainly had a sense that I was communicating with angels or with beings. Not so much with spirits who have crossed over – it was never like mediumship. It was just a very strong connection with the divine and a strong prayer life from a very young age, without being taught that. I didn't go to Sunday school and I wasn't really interested in religion, but I felt very close to God, God's source. Whatever it is that children are close to stayed with me quite a lot.

What was your parents' reaction? Were they intuitive too or were you different from them?

I was different. My mum is quite intuitive, but she's definitely a lot more shut down with it. My great-grandmother was a fantastic herbalist and lived till she was ninety-six. She wasn't on any of the doctors' books because she healed herself and, actually, the doctors used to go to *her*. But in my grandmother's childhood, she was teased that her mother was a witch, so she became quite ashamed of my great-grandmother and rejected whatever it was. So that affected my mother, although her gifts are still there. Now, whenever I have any readings, my great-grandmother comes through. I'm very closely connected with her in spirit.

I would say that my mum and dad are quite open-minded. My father was an army major and my mother was a teacher, so they were 'straight'. But they accepted me as I was, which was a huge blessing. My dad, who's very grounded, tells the story of when I was about two-and-a-half years old, when he was aware that I was too young to tell lies. He says, "You were sitting on my knee and we were watching the television. There was this panoramic view of a landscape – fields and trees. You'd never seen that before, but you turned to me and said very matter-of-factly, 'That's what it looks like, Daddy, when I go flying with God.'"

My dad then did a very cool thing – he accepted what I said. When I came down in the mornings and said, "I went flying with God last night," he'd say, "Great." I wasn't ridiculed for it or told off. It was just the norm that Kath would go flying with God.

When I was about four, I got very ill and it stopped. After that, I didn't have those dreams anymore.

What happened, Katharine, when you stopped getting those visions? Did you still feel different or did you somehow 'blend in' more?

I always felt different, but the truth is, Jane, my way to deal with it, though I wasn't really aware of this, was to become very self-destructive, at quite a young age really. I became disillusioned with life and people. Even though I loved people – I've always loved people – I ended up just seeking to escape, mainly through alcohol. Unfortunately, a lot of teenagers drink – that's our culture. And I'm an 'all or nothing' person – an extremist and very experimental, a leader as well. A terrible mix if you haven't got that under control. It can come out in all the worst possible ways, basically.

How did you come through that, Katharine?

I thought I wanted to act. I knew I wanted to make a difference, but deep down I wasn't very happy. So, I was more a part of the problem than the solution. I was very cynical and negative. Like a lot of young people, I thought I had all the answers. I had ideas, but to be honest with you, I was more interested in going down the pub and having a few drinks. I talked the talk, but I certainly didn't walk the walk. I had dreams, but I wasn't committed.

Yet you went on to university, Katharine.

Yes, and when I left university, I got a job in beauty PR. But it was very difficult for me in a corporate environment. I can remember feeling like I was dying. It sounds really dramatic, but I was only there for a couple of months and I was really struggling. I thought, *There is something majorly wrong with me because everybody else is just getting on with this and I can't do it.*

It was really, really challenging. Again, I channelled that by becoming self-destructive – staying out late and turning up for work hung-over. I used to get into trouble for signing my emails, *'love from Katharine.'* I couldn't really do anything right. I was *awful* at my actual job – which was quite low-end. It was about twelve grand a year and lots of admin, which is my worst thing. In my business now, I literally outsource everything to do with scheduling and admin because I am useless at it.

The amazing truth is that everybody does have genius. Everybody has talent; but if you're trying to get a round peg in a square hole, you're going to feel like a massive failure. You're going to feel useless. You're going to lose all your confidence because you're not actually doing what you're here on the planet to do. It's a completely vicious circle. You feel as if you're incompetent. So you don't rally yourself. You go on a downward spiral rather than the upward spiral, which is when you are working in your gifts. *Then* things start to flow and the doors start to open and you're doing what you're here to do.

But I resisted and ended up in the worst possible job for me. They needed someone who could stick the mood boards together and I'm not very neat. All my stuff would be wonky and hanging off. And I would be mailing things out to the wrong people. I used to actually hide in the magazine cupboard. I'd say that I was sorting it out, but really I'd be freaking out, not knowing what to do with myself.

After about two months, because the pay was so low, I got an evening job in a nice little gastro pub across the road. Lots of celebrities, journalists, writers, creative people and entrepreneurs went in there. So I started to make loads of great friends who found me really interesting because I was young and vibrant and had all these crazy stories and was always half-cut.[2]

It was brilliant. Journalists would ask me, "What are you doing, Kat?" and I'd say, "Oh, I'm working at this place and I hate it." I'd tell them my story. Even though it wasn't my job to do that, I'd end up getting the company a double-page spread in the Sun. That's the only reason they didn't sack me.

After a couple of months, I just couldn't do it anymore. I lost it. I was having lunch with Rupert, one of my friends, and he said, "Kat, you're wasted there. You've got to get out."

---

2   Drunk

"I can't. I'm terrified. I don't want to stay but I can't leave." I thought to myself, *I'm twenty-one. No responsibilities. What do people do when they hate their job but they've got a mortgage and children?*

Anyway, Rupert made me drink a glass of wine and said, "Go on. Go in there and just tell them you're leaving." So I did.

I then went full-time at the pub. I told the boss, "Robert, I'm just going to work here until I figure out what on earth I'm meant to do with my life," and he said okay. I couldn't pay my rent with the money I was making from the pub, so I moved in upstairs. I lived above the pub and I worked downstairs. I was twenty-one. I had a first-class degree. I had a place at Trinity College to do a Masters in Anglo-Irish Literature in Dublin. I had all these things, and I just decided to pull pints until I could figure it all out.

Around that time, I read my first self-help book – Allen Carr's *The Only Way to Stop Smoking Permanently* – and I stopped smoking.[d] It completely changed my life. Within a few months, I couldn't stay at the pub anymore because I had become so health-conscious. I'd started running and juicing and everyone at the pub now thought I'd gone mental. To them I was boring and sober – going to bed at a decent hour and getting up at 5 am. I didn't have any good stories anymore because I was meditating and getting on my path. So I had to leave there after a while as well.

That was me after university; a complete mess, basically. *[Laughing]*

But it's hilarious. Were there any other books or people who had an impact on you?

Yes. Something very specific happened, which catalysed me into a new life. I was still working in the pub. I was definitely a good-time girl. At the time, I thought all this self-help stuff was for losers and people who *really* needed help. I clearly wasn't one of those because I was so confident! But my confidence was masking a lot of stuff that was underneath. I hadn't dealt with it because I didn't know any different.

I was very much into mad experiences – still am in fact. I'd scuba-dived the Great Barrier Reef, skydived and paraglided. Just in the last few years, I've swum with wild dolphins, climbed Mount Kilimanjaro and lived with tribes in the Amazon jungle, working with shamans and medicine.

It was this passion for things that people consider slightly mad that saved my life in a funny way. One day, a woman came into the pub. She asked me, "Have you done Tony Robbins?" I remember the way she phrased it because I had no idea who this person was – I thought it was somebody local in Windsor who had been giving me a bad name around town. *[Laughing]* I looked at this woman with absolute daggers, "Who's Tony Robbins and what's he been telling you about me?"

She replied, "No, no, he's the Peak Performance person and he does these trainings. I thought you'd done the course because you're so happy and upbeat and friendly. Actually, if you're interested, he's doing a fire walk."

I was curious, so I wanted to know more.

"You walk over these hot coals and he conditions your mind so you don't feel the pain and you don't burn your feet."

I was like, "Hang on. You don't burn your feet?"

"That's right," she explained. "It's like a mind conditioning."

I was hooked – "Okay, I'm in." At the time, the ticket was about £400 and I was only on around £6 an hour, but I somehow managed to get the money together to go on this training course. It was there that I had my quantum moment when I realised, *This is really good. I'm meant to learn more. This is my path.*

I felt so excited and I actually felt, for the first time, like I understood something about myself. I had found my place that I'd been looking for when I felt so lost throughout my teens. When Tony Robbins was talking, I was like, *That's what I think. That's what I've been wondering about.* All these years, I'd known that life was not meant to be this way and there had to be something else, but I just didn't know what. That was my eye-opening moment into what that something else could look like.

> "All these years, I'd known that life was not meant to be this way and there had to be something else, but I just didn't know what."

What happened after that eye-opening moment, Katharine?

I took out a graduate loan and blew about twenty grand on his Mastery University three-day event. I was a totally skint graduate but I found a way. I got credit cards and loans and I stopped drinking overnight. I didn't drink for about five years – not even a glass of wine. Before that, I really did drink every single day. It was just normal. I went to army school in the middle of Britain and that's just the way it was. Now I have an occasional glass, which I really enjoy.

I found this whole new track. When I gave up smoking, got into the running and had to leave the pub, they all thought, *She's joined a cult.* But I just had to keep following my energy. The Tony Robbins event was so special for me because he actually called me on stage. I had to choose a moment where I had felt a very strong emotion and another girl had to mirror my moment. Tony put me into a hypnotic state. I went back to when I was nineteen, sitting on the steps of the Sydney Opera House in Australia. At eighteen I had promised myself I would get to Australia for a gap year before going to university. I worked for six months in a pub to pay for it. Tony took me back to this pivotal moment where I felt really proud of myself. I knew anything was possible, and I felt very expanded. This girl then mirrored it and everybody in the auditorium – around 1,200 people – all started laughing hysterically. Everyone was high because they were feeling my euphoria.

That powerful experience of having done something true to my being was anchored in me. It represented my desire for freedom and expansion, and for growth and travel and new experiences. Almost overnight I became a different person. I wasn't eating a load of crap. I was just respecting my body and myself a lot more. My energy was through the roof. I got into healing, meditating and transformational arts. I wasn't interested in going out and drinking and boys anymore. I was like a nun on a mission. I just became obsessed, *really* obsessed. I'd waited all these years to receive this type of wisdom, so I just devoured it. It was like water in the desert.

So, Tony Robbins was a massive catalyst. And then I evolved into much more, I guess, lofty stuff – *A Course in Miracles,* Marianne Williamson, Deepak Chopra and Abraham-Hicks. I just continued on that journey.

What did you see as your mission at that time, or were you just being a spiritual sponge?

Well, I was a bit like a balloon, Jane, to be honest. A deflated balloon with no air in it, but it's got all this potential. You can imagine. I was being blown up by all this information – getting bigger and bigger and bigger till I basically left the planet. You know, I lifted off the ground and floated off into the sky somewhere. So my mission wasn't grounded like it is now – it was like *I want to change the world.* It was a beautiful state that I was in, but I wasn't really in my body and I had to come back and re-manifest as a human.

> "I was a bit like a ... deflated balloon with no air in it, but it's got all this potential."

Anybody who's ever had a similar experience will get that; but anybody who hasn't will think, *What on earth is she talking about?* So I apologise, but you've got to imagine. I went on this fast track, Jane. I lost about three dress sizes in a few months. I wasn't trying to lose weight. It was just that my vibration was getting higher and higher. My body was getting more and more finely tuned, so I was like a dowsing rod. It was all new and exciting. I had to learn, *relearn*, myself, in the world now that I was so sensitive and attuned. Previously, I'd numbed all of that out. I'd dulled it out and I drank it all into oblivion. So, how did I now exist in the world as somebody who had all these gifts and was super-sensitive when it was like a whole new world to me?

How *did* you make that transition and ground yourself into your mission?

It took time. It didn't happen overnight. I did fall to the earth with a bit of a bump. Other people might relate to that as well. Almost like a burnout; you run into a wall at a million miles an hour and that really hurts. If you walk into a wall, you get a bit of a bump, but if you literally charge into a wall, you can do some damage.

So I had to pick myself up from that. I used to eat a highly raw food diet. It was literally affecting my body and my cycles, so I had to really take a look at things. I started eating more nourishing foods to ground me, which is especially important in Britain where we get such cold winters.

I basically had about a three- or four-year journey of learning – and learning through painful experience, I'll add. Not like studying, though I was still studying. I suppose this is when I began to study business more. It made sense that it would happen at the same time I was getting grounded because it's all very much root chakra stuff[3] – security and foundations, money and business – really getting into touch with my needs and desires.

I was getting my feet back on the ground while trying to integrate all of the amazing things that I had learned – about myself, life, the Universe, the nature of reality. I was also learning how to thrive, not just get by, in this dimension and on this planet – really applying the universal principles and making it work. I was being true to my soul, connecting with people again, singing my own song, but also being able to book a plane ticket or fathom out a business plan or structure – something in the real world – and see it through.

So that was a big, big journey. I think that's why I shortcut people now because I don't want them to have the same pain. I wish someone had just told me, very straight. I've got a real promise to myself that with my clients, I'm very straight, even if it's things they don't want to hear. It might be painful in

---

3   Chakra means 'wheel' in Sanskrit, the ancient language of India. The root chakra is located at the base of the spine and is associated with survival – health, wealth, instincts of self-defence and self-support.

that moment for me to say, "You're not grounded. You're being off-track here. You need to start like this. You've just got to do this first." I think to myself, *I feel really mean saying this to them because I don't want to crush their dreams*, but it's actually the only way to get there – to start where you are.

How were you surviving during those three or four years of your journey, Katharine?

That's a good question. You know what it's like; you get looked after, don't you? I wasn't *fully* on track with my purpose then, but I think that because I was willing and making so many strides and such an effort towards it, that I was rewarded in small ways. But the pay-off couldn't be too big because I wasn't in the right place yet. So I used to do a lot of copywriting and marketing. I had a retainer for a personal stylist to write all of her marketing materials. I was a good writer because I'd done an English literature degree. I was always good with words and I'd learned about marketing.

What happened that got you through that stage and much more consciously focussed on your path?

Well after a few years of writing and marketing for other people's businesses, the next transition was to bet on my own horse and start my own business. I like to say that I heard a 'call'. *[Laughing]* I basically listened to a free telecall – literally – but it was more like a deeper calling for me as well. It was a woman in America who specialised in life purpose stuff. I just knew that I had to be at this event. I sold my little Mini Rio on eBay and crashed it the same day – it was one of those bad moments. Luckily, I only damaged the wheel. So I ordered a new wheel off eBay, put the spare on so the buyer could drive off in it, and then sent him the new wheel a few days later.

With the car proceeds, I bought a plane ticket to Las Vegas where I'd never been before and made my way to the event at Caesar's Palace. It was a bit mad, but it was absolutely where I was meant to be. Like with Tony Robbins, this woman got me up on stage. I was a mess, crying, telling her that I was trying to blend spirituality with marketing and I couldn't really figure it out. I'd been doing all this work and working so hard. I wanted to help people like me – all the healers and creative people and sensitive people. I wanted to help them to make money and be in their power, but I wasn't in *my* power and *I* wasn't making money.

I think she just gave me permission – and some tools and training that I hadn't yet had. She gave me the confidence to build my own dream business. That was in June or July 2009. By the end of that year and the start of 2010, I started to get my first clients. I'd done so much work. I was so ready that they came thick and fast.

I couldn't go to a meeting or a group without getting a new client. It was just boom, boom, boom. The Universe was sending me people as if to say, 'You're in the right place now. You've done the foundation work and you're ready. We're using you as a tool.'

It was all just opening up and happening.

That's how *we* met, Jane, you and me. You were one of my first clients. Having sold my car and ditched my ex, I had to make all these massive changes. Around December, I ended up back at my mum and dad's in Shropshire. I was so gutted, really. But I knew it was the Star not the Tower.[4]

---

4   In Tarot cards the Tower represents major upheaval and chaos and the Star represents the call of Destiny to the better future waiting for you.

I knew I was being guided and I had to completely trust, completely surrender and completely let go. Then everything that I had asked for came in.

I loved – I still absolutely love – my clients. I get such a kick out of helping people. I went on to invest literally tens of thousands in different programmes and carry on mentoring because my clients were getting such great results. That's just so exciting and heart-warming for me.

When did you know exactly what your gift was, Katharine, and what Spirit, God, whatever you want to call it, wanted you to do?

It was more like a very blurry picture coming into focus bit by bit. I would love to be able to say there was this moment when I knew this was my gift and I had to do this for the rest of my life – but I didn't really. I had to take a massive chance – a leap of faith – and just start showing up. That was when things started happening. And the weird thing was that for my whole life, I probably had been using my gift. I just didn't know it because I wasn't getting paid for it and I didn't make a business out of it. But, certainly, at my boarding school I was the person who everybody came to. Even when I was just fourteen years old, the sixth formers would wake me up in the night with problems – sixteen to eighteen year olds wanting to talk to me.

It's maybe because you're an old soul, Katharine.

So describe to me what your gift is and how it benefits your clients.

When I spend time with someone, whether they tell me about themselves and their problems, or I just spend time in their field, I begin to receive a sense of who they are, what they're meant for, where their path is, how far off track they are. And then I help them get back onto track quickly. I also sense, if they say 'yes' to themselves and this calling, where they might end up.

So I actually see the heart of things very clearly. I get these very strong feelings. That doesn't always mean that these things manifest because oftentimes there are a number of factors that go into creating that outcome. The person would have to believe it and maybe go through some letting go and releasing, so that new experiences and a transformation could come in for them. If they're willing to do all of that then it happens very, very quickly, relatively speaking.

> "I had to take a massive chance – a leap of faith – and just start showing up."

For people to be starting businesses and making money within the first three years is miraculous really. Most businesses take at least three to five years to get on their feet. Yet I'm seeing people getting into profit within months in some cases. I think this is because when you step into your purpose, and with all the technology that we have available to us, you can have these quantum shifts and things take off. They always look like an overnight success – but there's no such thing because the people who that happens to did the work. They did so much more work than you could ever think, or more than you ever see on the outside. You can see the outside – they've done the nice website, they wrote that book – but the real work they did was inside themselves.

What have been your highlights over these last few years?

I did a speaking gig in November 2009 – just before we met – for about twenty women. And fifteen of them bought my offer, which was a one-month programme. I then spent a day with the woman who had run the event because she wanted some private time with me. As a result, she had a 3,000 per cent increase in her business within twenty days. And funnily enough, her husband had a big event he was organising too. So I was invited to speak there. I went from twenty women in a little theatre to 300 businessmen and women in an auditorium with Paul McKenna as one of the other headline speakers! I remember I wore a long, floaty goddess dress and no shoes. I really can't remember anything I said because I was so being guided and channelling, I guess.

"I was being guided. I wasn't making it up and I wasn't crazy. ... and just because it's an unusual path, doesn't mean it's not valid. "

I had a *sort of* plan for my talk. I knew what I was offering, but there were huge chunks of it that were just a total stream of whatever – just saying what I was meant to say up there. Afterwards, I had people coming up to me and saying that their whole bodies were vibrating. So there seemed to be a transmission going on. That was a big high point for me. It was also £30,000 in ninety minutes of sales, which was mind-blowing for me, really.

Within four months, I'd gone from nothing to six figures. It was just the most affirming thing to know that after all the work and confusion and doubts and praying and questioning, it was all taking me somewhere. I was being guided. I wasn't making it up and I wasn't crazy. This was my path and just because it's an unusual path, doesn't mean it's not valid. It was a massive confirmation that I had done the right thing to *not* get married when I was younger; to *not* take those jobs; and to have all my experiences. I'd learned tough lessons but I made the investments and it all paid off in the end. Starting my own business was definitely the right thing.

Making money was life-changing because of who it made me become, how it made me think and feel, and what I could do with it. I did some things that I've always wanted to do. I went back to the Amazon. As a retirement gift for my dad, I bought him a flight to Africa and the opportunity to climb Kilimanjaro with me. At sixty-six he took me up on it. We camped in a tent for ten days and he absolutely loved all of it. Now, we have the memory we can talk about. That's something that I'm very glad we did.

Those are just a couple of really high points that I'll treasure, and obviously, my son and being able to give birth in Ecuador. My son and I are now South American citizens. The world opens up when you get on your purpose.

What drew you to Ecuador, Katharine?

I did a lot of my own powerful transformation work with the shaman there. I had a special connection to that part of Ecuador with the jungle. My son was born in the high Andes. When my mum had asked me "Are you going to give birth in Bath Hospital or Bristol?" I had said, "Well, I'm actually choosing between California and Ecuador." *[Laughing]*

And you're a single parent, aren't you?

I am, yes.

I know from my personal experience of having two daughters with two parents, it was still really exhausting. How are you finding this adjustment to having a son and maintaining balance in your life?

I'm very lucky because my son is a literal angel. He doesn't cry a lot and he's very easy-going. That probably sounds a bit sickening, but I have a really lovely life at the moment and I've had the absolute gift of being able to work from home. I've got more white space in my calendar than I've ever had and more money than I've ever had. I'm doing absolutely what I love; I'm only working with clients that I really know I can help. I've a son I adore and his dad is a really great support. His dad's a wonderful father. We just didn't work out as a couple. We hadn't known each other for very long.

I'm also very keen on what I teach. I'm very clear that you do what you're good at and you outsource the rest. So I have someone do the housework for me. It drives me mental, and I'm not any good at it anyway. I try and clean the mirror and it's more smudged after ten minutes of me cleaning it than it was beforehand. I pay people – whether for cleaning or websites or whatever – if they're better at it than me.

> "I'm very clear that you do what you're good at and you outsource the rest."

The gift of leveraged income is what I would hope to share with as many women and new mothers – or old mothers – as I possibly can. Every woman and mother needs support. We used to live in tribes and get help all the time. It's no fun going it alone, and the truth is, I'm not going it alone. I've got a lot more support around me than a lot of mothers. I'm very, very aware of that and I'm very grateful. And I do believe that it's doable for anyone who really wants it.

What about the practicalities of life, Katharine, with all your travel?

I have one base in Britain, in the countryside near Bath in Wiltshire. I'm a bit of a country bumpkin; I like my wide open spaces. And when I go to Ecuador, there's a couple that basically are my son's godparents. They have three little boys and they're very special people in my life. They have a wonderful luxury holiday let, I guess you could call it, that I rent when I'm there. Otherwise, I stay in hotels. I took Ludo to his first hotel in January for a speaking gig I did in Ireland and he loved it. I'd been a bit worried about it, quite honestly, but he had a ball. We *both* had an absolute ball. We'd come back from Ecuador on Christmas Eve, so he was about four months old and he was an absolute angel. I really am blessed.

How lovely. From your experience, what would you want to share with readers that you believe would make a big difference?

I think for women and mothers, we're so good at many things. We're so talented, and for whatever reason, all of us doubt that at some level. If we could just stop and take a step back and ask ourselves – or put our hands on our hearts and ask our inner self, our inner wisdom "What do I want and what do I need?" we would get really clear on it. Just allow yourself to *see* what that is and begin creating it – because you can create life. You can do anything. You're really a miracle. Nothing is beyond you. There's no problem. There's nothing so big that it can't be solved and there's nothing bigger than God; there's nothing bigger than Spirit. So ask them for more help and guidance. Say,

"This isn't clear to me. I need help to make this more obvious."

And as women, I think we worry too much about what other people think. You've just got to block that out and think, *What would I do if I didn't care what anyone thought?* Start living your life for *you* and not what you think someone else is thinking of you. You can do that without being selfish as well. It's actually one of the most selfless things you can do.

I agree with you, Katharine. In your words, how can you explain how that's not being selfish?

Some of the most martyred women I meet are the most terrible to be around. They can't support you to save their lives because they themselves are full of bitterness and resentment and extremes and unfulfilled potential. Believe me – you're not doing anyone any favours by pretending you don't have any needs. You need to say yes to yourself and put your own oxygen mask on. Only then can you put anybody else's on and help others.

That's what I was saying right at the start of our chat. I was more a part of the problem than the solution because I didn't have my own shit together, at all. And I'm not saying that I have all the answers now, but I'm certainly much more present for my friends and family. When someone does need me, I actually have something to give. I have resources, I have reserves. I can show up in a different way than I used to be able to. That's because I became 'selfish'. I put myself first. I addressed what I needed to in my own life and did things just for me.

One time I had to choose between a friend's wedding and running a retreat. My soul said, "Do the retreat," and my ego said, "You cannot miss this wedding. What will people say?" I knew some people would be shocked, but I had to go with the higher, more powerful perspective. The truth is no one's actually thinking about you anyway. They're thinking about themselves, just like you are. *[Laughing]*

Looking ahead, is there anything in particular lined up?

I tend to start the year with some big intention setting and I didn't this year. Instead, I felt guided to have a reading – a sort of intuitive reading. As you know, I eat my own medicine. I have my own coaches and mentors and go to healers and guides and shamans and God knows what. I went to this particular person and she was amazing. I still listen to her reading and get something from it every time. I think it's the spring equinox[5] today, so things are starting to bud and have a bit more life in them, but basically, I've really allowed myself to have a winter – a fallow period. I've had a couple of on-going clients and I've started working on a book, but no new projects … because I've wanted to create space. I understand there's an ancient Amazon prophecy about human societies splitting into two paths, the Eagle (the mind, the industrial, the masculine) and the Condor (the heart, the intuition, the feminine.) The prophecy predicted the potential from 1990 of a 500-year period for the two paths to unite and create a new level of consciousness. We're in the time of that potential.

So, I don't know, is the answer; but I do feel very on track and available for whatever is next.

Just like you are ready for what's next too, Jane. You've done such a great job, by the way.

---

5   The date at which day and night are equal marking the first day of spring. Astrologically considered to be the first day of the new year and celebrated by many traditional cultures as a time of rebirth and renewal.

I've had such a nice time. I feel very relaxed, yet we've covered a lot of ground. I think doing these interviews is one of your gifts for sure.

Fantastic. Thank you, Katharine, for your encouraging words and for sharing your story.

I have much to be grateful to Katharine for. Without her intervention, I might still have been searching for my path – or my gift or money spot as Katharine would say. Sometimes we need a third party to help us. Katharine came along because I had asked the Universe for help. I then needed to be alert to clues – like the address change on just one email – but I was on to it. I contacted Katharine right away. I have learned to take action promptly if a hint appears on my radar.

Katharine believes in speed too. It shows commitment – to ourselves and our (often unseen) helpers. How many people would have sold their car to fund an air ticket to an event in Las Vegas? Katharine was so in tune with her inner guidance that she intuitively knew she was meant to be there. The same with the fire walk. That place of total trust comes from a place of stillness. Everyone can access that inner wisdom within the silence – but how many do?

When I was in the corporate world, I had little silence and even less peace. My mind was constantly buzzing. I knew I wasn't happy but I didn't know how to change. I was searching for something, though I didn't know what.

One weekend I attended a dowsing workshop run by homoeopath Bob Wooler.ᵉ With the help of a rough drawing he explained how dowsing worked and how we are all connected. It made perfect sense to me. When Bob mentioned 'The Quest', a correspondence course in metaphysics, my antenna rose. Nevertheless, I resisted … and left without speaking to Bob.

> **"I have learned to take action promptly if a hint appears on my radar."**

But my inner voice was persistent. I relented and asked Bob for more info. When it arrived, it looked like gobbledegook to me. I hadn't a clue what it meant. I certainly didn't think I had any spare time for it. Yet still I felt this nudging. I gave in and set the first of January 2005 as my first day of study.

I was ill over Christmas and New Year, so it was evening before I felt well enough to begin. The twenty-minute meditation felt like a lifetime! It was excruciating to do nothing – and yet I opened my eyes after exactly twenty minutes, without a timer.

The next day, the meditation passed easily. Once again, my eyes opened naturally after twenty minutes. Over the next few months my life underwent a massive shift. It seemed catastrophic at the time, but in reality it was the massive wake-up call I needed. In fact, I still start every day with a period of meditation and quiet reflection – testament to the value I find in this practice.

Like Katharine, I had resisted. But once you say 'yes', life changes. And there's no going back. You answer the calling and follow where it leads. As Katharine points out, it doesn't happen overnight, but it can appear to be that way. Your inner journey creates your outer journey, not vice versa. For me this is the way of my own pilgrimage – the journey home to who I truly am. Along the way I meet fellow pilgrims who enrich my experiences.

To me, Katharine's uplifting message is that everybody has genius. We just need to invest in ourselves to find it, whether that means time or money or both. Either way, it will require a significant leap of faith. This is our demonstration to the greater power – Universe, God, Spirit – that we are absolutely serious, we are committed and we will persevere no matter what. That is definitely Katharine. That is definitely me too. Is that you?

"Your inner journey creates your
outer journey, not vice versa."
JANE NOBLE KNIGHT

RACHEL ELNAUGH

"An entrepreneur creates value where none existed before."

Award-winning entrepreneur, founder and CEO of Red Letter Days, professional speaker and business mentor, Rachel Elnaugh is also author of best-selling *Business Nightmares – When Entrepreneurs Hit Crisis Point*. Rachel starred in the first two seasons of BBC TV's *Dragons' Den* where she was the sole female amongst four male 'dragons'. Rachel is a role model as to how an entrepreneur can hit rock bottom and come back up fighting and succeeding. She was awarded an Ernst & Young Entrepreneur of the Year Award in 2002 and was shortlisted for the 2001 Veuve Clicquot Businesswoman of the Year Award. Rachel also won the IAB Champion for Entrepreneurship in the UK Award for 2008 and was runner up for the SFEDI Supporter of Enterprise Award for 2009. Rachel lives in Bakewell, Derbyshire. She has five sons, Mark, Paul, Eddie, Michael and Jack.

www.rachelelnaugh.com

A Conversation with
Rachel Elnaugh

Business Alchemist

What would you expect from an ex-Dragons' Den panellist? When I attended a 'Women Who' luncheon organised by the Birmingham Chamber of Commerce in early 2007 where Rachel was the keynote speaker, I was expecting a rather hard-nosed, determined businesswoman. To my surprise Rachel was a delight – gentle, feminine and honest. I was totally charmed.

What particularly struck me about Rachel was her language. She talked about energy, flow and the Law of Attraction. I thought, *Aha, this is a woman on her path.* Prompted by Rachel's speech, I took three actions that day: I signed up to Rachel's updates; I suggested my daughter Rebecca check her out too; and as a bit of fun I set myself a little challenge to use the Law of Attraction to win one of the event's raffle prizes, specifically a presentation box of Harrods Wine – and I did!

I have continued to follow Rachel's blogs and progress. I thoroughly enjoyed her book *Business Nightmares*, which gave me fresh insights into her story. When I came to write this book, Rachel just *had* to be on my wish list. Some of her story is well-documented, but I suspected there was plenty I didn't know.

I sent Rachel an email inviting her to be one of my Pilgrim Mothers, and just forty-six minutes later she replied personally, saying she was happy to help. That's impressive. She invited me to call her so we could put a date in our diaries for a conversation.

I phoned Rachel two days later, just as she was launching her 'Business Alchemy Programme' at The Business Show in London to sell-out success. I'm not surprised. She bridges business nous and metaphysical wisdom – a formidable combination. Indeed, I went on to buy the programme myself to benefit from her expertise.

Rachel and I have had a few brief phone conversations prior to this Skype call. Nevertheless, I feel a sense of anticipation tinged with nervous excitement. After all, Rachel is someone I have admired as a

business celebrity for some years. I know this conversation, this moment to shine a spotlight on her as an amazing contributor and changemaker, will be an extremely important chapter in my first book. As we connect, I hear her familiar soft warm tones. I invite you to journey into the world of Rachel Elnaugh, Changemaker. I wonder what new things we will learn…

You say in your book, *Business Nightmares*, 'I always knew I would run my own business one day,' and you linked that to how you used to spend your school holidays in your dad's electrical shop. I can imagine it wouldn't appeal to many girls. What was it about the experience that you really enjoyed, Rachel?

Well, I grew up around business, generally. We lived above my dad's shop, so it wasn't just school holidays; I was always down there, pottering around. I just loved being around the business and counting the money. At Christmas, I would do a Christmas gift stall. My mum and I would make things for it, like crackers. It was just a very good entrepreneurial grounding. I think I got the connection between effort and money at that point.

I'd make something and then I would sell it, so it was like a little reward. I think business like that can get quite addictive – when you can get in that flow of creating something and then you make money from it. It's almost like getting hooked on business. I always knew I would do my own business one day but that it wouldn't be an electrical business like my dad's. I just had that entrepreneurial spirit. You don't know what and you don't know when, but sometimes in life, you just *know* it's going to happen.

> "I despair of our educational system…
> We turn out a load of victims who want it all on a plate as opposed to being enterprising and getting on and doing things and making stuff happen."

I hadn't thought about living above the shop in that way before – how the business becomes so much intertwined with your life. It's a real training ground, isn't it? Lots to learn.

Definitely, and it's just thinking entrepreneurially. So yes it was. I really enjoyed my childhood from that angle.

I went to a girls' grammar school, like you, and the career advice for me was virtually non-existent, just as you describe in your book. It was assumed you would go to university and study the subject you were best at. Do you think anything has changed in schools in general, or is it still the same?

Well, I despair of our educational system. I think that if we were to start with a completely blank canvas about what is the best way to equip our children for life, the British education system definitely wouldn't be it. We don't teach enterprise skills. We don't teach energy skills, energy management or mindset and positive thinking. I think those of us who have discovered all of those secrets have done it after we have left school, through chance, reading books, going to seminars and getting onto that path. It's a real shame that we don't teach that to our children. We turn out a load of victims who want it all on a plate as opposed to being enterprising and getting on and doing things and making stuff happen.

I agree with you on that. Do you think it's possible to train a young person to be an entrepreneur or is it, as you say, particular skills and things like self-esteem that should be taught in schools? If you were Minister for Education and did have that blank canvas, what would you do?

Well, I think being enterprising is a mindset, and it's not something you necessarily teach. But it is something you can bring out in children. The big problem with the education system is that it's run by teachers who have never experienced real life in terms of business. So I would try to bring much more experience of the commercial world into teaching and training. Not that it would be easy to do. A lot of teachers go to university, do their teacher training and then go straight back into education. They've never actually held a non-teaching job before or run a business – they've almost been institutionalised. So I'd completely change the way that education is delivered.

Absolutely. Can I ask you what is your definition of an entrepreneur, and would you say this is something different from being a businesswoman?

Well, I think an entrepreneur creates value where none existed before. I just love the way that, as an entrepreneur, you can take an idea, just the seed of an idea, and you can develop it into a revenue stream at its simplest. Entrepreneurs are the creators. With a businesswoman there is a different set of skills that kicks in when a business has got to a certain size and has become established. I have to say, I'm not a particularly good businesswoman, really. With that kind of managerial role, managing a whole team and all the structure, you need slightly more left-brain skills. I think entrepreneurs are more right-brain in that they are creators and initiators. You need a different type of person for when it gets established, and that was my real mistake with Red Letter Days; not having a really good team of operational people around me to manage the giant machine I had created, so to speak.

It's so refreshing to hear you say that you're more of an entrepreneur than a businesswoman. I think so many creators are. We need teams around us to do the nuts and bolts to get the machine working.

When you went to school, which wasn't an entrepreneurial environment, how did you create that bridge so that you did then become an entrepreneur in Red Letter Days?

I was in school and got onto that path that everyone in my type of school got onto, which is applying to universities. The difference was that I was rejected by all five that I applied to. Then I started applying to all sorts of management training programmes and was rejected by all of those too. Finally, in desperation, I saw this job in the local paper for an office junior for a firm of accountants. I applied and got that job. It was just filing and making coffee, but I was desperate by that point.

> "I learned to keep going and keep trying, despite rejection after rejection."

The interesting thing about that phase was how I learned to keep going and keep trying, despite rejection after rejection. I'm sure a lot of kids these days have that experience of 'no one wants you'. It's very easy to think that you're a failure.

I just got my foot on the ladder, really, in this little firm of accountants. And as it happened, I ended up specialising in taxation for entrepreneurs and small businesses. I worked my way up and ended up at Arthur Andersen in the City of London when I was twenty-one. I had all sorts of amazing entrepreneurs in my portfolio, so in a strange way it was the perfect grounding to go into business because I had seven years of learning about profit and loss accounts, spreadsheets, and the nuts and bolts of business – all brilliant things to have when you go into business. Most women in particular don't have that left-brain accountancy/numbers type skill.

You're right. I certainly have to work at it. You say in your book that there are three qualities needed by an entrepreneur – self-belief, determination and drive – and it often comes from a tough childhood. Now yours didn't seem especially tough, so how did you develop these qualities?

Well, I grew up with four brothers, so I had a very competitive childhood around these alpha male, win-or-bust types of energies. In that sense, I was used to being very competitive. Also, at that time, when I was in accountancy in the City, it was the 1980s when the City was booming and all these female entrepreneurs were floating their businesses on the stock exchange – Anita Roddick of The Body Shop, Sophie Mirman of Sock Shop and Debbie Moore of Pineapple. There was a lot of girl power around with Margaret Thatcher, and Lady Diana was on the scene. Overall, there was a surge of female energy, which was quite inspiring.

So what propelled you from Arthur Andersen to setting up Red Letter Days? I suppose you could have gone the accountancy route, having progressed to a big firm like that.

I know. And it was very tempting to stay in that kind of safe job. But as I progressed and my charge rate got more and more per hour, I was being drawn into doing much more detailed tax law work, and I just knew it wasn't really my thing. I could have stayed on that hamster wheel, but I just knew in my heart that there was something different for me.

I took the plunge and left Andersens, and I went off to go travelling for six months. Well, that was the intention, but after about six weeks of bumming around, I just got really bored and thought, *I'm going to have to get back and get on with something.* I'm a doer. I'm a real doer.

So, I came back to the UK and took a freelance job doing tax consultancy work, just to get the money flowing. That was when I thought, *Now is the time to take the plunge and create a business.*

> "What amazing stuff can we find? What amazing experiences are we going to create that are going to really wow people? That was the heart of the business – surprising and delighting people."

I've read the story about how you created the gift package of a jar of English mustard, a pot of curry powder, a cricket ball and a handwritten invitation with tickets to the forthcoming England vs. India cricket match for your father's birthday present. Do you think that there are all these seeds of business available to everybody, or do you have to have a particularly creative mind like you seem to have?

Well, the thing is, I was following my passion because I always took great care over gifts and giving things when I was young. I did the Christmas gift stand in the shop and I always made things with a lot of love and passion. So I had that creativity, and they do say in business that there aren't any new ideas; there are just old ones, repackaged. I'm a real advocate now of following your passion and doing something that you love because, really, the idea with that business was 'What do you give a man who has everything?' That was really it. 'How do you package it?' You could buy someone a voucher to go to Brands Hatch motor racing, but it seemed a bit loveless. I just thought there was a much better way to package and present it, and it became an umbrella brand for amazing experiences – the concept of Red Letter Days.

Then it became about 'What amazing stuff can we find? What amazing experiences are we going to create that are going to really wow people?' That was the heart of the business – surprising and delighting people.

I got a Red Letter Day for my dad for his eightieth birthday present. It was a flight in a vintage plane over London. He was certainly delighted. They were absolutely wonderful experiences. Did you go on any yourself, Rachel?

Yes. I spent a lot of my time doing all this amazing testing, so to speak. It was very exciting. It was a wonderful lifestyle of being invited to health spas and the Orient Express to Venice and hot air ballooning. I did a few of the scarier things like tandem skydiving, as well.

I quite fancy that.

It was *awful,* falling at 180 miles an hour, thinking I'm going to die!

Maybe not then. *[Laughing]*

But it was great fun, and the whole thing was just a big adventure, particularly for the first ten years. And then it got to be this huge machine that I started to get annoyed with. It was getting too big with crisis management and staffing problems, and I was just getting angry. Looking back – this is one of my big themes – when you're in a place of passion and love for what you do, you get into the flow and you make money. When it starts to become a chore and you resent it, and your energy shifts into quite a negative place, it ends up pushing stuff away. I'm a great believer that once the passion has gone, you have to move on. Sell out and move on. That's what I should have done before it got to the point where it was frustrating.

In your book you talk about the lack of ethics in big business and the terrible stories about its cut-throat nature. Do you think there is any alternative to this? Eventually, you lost control of your business. It's ironic that you, Steve Jobs and Anita Roddick created the brands and then were outvoted from the company – yet you were the creators. Is that what you were saying? That it's best to create a business and then hand over for somebody to run with? That's really difficult for a woman to do. As you wrote, we birth ideas, don't we?

When money starts flowing, it's amazing how much greed rears its ugly head. In the old style of business, it's really all about money, greed and power, so you do get what I would call 'the engineers'. They aren't creators; they couldn't create a business if it fell over them. These are the businessmen, so they are quite smart at seeing value and working out how to leverage it or steal it or grab it or coerce themselves into a position of power. I find it quite a dismaying thing. Business is changing, but there is still a lot of that old style, corporate, money-grabbing, greed stuff going on.

I think we are shifting in business towards a much more feminine, collaborative and ethical way of being, and what we're seeing is all of those old paradigm businesses crumbling before our eyes. You just wonder how some of the great businesses could crumble so suddenly. Something happens. It's almost like the monster is devouring its own tail.

It's an interesting time that we're living in because I don't think that old way is sustainable. It's caused a lot of the problems, with everything collapsing, and it's all because of the money, greed, power.

I worked for eleven years in financial services with Barclays. I always felt that I was an ethical person, but it's only as time has gone on that I have realised what an unethical business I was in. I really hope that is changing.

I will just go back slightly …

You were invited to join the panel of Dragons' Den for the first and second series where you described yourself as the 'token woman'. Why is it that women aren't represented on panels in the media in the same way as men? It is the same with Question Time, Strictly Come Dancing, The Apprentice and The Apprentice: You're Fired.

I don't know really. The BBC obviously had a very clear, creative idea with the Dragons' Den, which was to make it ruthless. Now it has two women and three men – but they've still chosen scary women. I think it's a bit sad, but at the end of the day, these guys are making a product and I guess, unfortunately, there's still a gravitas to having men judges as opposed to women. The women seem to be there for decoration.

Can you see a time coming where there's a more supportive business programme like those with Mary Portas[1]? I've noticed a slight shifting over the last couple of years, even in the popular programmes. Britain's Got Talent and X-Factor are becoming less cruel, and The Voice chose good singers for starters.

I do think there's a shift and the 'cru-ality TV' is starting to recede. I think the people behind these programmes are realising they have a responsibility. The Voice was a good example of celebrating talent as opposed to showing people being embarrassingly ridiculed. It was quite a refreshing change from that old paradigm of making fun of people. So I think there's a shift.

That's good to hear.

It's really important for women to have good role models, which is one of the reasons I'm

> "I think we are shifting in business towards a much more feminine, collaborative and ethical way of being … what we're seeing is all of those old paradigm businesses crumbling before our eyes."

---

1   Retail expert, known as Queen of Shops. Her TV programmes focus on helping retail businesses to be more profitable.

writing this book. Who were your particular role models?

Bigger influences were actually the mentors who came along at opportune moments when I was really struggling. That's one of the things ... I have always been open to help and receptive to getting good people on board. So that was more of an influence for me ... my mentors who taught me about marketing and branding, PR and publicity – and they were all actually men.

I think I've always got on better, strangely enough, with men than with women, probably because I had four brothers and I've got five boys of my own. I do work a lot from my masculine energy, less so recently now I'm more involved in metaphysics. But I still find that bit of me kicking in – that masculine energy.

In *Business Nightmares* you spoke about being at an event where Anita Roddick was speaking and the room was virtually vibrating with the amount of energy generated – 'an energy I have only ever experienced at female-only events.' Why do you think that is?

Well, whenever you do energy work, it's always amplified exponentially if you do it in groups. I find that women are far better at tuning into one another's vibration. There's less competition; there's less game playing. There's much more support and collaboration when women come together in a room for an event. It's a vibration – the combined energy of all the women who aren't there to judge and critique but are there to absorb and join in and enjoy. They tend to come at it from a different angle to men in an audience, who tend to be judging what's going on. Men tend to be much more into competition than collaboration.

So I think there's a natural joining and merging of energy when women come together. It's very intense at women-only events. I've been on the speaking circuit for seven years. I've done hundreds of events now and it's very, very noticeable that with women-only events, there's a much bigger energy in the room. As a speaker, it's much easier to do them because you can feed off that vibe. A room full of corporate males is my worst nightmare in a speaking gig because they're all sitting with their arms folded, judging, and it's like hundreds of inner critics, sitting in rows.

One of the Pilgrim Mothers in my second book is an actor who gave up everything at fifty to go to drama school and fulfil her dream. She talks about the importance of the audience when you're on stage because they're so much a part of the performance. Thank you for reminding me of the two-way process.

What I love about you, Rachel, is your openness. It's hugely inspiring because you share your challenges and your times of vulnerability. When you had this really spectacular collapse of Red Letter Days, it must have been absolutely dreadful, especially as you'd just had a baby. Do you think with hindsight that you may have manifested what happened in such an extreme way because your heart wasn't in it anymore and you were destined for better things?

Definitely. They say you live your life forward and you understand it backwards. Obviously, post-Red Letter Days, I worked through a lot of emotion and anger, resentment and bitterness. Then by doing more metaphysical work, I realised that everything is a mirror of your own energy. This idea of taking 100 per cent responsibility for everything that's happened because *you* attracted it set me on this path of thinking, *Why did I completely destroy that? [Laughing]*

I don't know if you've heard this story, and I can't even remember if I put it in the book, but in 2002 a friend of mine was training to be a life coach and she asked if I would be one of her guinea pig clients. I was like "I don't need a life coach but, okay, I'll do it to help you." She had me do all these exercises. One of them was a life plan where I had to plan my whole life through to when I was eighty-eight. After Red Letter Days crashed, I found that life plan. I was clearing out some old papers and I'd completely forgotten about it. I was horrified because on there I'd written that by 2006 to get rid of Red Letter Days, spend more time at home with my family, be creative and write. I'd manifested exactly that cosmic order, literally to the word, because I'd just got a book deal and I was working from home. It was really interesting.

One of the things that dawned on me recently (because you have these moments of breakthrough, don't you, with this stuff?) … When I was young, my mum was quite controlling and she always used to say, "Bad girls don't deserve *anything*." During the late nineties, my mum died suddenly of a heart attack. Then my dad was grieving and slowly lost the will to live over two years. He had a couple of strokes and my brother was looking after him back in Chelmsford. Looking back, I was so busy doing Red Letter Days and making money and the business was growing that I really didn't spend much time with him. I realised I was holding a lot of guilt for putting money ahead of him. I actually do think I self-sabotaged that whole business because 'bad girls don't deserve anything'.

> " … I do daily affirmations now – I always put in there, 'I deserve.' I deserve to be rich, I deserve to be loved, I deserve to be happy, I deserve to be successful."

Having realised that – because I do daily affirmations now – I always put in there, 'I deserve.' I deserve to be rich, I deserve to be loved, I deserve to be happy, I deserve to be successful. Because I think you've got to counter those very powerful programmes that you have had since you were a child.

Absolutely. In your book, you say 'enlightened observers' said you'd probably look back and realise this was the best thing that ever happened to you. Is that what you say now, and was it what you said then?

[With a wry laugh] What I realise now is that life is an adventure and moves in spirals. We're taught to go from A to B in a very masculine, straight line. But actually, the way the Universe works is through spirals. So to get to your higher soul purpose, you are going to be going via a route that you don't understand, and when you're on that route, instead of going straight ahead, you're going over here, to the right. You can't see round that corner to where it's leading you, and you just really have to have trust in the flow and in the adventure, that it's taking you to where you need to be.

I'm sure I'm on a path and I don't quite know the full picture yet. So many amazing things have happened for me post that meltdown. Obviously, it preceded the whole of the economy collapsing in 2008, which coincided with my book. *Business Nightmares* came out in 2008 and literally, several months later, everything collapsed; so it was almost prophetic in that sense. Being set on this path of going out to speak at events and facing my fear of public speaking, as well, was a major thing for me. And it's just led me on this whole metaphysical journey.

Now I'm working with Barefoot Doctor, who is an incredible mentor. You couldn't work with someone more inspiring and fascinating. He's a real magician. When you're used to controlling everything and making stuff happen in a very masculine way, it's a very different way to work – trusting in the flow and going with it. Living life as an adventure and allowing yourself to go with that flow as opposed to keeping on swimming. Often we swim really hard, completely against the current.

So did your metaphysical journey start after the collapse of Red Letter Days or, looking back, were there certain clues throughout your life that you had intuitions or similar?

When I look back, I realise that my spirit guide had been knocking on my door for decades and I just hadn't been answering. Through a bizarre piece of synchronicity, I met a coach who took me on this journey to meet my spirit guide, who turned out to be St. George. At the time I was thinking *What's this load of bonkers stuff?* It was just really weird, and then I thought, *Oh my goodness....* So much of my life then made sense because my mother's maiden name was Knight. You're a Knight. You're a *Noble* Knight.

[Laughing] Yes, I genuinely am.

My mother's side of the family were Knight, and one of the few things I have from my mother is a sovereign pendant and on it is St. George slaying the dragon. It's a 1962 sovereign, which is just before I was born. And then of course, Red Letter Days ... a Red Letter Day is a saint's day, and its logo was red on white.

All sorts of things happened. For example, after Red Letter Days crashed, I was invited to do some consultancy for a company in Barcelona – an experiences company. I went over there and it happened to be St. George's Day, who is the patron saint of Barcelona, and I was given a red rose, which is the symbol of St. George. Just so many signs… I could sit here all day and tell you about all these signs that I was completely blind and oblivious to. I just really, really believe that I am on some kind of journey. The more that I tune into that and I follow the guidance, the more magic happens because you can easily turn off that tap when you think *you* know best.

Here's a bizarre story that actually happened on St. George's Day this year – which is really weird. The day before, which was a Sunday, I'd gone through a bit of a meltdown. I had been in a state and I said to God, "Why are you putting me through this?" Then suddenly, the church bells started ringing, literally within a minute. I thought, *It's a sign. I've got to go to church.* Then I thought, *Oh no … I'm not particularly religious like that.* The next day was St. George's Day and I was due to do a speaking event in Doncaster for a women's Chamber. When I got there, they said, "We've decided you're going to do your speech in the Minster."

I said, "Oh, right. Okay. Can I see the venue?" and I walked into the church – it was a big, black cathedral-type church – and there was this massive statue on the wall of … St. George and the Dragon … *and* it was St. George's Day!

Directly, from that day, I had this divine guidance to create Business Alchemy, my latest

"The more you align with those messages, the faster you can go on your journey and the more you can get into that flow of magic."

programme – material I'd been sitting on for well over a year and had not got my finger out and done anything with. From the energy of that event, I was determinedly thinking, *Rachel, you have got to get this work out into the world and make it available.* I literally scoped the whole thing, filmed it all that week and created it. It's actually my most successful mentoring product ever.

So it's like following divine guidance. It's a very subtle thing. You've got to tap into it, but you can't force it. The more you align with those messages, the faster you can go on your journey and the more you can get into that flow of magic. I could go on forever about this.

Wonderful. Inspiration from a gathering of women in the Minster with St. George and the Dragon!

That's right, it was. It was. And yes, a lot of magic happened that day, and when that happens, I just think there is definitely an 'I'm being told something, here'.

Yes. When that sort of thing happens, it's quite mind-blowing, isn't it? You think, *Oh my goodness. How on earth has all this come together?* I was getting goosebumps when you were talking about St. George!

It's really strange because if ever my mind goes into thinking, *I'm going to give this up. I'm not going to do the mentoring anymore, I'm not going to do the speaking* – for example I might be on a train going to a venue and think, *I'm going to give up doing this* – what happens is I then look out of the window and see a St. George's flag flying somewhere. It's like a message – 'No. Keep on the path.'

It's about being aware of those signals as well, isn't it? And the signs of encouragement that are there.

Now, I wanted to ask you about your blog you wrote just after Steve Jobs died in October last year. You actually mentioned St. George and the Dragon. You wrote, 'When shrines are created for a corporate leader, you know that we have entered a new era for business, an era where business is about more than making money and where entrepreneurs are the visionaries who have the power to change the world.'f

You call yourself a 'changemaker', Rachel, and I totally agree with you. So, what vision do you have for the future?

[Laughing] That's a big question. I just thought the whole Steve Jobs thing was very interesting. I did a mixed event up in Newcastle – half men and half women – so it was very balanced. And for the first time, there was like a conversation and the audience was asking me questions as opposed to me doing a speech. Many of the men were really leaning forward and interested in metaphysics. One of them asked me whether business was the new religion. Steve Jobs had died not long before and it was just really interesting to see that shift.

I think that we are at a stage of a big quantum leap. They're saying that 2012 is the year of the shift in consciousness and that evolution moves in quantum leaps. I think that the traditional leaders – the governments, presidents, prime ministers, bankers and all the politicians – are busy trying to maintain and preserve the status quo, and yet the energy is completely moving towards breakdown. They're desperately trying to keep the Euro afloat, but natural forces are tearing it apart. I think that it's the entrepreneurs and the changemakers who are the ones who are going to lead us out of this mess. It's not going to be the establishment because their remit is to preserve the old way, but the old way is breaking down so rapidly now.

It's interesting because when we were working on an online TV project to showcase Lightworkers, quite a prominent business astrologer said to me that there was a very rare planetary conjunction that happened for everyone who was born between 1963 and 1968. I was born in 1964. It's basically Uranus conjunct Pluto in Virgo and mine is added to because I have Mars sitting on top of it as well. It's like this changemaker energy, and she basically said, "You are the people who are going to be the architects of the new paradigm when everything is broken down".

> "I think that it's the entrepreneurs and the changemakers who are the ones who are going to lead us out of this mess."

The funny thing is so many people in my orbit are born in that period of time. It's almost like the architects are all gathering but they don't quite *know* what the job is. They don't quite know what the brief is, but they're all kind of assembling, ready. It's really weird. So, I can't say what's happening, but I do think massive change is on its way, and I think there's a real opportunity. But as you know, things have to break down before you can have a breakthrough, and out of that destruction or catastrophe, I think, will come something very wonderful. But the old has got to break down before the new can come through. It's the classic cycle of life, isn't it? … of creation, sustaining and then destruction.

Yes, absolutely. Is this the time of smaller businesses coming to prominence and more influencers maybe?

Well, I do think that the big corporate world has got a lot to answer for in terms of their part in everything that has gone wrong. Unfortunately, the bigger an organisation gets the more power it wields, and I do think that there is a complete shift. This is where the government have got it so wrong. They keep saying we have to get back to normal, and they think the future for our children is in employment and creating jobs.

Actually, I don't think the future is about that at all. I think the future is about people being enterprising and understanding that in the future, there are no jobs. It's everyone doing multiple projects and having multiple revenue streams. Certainly, I live like that now. I can't imagine those days when I just had one job where I commuted into work 9–5 every day on the train. It's just so *completely* different to my life now where I just work from wherever I am. My system is in the cloud and I just create revenue streams and help others create wealth and prosperity. That's my life, really, and I can do it from anywhere. It's an interesting life.

From what you're describing, leaders are going to have a mixture of spiritual and entrepreneurial qualities. Yet so many spiritual leaders seem to be American. There are very few big names in the UK.

I just think that the American so-called spiritual people are much better at marketing themselves than British people. Particularly in the UK, there is still an embarrassment around making money, whereas the Americans don't have that.

It's really interesting because I did two shows recently. I did the Business Show in May and I did the Mind, Body, Spirit festival last week, and it was just like absolute chalk and cheese. Really, so noticeable. It was two completely different tribes of people with *completely* different values in life – the very poverty-conscious world of Mind, Body, Spirit and the Business Show, which is much more prosperity-conscious. And I do think it's important that we get back into *prosperity consciousness,* which actually doesn't have anything to do with how much money you have. It's about living in a place of abundance and flow, giving and faith, and positive energy around money.

Absolutely. That's definitely the way forward.

I have to say, Rachel, I'm totally in awe of all that you have achieved, with five sons as well. How on earth have you managed it? They were young when you were in the Red Letter Days business, and after that. Any secrets for mums who want to go into business? How do you balance, or don't you?

"... it's important that we get back into prosperity consciousness … It's about living in a place of abundance and flow, giving and faith, and positive energy around money."

The key thing is I could never have had five children and had that kind of family if I had been an employee for someone else. Because when you run your own business, you completely create your own rules. These days, I go totally with my energy flow. So, if I feel like working, I work, and if I don't, I don't. I've got a good structure around the children, and I do have a nanny who has been with them for four years now. So she's part of the family, like a surrogate mother almost. So I think you just have to create the support system around you. Yes, it's good.

I've had a large family and the funny thing is, everyone says, "Five children! How do you cope?" Actually, in some ways, it's a lot easier to look after them because together they're like a little tribe that amuses itself. When I had only one or two, they took a lot more of my energy and time and attention, whereas when you've got lots, they do their own little adventures and play their games and whatnot.

My mother's one of twins and her mother said that once they got to eighteen months, they were much easier. It was hard work till then, but then they just occupied each other.

What would you say for someone who isn't at the stage of flow that you're at, but is perhaps a would-be entrepreneur or somebody in the early stages of business or maybe experienced but having tough challenges at the moment?

Gosh, well, *[Laughing]* I'd get them to sign up to my Business Alchemy programme actually. I only put a price tag of £8 on it because I wanted to make it really, really affordable. I want people to understand that the results they are getting are completely matched to their vibration and to the energy they're putting out – most people just don't get it. I get letters and emails all the time from people who are in a dark place. They're in full-blown victim mode. This happened and then that happened, and this person came along and stole all my money, and then my partner left me and ya-da-da-da-da-da-da *[like machine-gun fire]*... They don't understand that they are in complete victim mode, having completely given all their power away to these characters that have shown up as a match to their own broken energy.

When you really take on board that *you* are the point of attraction and you start to really shift that vibration – and it's quite easy to do, through affirmations and energy work – you start to get a totally different set of results. It's very magical and it's really powerful. I just wish we would teach everyone these basic skills because they take you out of a place of lack and despondency into a place of where you're working with joy and passion. I do think everyone is being drawn to their higher soul purpose.

What people have to do at the moment, what everyone is being forced to do is let go of the stuff that isn't working to make the space for the new to come through. But they are reluctant to do it. We're very stuck because when we're in a place of fear, we don't want to let go. That is the big challenge at the moment – letting go and allowing the new energy to come through.

A lot of people are resistant to change and are frightened of it, but when they understand that the whole Universe is flow and change and relentless, they can understand that nothing ever stays the same.

And when you actually have that big letting go, when you do something that seems scary and there just seems to be no alternative, and you do it ... then there is that release and the feeling of bliss ... You think, *My goodness, why was I resisting?*

Yes, definitely. Exactly, and we do live a lot of our life in resistance. But when you get into that magical place – and it's easy to lose that connection with it – it's really fun ... and life becomes a real adventure.

At the end of Rachel's *Business Nightmares*, there's a section called 'Contact Me'. There she has written 'If I can help you in any way I can, I will. All you have to do is ask.' That's very easy to write, but less easy to put into practice. Yet Rachel is true to her word – both before she wrote those words in the book and after.

Around April 2007, my younger daughter Rebecca finished writing the first draft of her book *POW Habits*.[h] As she and I had no experience of the publishing world at that time, she looked around for someone she felt drawn to who could give her feedback. Rebecca chose Rachel, one of her business icons. She was absolutely thrilled to be invited to Rachel's home in Derbyshire.

Rebecca wanted to show appreciation for Rachel's kindness and reflected on what gift she could take. On discovering that Rachel was born in the Year of the Dragon, she decided on a dragon wind chime ... hmmm, perhaps that's another one of those 'weird' things Rachel spoke of ... It was surely no coincidence Rachel was on the first two series of Dragons' Den. Maybe it was not just St George who was looking after Rachel then!

Rebecca will never forget the warmth and generosity shown by Rachel to a young unknown writer. It is so important to have positive role models.

I was therefore not surprised when I received such a prompt, positive response from Rachel to my request for her to be one of my Pilgrim Mothers – but I was delighted. I find it interesting that in all the stories told in my book, each woman experiences a time of great lack or loss – whether financial or emotional or some other way of feeling dispossessed. Rachel is no exception. Yet from this depth of despair and deepest challenge comes the greatest learning and insights. It's as if it teaches a sense of humility and a trust in a force beyond one's own physical limitations. I've known that feeling of desperation till I've been forced to let go of what I was clinging to – relationships, house, money, possessions, whatever.

In that moment of release there is an overwhelming sense of relief. You break free of your shackles, let yourself be called away from the humdrum and move on to your next adventure.

Rachel has answered her calling. I absolutely know she has an important role to play in the dawning New Era of business – a Business Alchemist who is showing the way for others. We each have our path. Are you following yours?

"… from this depth of despair and deepest challenge comes the greatest learning and insights."

JANE NOBLE KNIGHT

GILL FIELDING

"My purpose in life is to light the spark of financial possibility for as many people as I can get to in my lifetime."

Secret Millionaire and 'Money Mum', property investor, FSA regulated Chartered Accountant, public speaker, writer, TV and radio presenter, and author of *Riches – The 7 Secrets of Wealth You Were Never Told*, Gill is a wife and mum whose humble roots were in London's East End. A self-made millionaire who featured on TV series *Secret Millionaire*, Gill is passionate about educating and giving families financial tools, such as the Financial Five a Day, to secure their future through the Fielding Financial Family. Gill is married to Martin and lives in Sussex with their three wonderful children and a menagerie of rescued animals.

www.fieldingfinancialfamily.com

A Conversation with
Gill Fielding

Money Mum

I bet that if I were to sing the line from the song of the same name from the musical *High Society – Who wants to be a millionaire?* – most people would respond with 'I do' not 'I don't'. I know I certainly would. I'm fascinated by self-made millionaires. I love hearing their stories and how they got to be where they are today. I suppose that's one of the reasons why I love Channel 4's *Secret Millionaire*. Another reason is seeing how profound the impact is on both the millionaires and the people they help. Gill Fielding appeared in one of my all-time favourite episodes in Series 2. She blended back into the East End where she grew up and demonstrated clearly by her actions how she was able to succeed despite the poverty.

In September 2009 I was due to attend a Triumphant Event in London. Initially I had been drawn by the appearance of Peter Thomson who was billed as the UK's leading Product Creator. Gill was a later addition to the speakers. I was actually away that week at my French friend's house in the Ardèche and was not due back till the early hours of the day before. With all the usual demands of a first day home after a holiday and the very early start needed, I was talking myself out of going. However, something was calling me. So I followed the call.

Gill was the first speaker in the afternoon – the traditional graveyard slot. Not today! Gill was electrifying. Her presentation was based on questions people asked her about *Secret Millionaire*. I found answers to questions I didn't know I had! Gill's CD programme 'My Daughter Wanted a Pet – So I Bought Her a Greyhound' was included in Peter's programme, which I had invested in. So I listened to Gill's advice regularly on car journeys.

I subsequently met Gill on about six occasions when she ran various workshops in connection with a financial programme I later joined. She was always the same – bright, breezy, laughing, smiling, poking fun at herself and others. Her shoulder-length, blonde, wavy hair was as informal as she was – her clothes as colourful. Refreshingly, Gill has retained her East End accent unlike some successful people who end up with strange hybrid accents – which to my ear just sound unnatural.

I hear Gill's familiar voice as we connect on Skype at 10 am on the dot. It is exactly the precision I would expect from accountant Gill. She then tells me she forgot to charge up her wireless headset overnight, so she has just plugged it in. Human too – phew! We begin the call with Gill's old headset, but the sound quality is unclear. Thankfully, when Gill switches back to her partially charged headset, there's enough juice for us to finish our conversation uninterrupted. I listen, thoroughly entertained, as Gill responds to my questions quickly and fluently.

Gill is definitely not the 'daft tart' she calls herself – as you will discover. Join me in finding out more about her genuine 'rags to riches' story...

You're sitting there now in your home in rural East Sussex, Gill. It's a far cry from the backstreets where you grew up. What was life like for you as a child?

Well, my start in life was very odd, but in retrospect it was the formation of me as an entrepreneur and as a character. I was born into a very poor family in the East End of London. We lived in a terraced 2-up 2-down that backed onto the sewer's bank. I was quite old before I realised that sewers normally went underground; but in the East End of London they were up there on the streets, stinking away. So I grew up surrounded by smell and pollution.

We were quite a close-knit family. I was the youngest of three children. Unfortunately, the middle one was born completely mentally handicapped. He's still alive today and he has a mental age of about six months. In the '50s there wasn't much help for families with a disabled child. So my poor mum and dad – my mum in particular – spent all their time looking after Raymond. I think actually she forgot that I was there. Subsequently, she did have a nervous breakdown and Raymond was taken into care because of the strain on the family. It meant that from my very young days, up until I was around thirteen, I was completely isolated and left alone. I had no money and no anything. I had the door key around my neck so I could let myself in and out as I went to and from school. My mum would take Raymond to a day centre and forget about me. I would sit in the gutter outside the house and neighbours would take me in and give me a bit of lunch and a bit of tea.

So it was very weird. In today's society, I would be whipped into care in the shake of a dog's tail. But what it meant was that I had no support and I never actually felt anyone was *ever* on my side. As a young person, that was very hard; but as I've got older, that's become a big strength for me – I don't really need anybody. I mean I love my family – I love my husband dearly, I adore my children, I work with very supportive people. I'm just amazingly resilient.

So, no love, no support, no money, no nothing. But I sat in the gutter outside the house and became a people watcher. I'd watch the world go by. That has been a godsend because I'm now very good at intuitively picking up people's moods and what they're up to.

Did you have any role models when it came to making money in such a poor background?

Funnily enough, I struggle with that question because I don't think I did have any *financial* role models. But I know quite distinctly that I had two very strong role models – my Auntie Em, who was my mum's older sister, and my Uncle Dennis, who was my dad's younger brother. They taught me about the *emotional* belief in wealth and money and abundance. I actually believe that being wealthy is two-faceted. You need both the technical knowledge and the belief that it's possible *and* the emotional stuff. I call that the Scales of Abundance.

So, although my two role models didn't have money per se, it was interesting that they were both single people. My Auntie Em was a widow and my Uncle Dennis never married, so they just lived for themselves. Whatever little they earned, they spent and enjoyed. I can remember my Auntie Em taking me up to London to the theatre. This was a massively flamboyant gesture. Auntie Em taught me that money is good. Money flows, money comes and money goes. She squirreled a little bit away and managed to buy her own house and all of that kind of stuff. So it was wealth on a relatively low scale in today's terms; but more importantly, she had this spirit of abundance and joy with money that was really important to me as a child.

> "…money is good. Money flows, money comes and money goes."

And likewise, Uncle Dennis. He worked for the local council as a road-sweeper and he lived in one of these prefab houses – a corrugated iron shed provided by the council. So again, very little money but incredibly abundant in his love, support, generosity … this sense of everything is okay, particularly with money. Uncle Dennis and Auntie Em would give me money for sweets. My Auntie Em, particularly, would buy me a book – a *whole* book every time I saw her. That was 7-and-6 [seven shillings and sixpence] in the old days in old money. A *massive* amount.

Then of course Uncle Dennis gave me my first ever £5 note when I was about seven. These two people instilled in me the sense that money is abundant, money flows, money is exciting, money is funny, money is to be enjoyed. I'm quite certain that all these positive beliefs I have about money are why I'm wealthy.

I can totally see that. I believe you've still got the £5 note, framed.

It's not the original, unfortunately, because when I was a teenager, I became a devotee of something called 'the building society'. Before then I had the £5 note hidden in a book in the cupboard. I had one of these regular savings accounts where you could get extra interest each month. I can remember being parked on the doorstep outside the building society on the first of each month, just desperate and itching to pay my money in to get this extra interest.

So I paid the first fiver in there, but very soon after – those big old fivers had gone out of use by then – I bought a 1964 £5 note. *That* is the framed one on my wall. Sadly, not the original but very close.

Indeed. Now you've always been a grafter, Gill. You left school at sixteen with two CSEs and yet you went on to university and to be a Chartered Accountant. How did that happen?

Funnily enough, I went to one of the old-fashioned grammar schools in the East End of London because obviously I was quite bright – but you wouldn't know it from the way I was treated. When I look back, the fact that those teachers couldn't even get *me* – who I have to accept is quite bright – through an O-level is absolutely despicable. I'm very glad to say the school has now been closed down. But the school didn't like me. I didn't fit for whatever reason. I don't know why. I guess I wasn't a *standard* person and they encouraged me to leave school at the age of sixteen. I was very happy to do so because I hated them and they hated me. So there was never any concept of further education.

After a few bizarre jobs, I ended up working as a junior in a library where my role was to put the books back on the shelves in alphabetical order. Sometimes I did and sometimes they got put back higgledy-piggledy because I guess I was a bit of a rebel. But the Head Librarian there obviously saw a spark in me and said, "Why don't you go and get yourself educated?" I was at that 16–18 year old stage, with all this independence and resilience I'd had as a very young child kicked in. With her guidance, I knew that *unless* I got myself educated and *unless* I got myself sorted and *unless* I got myself a decent job, I was going to be stacking shelves forever.

I had friends who were on the streets, literally. I had friends whose parents – fathers in particular – were in prison. I didn't want that for me. It wasn't really a conscious thing that I wanted to fight my way out of the gutter – it was quite an organic, natural thing for me to do. I knew I wanted a better life. The librarian basically said, "Off you go and do A-levels in a sixth form college." Although her support was indirect and subconscious – in a way, subliminal – it was obviously enough, with my drive, to get myself back into education.

I did a deal with the sixth form college where I could sit at the back of classes, as long as I kept quiet and didn't disturb anyone because I wasn't bright enough, so they thought, to do the actual courses. But it was a new college and they needed the numbers to get their grant from the government. Within a few weeks I'd turned myself round. I came out with grade A A-levels and went to university.

All the time I was working very hard. I've always worked in pubs, pulling pints. I've always done cleaning jobs. As you say, graft, graft, graft. When I decided I wanted to go to university, I set myself a target to earn enough money in about eighteen months to be able to buy myself a house. I knew that the biggest expense was the accommodation. At the time, the state paid the fees and I always knew that I could do pub jobs and stuff to earn food, but the accommodation bothered me. So I worked full-time for the VAT office during the day and then I'd walk from there to what was one of the first ever David Lloyd leisure centres. It was big, with a casino and a restaurant and everything, in Essex. They would give me my tea and I'd work till midnight, and because I was a late shift worker, they would pay for my taxi back home.

I'd then get up at seven the following morning, walk to the VAT office and start the 24 hours again. Even during my lunch breaks, I took on a job delivering leaflets. (I was working for the civil service, so we had the formal one-hour lunch breaks.) As soon as 12 o'clock came, I'd grab my pile of leaflets and shoot out the door and start delivering. And then I packed in the weekends with a couple of cleaning jobs and working in a pub.

That's incredible, Gill.

It seemed like great fun at the time. I've always been very good at combining moneymaking with fun. I *loved* doing the late shift in the leisure centre. I was young and fancy-free. I'd get all the men buying me drinks and then I'd inevitably pick one so that when I finished my shift, if it was a weekend, he'd take me to dinner in the restaurant downstairs. So I managed, through this cycle, to get myself completely fed and watered on a daily basis by a combination of my employer and the men I picked up in the bar. *[Laughing]*

I had a fantastic life, lots of friends. In my free moments on Saturday nights, I'd also be shaking my stuff down in the nightclub as well. It became my life, and, of course, the more you interact with customers at that level, the bigger the tips are etcetera, etcetera. So I learned back then that if you really pander to a customer, they give you lots of money, which was useful later on.

You saved an amazing amount of money to buy that first house at the age of nineteen.

I did. I managed to save about £4,800. The house itself only cost £7,490, so I only had to get a small mortgage of £2,000 and a bit, which I managed to get fairly easily, funnily enough, because I had such a *massive* deposit. So, I had a tiddly mortgage and threw myself into university.

As soon as I got there, I went round all the coffee bars and said, "Can I work for you for free in return for food?" I got myself a job doing a shift in one of the coffee bars and then I could take a sandwich and stuff for my lunch. An elderly lady was running the coffee bar. After a while she said, "Do you mind banking the money as well?" Within about six months, I was doing a shift, doing the accounts, looking after the cash and feeding myself permanently there. So that was the start of *another* entrepreneurial business where I learnt that if you put the buns out early, you generate more cash and so on. Of course, I got used to banking the cash and doing the accounts and managing the money, which again was a real good learning for later.

What were you studying at university, Gill? Was it related to maths and finance?

No, not at all. I was completely *un*directed and *un*guided and I don't know why, but I applied to do English Literature. I liked Shakespeare; I liked Hamlet, which was where I'd hidden my original fiver. When I got to university, I studied Hamlet again because it was a thing that I was comfortable with. Sometimes I think, *If only I'd done Business Studies... if only I'd done this... if only I'd done that...* but actually *I* believe that people perform best when they are multi-disciplined. Doing a degree in English didn't stop me going on to be a Chartered Accountant. I got into Price Waterhouse on the back of talking to the partner about ballet. I never mentioned business or maths at all. I thrived at Price Waterhouse – despite the fact that the night before I started training, I sat at home crying because I couldn't even work a calculator *or* work out a percentage. I was totally backward in those skills at the time, but I grew to love the numbers and all was fine. So I'm glad I did an oddball type of degree, really.

What happened next, Gill?

Well, funnily enough, again, not really very scripted, but I'd started buying properties at nineteen. I bought the original one for £7,500, sold it for £30,000, bought one in London for £40,000, sold that for £160,000. I was working for Price Waterhouse at this time. Once I sold the second one for £160,000, I had a light bulb moment. If I bought another house for £250,000 in the early '80s, it would be a mansion with a swimming pool. I realised I didn't need any more houses. So I sold the one for £160,000, bought one for myself to live in and bought my first ever investment flat in Tewkesbury.

I made up my mind that every time I sold one, I would buy two. So the property portfolio got off and running while I was working for Price Waterhouse. My wealth was accumulating in the background without really any big input from me. Then I met my husband, got married and had my three children. When I had my third child, I worked throughout the whole thing. I was Finance Director of a bank and then I went on to be Chief Executive of a financial services company. But when I had my third daughter, I just got exhausted – probably post-natal depression – and decided that I didn't really want to go back to work, much to the annoyance and distress of my Chairman where I was working at the time. They offered me loads more money to go back, but it just didn't feel right.

I stayed at home and slept for a couple of weeks and righted myself. Then one day I sat at my computer and thought to myself, *Okay, what shall I do now?* I was piddling around on my spreadsheets and realised that with all the properties I had, I was already a millionaire. I thought, *Well, that's all right then. I'm not going back to work.* That was the start of my path educating other people because it was such a natural thing for me to become wealthy. I'd done it inadvertently. Even though it had taken me twenty years, I had accumulated my first million.

I then started to write articles about wealth, and that's where the current career path took off really, when my daughter was born. That was fifteen years ago.

That's an incredible story. What would you do with the current education system to encourage a healthier attitude to wealth?

Oh gosh. Well, about 197 things I want to say there, so you might have to stop me on Tuesday week. But we are not educating our children, *at all,* to cope with financial life. We teach them how to dissect a frog, what an oxbow lake might look like, what Henry VIII did. We teach them some fantastic stuff, and I don't deny any of that at all, but we don't teach people the fundamentals.

I think there's a financial five-a-day that *everybody* needs to be taught as a young person – and older people as well – because people just don't get it. Number one is *understanding what a bank does* and how to physically transact your money. Most kids come out of school and don't know how to choose and open a bank account.

Number two is *understanding debt and credit* and how to cope with it, get rid of it, love it, maintain it and so on.

Principle number three is *understanding how you spread your money out* from one payday to the next, or even one benefit day to the next, because people don't have any sense of budgetary skills nowadays. They get their money on Day One and by Day Two, it's gone, and so by Day Three, they're at Payday Loans, looking for ridiculous borrowings to last them to the next payday. Let's teach people how to spread their money over the given period.

The fourth principle is about *understanding some future sense of money* and perhaps saving a little, or your future is very, very bleak… As we know, the government can't afford the current pensions regime.

The fifth principle really is the most important one, and that's *a sense of purpose and independence.* We need people to understand that they are responsible for their money. It's not the state. It's not social services. It's not somebody else – it's *you.* And unless *you* do it, you are never going to have any money. The state's looking at a national budget. They don't care about individuals.

So we *have to* get this 'Financial Five a Day' out to the world and talk to everybody. This last one about self-reliance and independence comes partially from belief because our young people, particularly, don't believe that wealth is possible for them. They think *fame* is possible via X Factor and all these other things. They see the fame gig and, I suppose, as a knock-on from that they see that wealth might come. But no ordinary sixteen year old on the street understands that they are capable of becoming wealthy if they just choose to follow the fundamental five, like I did.

They are basically the skills I learned as a child, sitting in the gutter. But parents, culture and the education system knock out of kids any joy with money. Most kids have a natural joy playing with money, saving money, playing with coins. It's magical, it's sparkly, it's lovely. Most parents unfortunately start to tell their children that love of money is bad, in some way or another, and certainly schools do that. When my youngest daughter was at school, her *geography* teacher told her that credit cards were bad. In some circumstances, they're bad, but in some circumstances, they're good. It's not the love or dislike of credit cards that's important; it's understanding them, being educated about them.

I always say financial education is just like sex education. There's no point saying to children, or anybody really, "Don't do credit cards" because everybody's going to do it. What we need to do is, like sex education, teach children to do it safely and to protect themselves. *That's* what it's about and, unfortunately, our government just doesn't get that. Although I bash down the government's door periodically and they *get it* when I talk to them one on one, basically they don't care because a government is only interested in getting re-elected in five years' time. Unfortunately, some of these educational things, like pensions and so on, are a forty-year gig.

> "Mothers, particularly, are the world's educators."

Governments aren't interested in forty-year gigs. They're interested in five years. That's why I'm now the self-appointed Money Mum. Anybody reading this can go onto www.moneymum.com and see what I'm up to. I have a campaign for cash commonsense and I'm collecting signatures to go back to the government with. Mothers, particularly, are the world's educators. We are ideally positioned to teach, when the babies are at our knee, these fundamental things, and then they'll be safe and secure going into the future.

Financial education's a big, big passion, a mission, for me. I thought somebody needed to do something about that, and in all honesty, it's got to be me, it's got to be you and it's got to be the mums.

Good for you.

Your three children have been brought up very differently from the way you were. How have you instilled lessons of financial independence in them?

In a word, I haven't. I've brought them up in a spirit of abundance for sure, but I haven't been in their face with wealth creation. Although I can tell their friends how to do it and they listen, kids don't really listen to their own mum. No matter how famous I am or whatever I do, I'm still only their mum and I'm in the way when they want to watch the telly.

However, I've taught them basics. I've taught them that when they get money from their Nan or whoever, to save half and to spend half. So they've all got their building society savings accounts. I was looking at my seventeen-year-old son's account yesterday. He's got £7,000 in the building society and £2,000 in the bank and so on. So they do get it at that level. All of my children like playing with money. If you can make money fun and exciting, and stop this negativity, then they will grasp it themselves.

If you make *them* go down to the building society to get the book updated, they see what interest they have. It's like a bonus. From a very young age, my kids have been very attuned and used to talking to the lady behind the counter about their money. I'd also get them to play games and estimate how much the interest would be.

We invite our personal bank manager round to our house for lunch when the kids are there; they listen to conversations about overdrafts, mortgages, etcetera. It's about letting the information be freely available and, with their natural curiosity, they'll pick it up. Our eldest daughter, who's twenty-two, is going to buy her third house in the summer because *she* gets the house thing. My son gets the investing thing, so he is very interested in share and currency trading. The youngest one is interested in spending her money in Top Shop, but that's another story…

They all get there in different ways at different times. If you overforce children – we all know this – they'll deliberately do the opposite because that's what, particularly, teenagers do.

You also refer to people who join your programmes as 'your family'. Where does that idea come from, Gill?

It probably comes from my own personal need to be connected to groups of people because I never had that for myself. Wealth is a team sport – quicker, easier and better if you share with people and support each other. On your own, it's really hard. I always say, "I'd rather have 50 per cent of something than 100 per cent of nothing." So I'm very keen to joint venture with people.

So many people would say, "I really wish I was a member of your family," because I would tell stories about my kids and their dad and things I was doing with them in terms of money. I suddenly realised a few years ago that they *could* all be members of my financial family, even if they're obviously not my biological family. The more people I help, the richer I become. Bizarrely, a lot of people think that if you help other people become wealthy, you're less rich. That's baloney. It's nonsense. I believe in this massive ocean of money. Everybody can contribute to the sea and everybody can draw from the sea. It's just a choice thing – how much you want to have.

I believe passionately in this massive, unified financial family. I see my role in life is to support people and to *show* them that wealth is possible. I really am very emotional about that as an issue.

In your DVD, *Riches*, you say that 75 per cent of self-made millionaires are rags-to-riches entrepreneurs. You're one yourself, Gill. Why such a high percentage?

The stat is absolutely right – three quarters of millionaires are self-made. They do it themselves from the gutter up or from wherever they start up. I think that's just a natural, evolutionary thing. The other 25 per cent are inherited wealth. That too has its challenges because when you get given money, you haven't had a chance to build up your own beliefs about money. Your scales of abundance – this two-sided thing I mentioned earlier – aren't in balance. So, inherited wealth is very easy to lose. You didn't do anything to get it, so it's quite easy to let it go.

Also, you might not believe that you deserve it, so you will contrive to lose the money. We've seen lots of really high profile, wealthy people do that.

The self-made stat is a fantastic endorsement of everything I've been saying because *anybody* can become a millionaire if they choose to. People who are self-made are much better at it. It took me *twenty years* to make my first million, but every subsequent million has happened quicker and quicker. It's like any skill – once you learn the skills as an entrepreneur, you become rich very quickly.

In fact, it wouldn't surprise me if that split of 75/25 per cent didn't get bigger where the 75 per cent becomes 80 or 85 per cent over time because evolution will promote the entrepreneur and will minimise the inherited wealth. So it's an interesting stat.

I always think of government as being like people who inherit money or win the lottery. They haven't had to earn it, so they're frivolous with it rather than careful.

That's a fascinating thought, Jane, and it's not only *that*. The government are dealing with what I call 'macroeconomics'. They're talking about gross domestic products and M4 and M0 and loads of stuff that most us haven't got a solitary clue about.[1] The biggest problem with any government is that they're looking macro. I'm not party political at all, but what we need is a Chancellor who looks at micro, at budgeting, at what's in your purse, at your fundamental Financial Five a Day, and who interacts with Money Mums.

I think history will show that Gordon Brown was a fantastic Chancellor of the Exchequer at a macro level. But he knew absolutely *nothing* about what people need and how to get £2 in your purse – this micro, fundamental grassroots thing. The government approaches all of our country's financial challenges from the top down and the only way we will solve these challenges is from the bottom up. The sooner we get this campaign for cash common sense out there to teach people the Financial Five a Day, the quicker this will happen because people will be doing it from the bottom up.

That's really interesting, Gill, because you break the mould of the archetypal introverted accountant. You're a self-confessed people person. And as a mum, you see finances in a different way to an awful lot of politicians.

I guess I do, but that's because I look at money from the gutter. I can remember the joy and pleasure I got from looking at that first £5 note and how I enjoyed playing with it and adding to it. So I know that what impacts real people is the small tangible stuff. Even as I'm sitting here in my office, I've probably got close to £2,000 in notes just littered around because I think money is joyous. I think it's funny, powerful, sexy, amusing, brilliant, awesome. Every time I save another £5 note or I put another £10 note in my drawer, it's a real boost to me personally. That fun with money is lost on most people and certainly I don't think governments get it.

> "I think money is joyous. I think it's funny, powerful, sexy, amusing, brilliant, awesome."

People say to me, "You hang on to your working class roots." Yes I do because being in the gutter with a £5 note is the important bit as far as our country's economy is concerned. It's that basic, raw, starting money. Not some macro gross domestic product nonsense that's a trillion pounds with five noughts on it.

What impact did going back to your roots in *Secret Millionaire* have on you?

Well four and a half years on, I'm still totally committed to all of my people. I still pay for the dance school, I still pay for the little girl etcetera.

---

1   M0 and M4 refer to different measures of money supply. There's also M1, M2 and M3.

The programme was a real epiphany for me. I'll be honest; I wasn't really interested in making it. I went with the intention with getting it over and done with very quickly, but they took me back to the East End of London, very close to where I was born. From about day two, the sledgehammer started to hit me square in the face. I was actually working in a greasy spoon café in a market with some women that could have been me. We were born in the same area – one of the women even went to the same school as me. It was like looking at myself in a different pinny.[2]

I went home and sobbed my heart out because I realised how far I'd come, how much I knew and how powerful that was. I was actually overwhelmed because I realised, meeting and working with those women, that I'd made myself financially free since I left the area. Not only that, I knew exactly how to do it again. I was allowed to earn £10 a day, so £100 for the ten days' filming because you're meant to be living on the statutory minimum wage. By the time I had finished, I had £83 invested, I'd started a small business and I'd got an idea for buying a property. All from the minimum wage in this country. The film crew just *could not* believe how powerful and energetic I was because I immediately reverted to type. I wanted to work extra shifts in the café. I did deals with the café owner. "If I clean the toilets, can I take home a piece of bread pudding and a newspaper?" I immediately went back onto a barter-type mode of getting what I needed for no money.

The producer said to me, "If *you don't stop* all this other stuff," because I'd gone off on a completely different path, "we're going to lock you in at night!" *[Laughing]* I was getting up early to sort out the newspapers in the local newsagents and while I was waiting for the film crew, I'd walk the streets, looking for coins on the floor. I'd pick up pennies, two pence pieces … I even found a pound one day. And of course, when you're only earning £10 a day, a pound is a *massive* amount of money.

I was getting used to feeding myself and living from tips in the café and stuff that I picked up off the floor. It drove the producer absolutely nuts, so one day when I'd earned £20, she stole £10 of it, saying, "How do you feel now?" I looked at it and then her and said, "That's absolutely fine. This is plenty for me. I'm going to be wealthy off this £10 note." The next day, she cut the gas off so I didn't even have hot water. It absolutely drove the film crew mad that I was so happy on £10 a day, still creating wealth.

It was an amazing programme for me – a big, big event. It all happened in two weeks of my life. I went from being fairly naïve about wealth creation to being incredibly focussed because I realised that I *had* started the wealth journey all over again. I was probably only eighteen months away from being a millionaire again, starting with £10. So I came home and cried for a fortnight because it was so shocking and powerful. Then I sat down and thought, *Okay, if you know what the path is, if you know what the formula is, write the darn things down.* That's how the film *Riches* got made and the book *Riches* got written. It was about the basic things that I do *naturally* to create wealth.

Brilliant. Out of the fifty-nine millionaires that they've had on the show in the UK, just twelve – 20 per cent – have been women. Yet you and Dawn Gibbins have been two of the most generous by a long way. Are women more innately generous?

I happen to know Dawn. In fact, I know most of the women Secret Millionaires. I think it's not so much that women are *more* generous, but men, generally, are *less* generous. Men have this

---

2   Informal form of pinafore. Apron

competitive thing that women don't have as strongly. Men want to be better than the next man, so it encourages a sense of scarcity – this holding on tightly to everything you've got, just in case the bloke next door gets some of it and gets bigger than you. Unfortunately, testosterone stops men from being as open and as generous as they could be.

I think men do a lot more willy waving. They want to be the biggest and the best. Women are much more open and giving than that. As a mother, as soon as you have your own child, you realise that there is somebody else in the world far more important than you, and that's your child. Even if you don't have children, as a woman you have some kind of maternal love for another thing, whether it be your cat or your dog or a baby. Women are naturally much more loving and want to support other people. I've been deliberately diverse here to prove a point – men are much more ego-driven than women, and that results in them not giving as much money away. Once you get to a certain level, like Bill Gates and Richard Branson, the floodgates open. But for the level you're talking about, I think women are much more prone to being generous.

What other qualities do women entrepreneurs bring into the world of business?

Lots and lots. We know that women actually perform better than men, given the same circumstances. Statistics from the US prove that women-owned businesses do much better than men-owned or mixed businesses. So women, we know, are very strong. We also know that if a woman invests in shares, she will outperform a man doing the same thing.

There are lots of reasons. First of all, to take a very simplistic level, I'm going to talk recipes – this is a very sexist, minor example. If women have got the recipe for a cake handed down from their grandmother, they just re-run the recipe again and again. They're very good at following formulas, while men are not. Men will say, "This is a fantastic cake, but I can make it better. So I'm going to start tweaking it."

Men *will fiddle* with every success formula because in the main, men think they can do it better. I'm deliberately being very sexist and generalising here; but as a rule, women are much better at saying, "I'm going to stick to this because it works." Women are multi-tasking all the time and they want to do something that's quick and easy. If they can follow the same recipe, whether that be for a cake or for wealth creation, they will do it. So I think that's number one.

Secondly, women are much more aware of the outside world. They have less ego to bring to it, so they're much more aware of customers – customer needs, customer service and communications. It's a proven fact that women have got far superior communication skills. Research on babies shows that by nine months old, the communication part of a baby girl's brain is developed far beyond a boy's. It's a hormonal, chemical thing. There's no point being silly about it; it's just a fact. So women are much better at communication skills and that's vital in business.

Thirdly, I think women are happier to embrace a sense of intuition – a gut feeling – a sense that it's the right thing to do. This tends to lead to honesty, to transparency. I'm not saying men

> "I think women are happier to embrace a sense of intuition – a gut feeling – a sense that it's the right thing to do. This tends to lead to honesty, to transparency."

are dishonest, but men are not quite as open and most certainly don't embrace intuition. Richard Branson does. He would say, very publicly, "Most of my business decisions are based on intuition." So actually, some very successful men do use intuition. Generally, I will go with "That feels right to me," whereas a man will say, "I want to see the spreadsheet, I want to see the facts, I want to see the research; I want to see the return."

I *also* want to see that, but sprinkled with a sense of 'What's my gut telling me about this as a business opportunity?' So I think women, naturally, have some really powerful skills and, if we can just get the knowledge out to them, given the opportunity, women will beat men in business every single day of the week.

That's excellent news. Now you've said yourself that you actually don't need to work anymore, Gill; so what really fires you up to continue?

I think this eventually comes to everybody. For 99 per cent of the population, their purpose in life is to get up, to go to work, to earn enough money to pay the gas bill, feed the kids, and that is actually, by habit, very purposeful. When you don't have to get up in the morning because you don't need the money or you have to retire, your life takes on a very bizarre twist. Suddenly, your purpose in life has gone. You have a choice. You either stay in bed and rot, be miserable and paint your nails and do nothing of any meaning, or you start spending your life on something purposeful.

I actually had that dichotomy quite a few years ago. Suddenly, there wasn't any purpose in my life. I spent a lot of time working out who I was and why I was on the planet. To cut a very long story short, I realised that my purpose in life is to light the spark of financial possibility for as many people as I can get to in my lifetime. I believe my whole life has been gearing up to that from the start in the East End of London.

I was born in exactly the same room as my father thirty-two years before. My father, Reg, is eighty-six and he's poor. He's living off a state pension. Yet I was born in exactly the same room, same genetic make-up, the same start in life, and I'm a multi-millionaire. I actually think that I was born in that room so that I could prove the point that it is possible for *anybody*. And it's what flows to me. It's where my energy is. It's where my intuition is. It's always about giving this sense of financial possibility.

Of course, this mission leads to an *amazing* life that is fun and energetic and so on. When I'm not on purpose, sometimes I think, *I'll have a couple of days off. I'll knit and chill out and watch the telly.* Within about an hour, I start getting morose and lethargic and depressed, and the cycle starts going the other way. So for me, this isn't work. This is my life. This is who I am and I'm the best possible me I can be when I'm lighting the spark for people. That's when my life works and everything starts to go on fast forward and the joy and money comes. I'm lucky enough to know my life mission. A lot of people go through their lives never discovering their true purpose, never being the best them they can possibly be, and that breaks my heart because I know what a difference it makes to me personally.

I am lucky enough to live my mission every single second of every day and what a joyous life that is.

Fantastic. And what legacy do you want to leave to the world, Gill?

I'm very passionate about a legacy. I started building a legacy for my own children because your love for your children as a mother is so overwhelming; I wanted them to have everything forever. I can't be there forever because I'm going to die. Suddenly, when you have children, all of those thoughts occur to you. That's when I started recording my material onto DVDs and CDs and writing it all down because I need to know that in fifty years' time, when I'm long gone, my kids can sit round a kitchen table and say, "What was it Mum said about property investing?" and they can get access to it. They can re-run the DVD and play the tapes and so on and actually see what it was.

"On my gravestone I want you to write, 'She lit the spark'..."

I think it was Stephen Covey who said that the purpose of any life is to live, love, learn and leave a legacy.[h] I live life to the full. I have plenty of love, I'm always learning and a legacy is very important.

So it started for me with my own children. If I can leave the legacy of this financial possibility, if I can leave the concept of Money Mum, if I can leave the concept of the Financial Five a Day, if I can leave the concept of the financial family, then that will live on after me. My mission will continue long after I've gone.

That's an incredibly powerful thing. I have said to my husband already, "On my gravestone I want you to write, 'She lit the spark' ... because that's the point for me.

Gill is a real live wire, so it's 100 per cent appropriate that she should be lighting sparks. And what a great inspiration she is. She proves that whatever our starting point, we can all become millionaires – if we want to be. Gill demonstrates clearly that there are certain good habits that we can cultivate in order to become more abundant – in health, wealth, happiness or whatever – starting right now.

One is to be grateful for *everything*. It is probably easier to be grateful with hindsight, just as Gill appreciated her early hardships because of all the benefits she gained, such as independence and resilience. However, Gill's story also shows the importance of gratitude, regardless of our current situation. Despite her poor home circumstances, Gill appreciated the gifts she was given as a child by her Auntie Em and Uncle Dennis. She focussed on positives, not negatives; so positive experiences flowed to her.

I remember myself being in a very bleak place a few years ago when I was finding it hard to see positives in my situation. Then I came across the idea of a gratitude journal where every evening I wrote down what I was grateful for that day. The first attempt was really difficult, but then each day became progressively easier. Within days I was covering pages with my thanks, and lo and behold life improved for me. What you focus on, you attract.

An equally valuable gift Gill received from her auntie and uncle was the sense of joyousness and spirit of abundance around money they engendered in her. Money was to be enjoyed. I could feel, see, hear, smell and taste the pleasure Gill gets from money. There are absolutely no negative connotations for her where money's concerned. So money loves her. It flows to her. There is no limit to her abundance – or ours. As Gill says, there's an ocean of abundance. We just have to choose abundance – in limitless oceans, not tiny puddles.

Whatever Gill has achieved, she totally deserves. The responsibility she took for herself from a very young age is truly impressive. She focussed on what she wanted and followed through, one step at a time, with great perseverance. I love how Gill described her life as fun, even when she was working all hours for eighteen months to buy her first house. I can imagine these circumstances being related by some people with a sense of weariness and drudgery as an example of how tough life has been – but not in Gill's case. Moneymaking and fun are Gill's lifelong buddies.

Gill lives every day fulfilling her mission. Her life is exciting and joyous as a result. We all have a mission in life. The good news is that it's never too late to discover it. Look for what makes you come alive… and do more of it. Therein lies your gift to the world – and the key to your happiness.

"… there's an ocean of abundance. We just have to choose abundance – in limitless oceans, not tiny puddles."

JANE NOBLE KNIGHT

PENNY POWER

"I'm driven to ensure that there is some corner of this Internet world that feels good for people who are very values driven."

Social networking expert, author of *Know Me, Like Me, Follow Me*, entrepreneur and popular public speaker, Penny, with her husband Thomas, founded Ecademy in 1998. UK's first online social business network, Ecademy is a global operation, which, at its peak, supported 620,000 SMEs to migrate to the digital world in over 200 countries. Penny is also founder of Frontier Digital Coaching and Digital Youth Academy. Penny has been married to Thomas for twenty-two wonderful years and has three children. They live in the countryside in South East England. Working with her husband is Penny's "…dream come true … We laugh a lot together, we travel a great deal to meet members all over the world and we love our family time."

www.pennypower.co.uk

A Conversation with Penny Power

Internet Mummy

How would you picture a 'triumphant event'? I certainly imagined a positive experience. And so it was when I joined hundreds of others one Wednesday evening in January 2008 to listen to Dr John Demartini at a packed-out venue in Central London. I had to concentrate on his every word as I had never heard anyone speak so fast while staying articulate. I was duly impressed and went on to attend many more Triumphant Events.

I have their founder, Daniel Priestley, to thank for introducing me to Penny Power, who I saw speak at two Triumphant Events. I was struck by the contrast between her and the other speakers – not just because they were mostly male, but also because Penny exuded a definite feminine energy that was very gentle whilst totally professional. Her rather understated style was very different from Demartini's. She stood behind the lectern and read from her notes, whereas he paced about energetically with lots of gestures. Both spoke from the heart. The audience was equally enthralled. We hung onto Penny's every word. When she read her poem about social networking, I sat there with tears flowing down my cheeks. I wasn't the only one. For me, Penny's sentiments came from deep within and expressed her values and vision perfectly.

I subsequently saw Penny speak again at an Entrepreneurs' Business Academy event in 2010. The lovely Bev James had very kindly sent me a complimentary ticket. While I waited at the end to thank Bev for her generosity, I noticed Penny standing alone briefly. I took my opportunity to thank her for being such a brilliant role model for women and mothers. I found her to be gracious and modest about her achievements.

When I emailed Penny a request to be one of my Pilgrim Mothers, one Sunday afternoon in late February 2012, much to my surprise and delight, I had a positive response from her just three hours later, expressing her honour that I saw her as a Pilgrim Mother – and I absolutely did!

And so on a rainy St George's Day in London, sheltering under my bright red umbrella whilst avoiding puddles and people, I make my way along wet, shiny pavements to 9 Adam Street, the private club just off the Strand where I have arranged to meet Penny. And there I find her, sitting downstairs in the busy bar/meeting area with her PA, Mel. There's a buzz and a hum about the place; in fact, this enclosed space reminds me of the proverbial hive with comings and goings and conversations.

Penny is easy for me to spot. She looks exactly like her photos – dark eyes and blonde, straight, chin-length bob with full fringe. But it's not just her appearance that's the same – it's that spirit of authenticity about her. Her eyes look directly at you. There's no subterfuge. Every time I see her, I get the strong impression that what you see is what you get – and this time is to be no exception …

When I heard you speak and read your book *Know Me, Like Me, Follow Me*, I thought, Penny has got to be one of my Pilgrim Mothers.

Are *you* a mother?

Yes. I've got two daughters in their early thirties.

Oh, how lovely. Are they mums yet?

Not as yet.

They're all doing it later now. Hannah had gone back to uni and my son and I were talking last night over the Sunday roast. He perceived that Thomas and I had been so young when having children, but we didn't see it that way at the time. Now people are having children much older. There have been such strides in the last fifteen or twenty years in medicine. If you know you've got longer to live like this generation does, you don't have that sense of rush that I had.

When I got married at twenty-three in 1975, the average age for women getting married was twenty-one. So I was actually old when I got married.

I wasn't perceived as young when getting married at twenty-six. As you get older, you become more aware of who you are and there's a danger that you become overly selective when choosing a partner. At twenty-six, it was just lust and love and 'this feels right.' I knew I had to go on a journey with someone and thought this person looks like they could go on a journey with me to find out who I am.

When you started out in life, did you have a mission to do something?

That's an interesting question. I'm the last of four. My siblings were all born in Scotland. My parents moved south about two years before I was born. I was an accident. In fact, my godmother met my mother in a playground, crying, because she'd discovered she was pregnant with me. I've got great parents, but by the time I'd got to twelve, my mum had been a mum for twenty-four years. You have to see it in that context. That's quite a lot of years. She had her first son quite young, so she hadn't had a lot of life to herself.

I did grow up in a really loving family, observing a very busy family life. When I got old enough to take part in it, my siblings had all grown up and gone. We lived in quite an isolated village, so I do remember feeling a sense of loneliness when I was young.

I went to an all girls' convent school. My parents were a classic, hardworking, Scottish couple, but I went to a school in Newbury that was of the wealthy set. My best friend's father was Joe Mercer, the jockey. I remember being on her horse, Tally Ho, but I wasn't from a horsey set. So my social life was fairly disconnected from the school because I didn't do the gymkhanas and horsey things at the weekends.

When I was about ten or eleven, a family moved in next door with a little boy, Toby, who had very severe cerebral palsy. Toby couldn't feed himself and couldn't hold himself up. He became a really big part of my life. My time with Toby was quite a turning point in my self-esteem. I always thanked his mum for letting me see him. I didn't actually realise that I was doing his mum a favour. I always thought she was doing me a favour, letting me come and play with Toby. But I suppose, looking back, it must have been quite a relief for her that somebody visited him. During school holidays, I spent a lot of time at the hospital where he went for day care, and I got to know all the other children there.

What was it about Toby? There was obviously some heart connection there.

I don't know. I think he wasn't lonely – *I* was very lonely. At school I ran a charity event to raise money for Stoke Mandeville Hospital. I really don't know what sparked it, but there was something in me that wanted to try and make a difference to people from a very young age. In a way, I'm cautious of saying that because it sounds so egotistical, that you could go down a path thinking you could make a difference. But I just didn't want the world to be about my own personal gain.

I think it's actually the opposite of egotistical because you've got a wider purpose for good in the world. But I know there are cynics out there.

Yeah, I know. I think, also, there was my situation of growing up the youngest in my family. I'd hate my sisters to read this, but I realised I got attention if I gave. I was always there to serve. I wasn't able to receive a lot, so I liked making them happy and getting attention in that way. I don't know whether that was a deep-rooted thing.

I think it's also a woman thing. It's part of our hard wiring to give and be of service.

Exactly. Absolutely. The joy you get back from that.

Someone quite early on in Ecademy said to me, "You're a servant leader." I'd never heard the phrase before, so I researched it. I liked the idea. I prefer to lead by serving rather than others serving me. With Maslow's Hierarchy of Needs, people used to say you can start serving others once you've served yourself; but I think you achieve more when you *do* serve others and serve their needs.

Anyway, I ended up wanting to spend my career with cerebral palsic children. I put myself down to become a physiotherapist, but I didn't get in. Unfortunately, my school wasn't academic. We were taught things like needlework and domestic science, so I had a bit of a shock when I got my results. I thought I was quite bright until then. Of course, if you don't follow a curriculum at school, you don't have a chance answering the exam questions.

Then I transferred and spent three years in a Sixth Form, which was brilliant. However, trying to catch up so much, I ended up not having enough qualifications to go the academic route into physiotherapy. So I had an enforced gap year. I worked in a pub and also at a school as a welfare assistant.

A recruitment consultant called Barbara Allen came into the pub and said to me, "You should be in sales." At nineteen-and-a-half, I knew nothing about business. I didn't know you had finance, marketing, sales. I'd never even given business a thought. She convinced me that it would be a much better way to save up money for going to university, where I planned to study psychology and go that route to helping children.

So I joined a computer distributor company. It was 1983, just at the wave of the computer industry. It was very heady and successful. I joined in the February and when I resigned in the September to go to uni, I was taken to the company's CEO, the big cheese, to be convinced that I shouldn't leave because I was really good. That surprised me because I wasn't the classic open-and-close salesperson.

From there I went on a career path until I left the industry at twenty-eight to have Hannah, my first daughter. I met my husband Thomas in that period when I was Sales and Marketing Director. I had a beautiful Mercedes and my own house. I wouldn't have known what was in my bank account. Money didn't even mean anything to me. I had risen through various companies, but I actually came back to the original company to take them through quite a rapid growing stage. Thomas had a contract with one of the manufacturers, so he came to try and get some of my marketing budget.

He used to find it hilarious that I didn't really know what the products did and I couldn't have read a P and L (Profit and Loss). I just loved people. I loved the relationships with our suppliers and the customers and our staff. There was nothing clever about what I did.

Anyway, I left at twenty-eight and had my three gorgeous children. I was determined that I would be a full-time mum, and I really thought I could be. I loved being with them, but there was something about trying to stimulate my mind that was really important to me. However, I was determined not to go back into employment, which meant it was quite a financial strain for Thomas and me at that stage. But both of us believed in that.

During that period that I was out, '92 to '98, the Internet emerged. Everybody was getting excited about it. In fact, before eBay, Thomas and a team of people sold the world's first auction software system to Mercedes for auctioning old cars. I said to him, "I really see this Internet as a shift in humanity where people have a voice and can communicate across the world, and where the good can rise to the top." I'd seen a lot in business that I wasn't keen on, and I just saw this as a chance for people and business to come together and the good would emerge at the top.

> "I really see this Internet as a shift in humanity where people have a voice and can communicate across the world, and where the good can rise to the top."

I could see that there was a rapid increase in people starting businesses from home and more people like me, as a mum, wanting to combine their life with children and business. When I started Ecademy in 1998, I had no idea of the journey I would go on. There was not even a back-of-the-fag-packet business plan.

Very quickly, within about two weeks of the idea, somebody offered to invest a quarter of a million pounds in Ecademy. This person had known me previously in the industry and said I was really onto something. In fact, he saw what I was on to better than *I* could. For him it was an economic investment. That was to be a real lesson in my journey – to make sure you invest with someone who has similar passion and drive for what you're doing, plus values – I'm very values-driven. He was a great guy, but he was definitely in it to make a financial return, whereas *I* wanted to build a community. Every member that joined Ecademy, the first 3,000 members, I got to know. I chatted with them, we ran events, we met them – these are really important building blocks if you're building any community.

I've often said that if you look at companies that start with venture capital income, it's basically an idea put on steroids. It's like building Basingstoke or Milton Keynes. It's very hard to backfill community into new towns, whereas if I look at Farnham, where I live now, it goes back to the seventh century. Its community has been built slowly over time, based on the values of those people. I very much believe communities are built by the early people who have the passion for it and then they invite the next person in.

Anyway, this shareholder wanted to float Ecademy on the stock market. He got it all the way through to six weeks of flotation. At that time, Thomas and I were worth 22 million pounds on paper with our shareholding. I remember lying in bed next to Thomas and saying to him, "This is just obscene and wrong because there is no substance to this yet. There's no volume of any consequence." It was just an idea.

The last company to go out onto the stock market, on that round of investment, was lastminute.com with Martha Lane Fox and Brent Hoberman. Then literally the market crashed. There were loads of very big victims, but we were one of the victims that didn't float in the end. The shareholder then lost his interest and his money. Thomas and I had to raise money to buy back the shares from him so that we could own it again. And then, since 2001, we've been on a big journey, developing an organically built community.

> "They know how to communicate their message as a thought leader and a changemaker, as opposed to someone who knows how to sell."

We have been learning from the inside. On the one hand, watching and observing people who want to use old business values but apply them to modern technology, as opposed to a big cohort of learners who are coming in and are actual changemakers who want to use the Internet as a way of communicating shift. They know how to communicate their message as a thought leader and a changemaker, as opposed to someone who knows how to sell.

I'm seeing the clash of values now inside the Internet. It happens at a small level – two people communicating on Twitter or Facebook or LinkedIn – and on a grand level, the values of Facebook and Google and these large, invested communities. If you Google these big names and their values – 'What are Facebook's values?' – the response is clearly about the 'shareholder value', not 'the values of this community that we stand by'. I think we sit on a cliff edge right now. In ten years' time, will we look back at this point and say, "The Internet has become Mad Max and the good people have actually withdrawn from it," or are there enough people inside it, pushing for the Internet to be a force for good? There's a lot of destruction and a lot of companies just wanting to own and control, which is no different to the old world. I hope I'm one of the voices that say this actually could be something amazing for humanity.

When you look at that issue, where do you create the shift? I believe you create it at grassroots. So I'm now creating a youth community – Digital Youth Academy – and a qualification around social media that will embed young people into companies through an apprenticeship programme that is very much values driven. Those young people understand what it means to be social and to have a friend online as opposed to just the old way of selling, using new technology.

Do you think communities and businesses need to be smaller and represent joint values? What about a Social Contract like the 'Mayflower Compact' that the Pilgrim Fathers created?[1]

Well, we're certainly seeing a shift from the industrial revolution where all the power was with people who got the power first. It worked on an employer principle – if we employ you, we own you. These businesses have increasingly become not just about owning your work time but owning your leisure time as well – and owning your mind. I think we're now seeing a shift to the individual owning the Intellectual Property (IP) and the communication.

I talk about *social capital*. We have *human capital*, which is our knowledge and our IP that we have maybe created. We have our *financial capital*, which is our assets that allow us to make choices, and we have our social capital. As individuals, we are in control of our own social capital.

When I'm on Facebook or Twitter or LinkedIn – and these are *huge* communities – it's up to me as an individual to create my own circle of community around me and make the choices as to who I want to be associated with and what information I want to flow outwards from me. In doing so, rather than controlling or commanding people, I am attracting them towards me by my values and message. Instead of coming from a world where I went out with a fishing net and tried to entrap people, and it was 'Suspect, Prospect, Customer', it's moving to a world where I just have to become a magnet and decide what sort of people I want to attract to me.

> "... rather than controlling or commanding people, I am attracting them towards me by my values and message."

I think you have to learn to play the long game. I mentor a group of ladies in a mastermind group. I was with them last week for a couple of days and I got this sense of a gold rush feeling. There was a real panic in them that everything has to be achieved fast. But the danger with this is you lose the ability to build depth and relationships and real context around you. I'm mentoring these ladies for a year. I want them, in a year's time, to have got to a point where they feel they can be successful. So I'm actually having to slow them down and almost *reduce* their ambition; calm them down and then help them to build from *that* place of authenticity, as a lot of them are building on very rocky foundations. They haven't centred themselves; they haven't really worked out their own voice. I love this quote by Mark Twain, 'The two most important days of your life are the day you are born and the day you discover *why*.'[e] A lot of the women haven't really discovered themselves, so they can't build social capital around themselves yet because they haven't

---

1   The Mayflower Compact is often regarded as the first written North American constitution. The forty-one adult males who signed it served as the initial government of the colony by electing a governor, enacting laws and admitting others to membership as they saw fit.

worked out their vision, their values and their purpose. So there's a dichotomy in many of their activities. They're saying, "I wish I was doing this, but I'm making my money this way." It's almost like stripping it down.

I think a lot of people in business now have to stop this 'connect for connect's sake' and 'broadcast for broadcast's sake', and just centre themselves and say, "If I want to build *social* capital in my life and around my business, how am I going to do that as an individual, rather than as a brand?" It seems that most people have thought about building company brands, but they've not thought enough about building their individual brand.

Have you heard of the Slow Movement? Slow food?

Yes. I lived near Ludlow for fourteen years, which is the foodie capital of the UK. It was the first Cittaslow town in the UK. [2]

I think there is going to be 'slow media' or something similar because there is a need for people to calm down and just consider. We've all got our own profiles. James Knight has developed this system called iMA about the four communication styles.[3] I sit in the 'High Blue', which is classically the person who wants to deliver a purpose and have deep relationships. That's my set of values, so there's a danger that people reading this interview will say, "Well I don't identify with that because I'm in a different communication space."

> "To me, connecting online is about friendship and that's why it's called 'social.'"

To me, connecting online is about friendship and that's why it's called 'social.' If we take ourselves into that friend space and say, "Who am I?" at my best I'm usually being a friend. That means I'm being open, I'm being very random in what I'm willing to talk about and I'm being supportive. The old world comes from being closed, selective and controlling – its business comes from that concept that is about me, my knowledge; I'm keeping it close to my heart; I'm being selective about who; I'm being targeted about where I'm wanting to go; and I'm being very controlling about the outcome.

When we're online, the more that we can go into this open, random, supportive space – which is the true value of being a friend – the more we can understand the shift that's taking place. And that might be more 'Blue' behaviour because 'High Blue' behaviour is about depth, about friendship, about purpose. And also Blues want to take life a little bit slower.

Now I can multitask at an unbelievable rate. I watched the film *How Does She Do It?* with Sarah Jessica Parker and, like most women, I was thinking, *Yeah, and?...* It's not about the ability to be fast-paced; it's not about the ability to multitask. It's about getting value in each day and appreciating the moments with people and taking time – but it is a long-term view.

I so identify with that, but I find that it is a fine line. I can be very driven, like in getting this book finished, and then circumstances may happen to slow me down. I can get very frustrated by

---

2   Cittaslow is a movement founded in Italy in 1999 inspired by the Slow Food organisation. Its goals include improving the quality of life in towns by slowing down their overall pace.

3   James Knight describes iMA as a universal colour-based language designed to maximise connectivity.

the delay, but it makes me question why. Often there's something important that I'm missing. So I have had to learn patience when this happens and take things one step at a time.

And for me, it's also about knowing whether I'm in my *head* or in my *heart*. I did what's called my 'Core Process'.[4] It's a coaching method whereby you discover two words that you really connect with about yourself. It's an interesting process you go through to find them – mine are 'connecting hearts'. My belief is that the Internet should connect at that cerebral level because it's about sharing knowledge, especially the *way* that knowledge is shared and what the intent is.

> "… it's also about knowing whether I'm in my head or in my heart."

I'm very much a living, breathing, pulsating businessperson now. I believe in the importance of business and creating wealth. People call me a social entrepreneur, but I create commercial organisations for wealth, and for people working with me to make wealth, because I do believe money is a form of energy and it's important.

This philosophy then translates into 'how do companies *learn* how to go into that space of creating wealth and still please their shareholders?' I was talking with my daughter, who's nineteen. She was talking about a company, a brand, that have let her down and she said, "Why don't companies spend more time caring about communicating and engaging?" I was saying that they just can't see the return on that yet, and it's almost like there needs to be an index at shareholder level that measures that social engagement. As I said before, it takes a long time. CEOs don't have a long time and this is the big problem now for companies.

You could get a CEO who would sit here and agree with us, but he won't have the time to implement that. Maybe that would mean you end up having to create an underground movement where large companies evolve. What's interested me is that Facebook and Google and LinkedIn – these companies that have grown up with the new philosophy of connecting people – have actually built their business based on shareholders (a lot of Russian and Chinese money) and haven't been able to implement that new philosophy in the way they've structured their *own* companies, the way they treat their own employees. They're still monopolistic; they're about control. They're all about the value to the shareholder again, which is a real shame. I'm interested to see what companies emerge that actually truly reflect this shift toward individualism.

I love the story you tell about Hannah's generosity when, to save her friends' stress one January, she shared with them her mock exam notes that she had spent her Christmas holidays writing, even though they hadn't put in the same effort. It was just so heart-centred of her. You talk and write very touchingly about learning from your children. I think more parents would benefit from learning from their children. What are your hopes for your own children? Can you see them working with you in Digital Youth Academy?

It's interesting because Hannah's gone off classically. She's in her first uni year, doing Law at Warwick, and it's very high pressure. She came back at Easter – she just went back yesterday – and she has worked a bit with me on Digital Youth Academy. She interviewed

4 Core Process was developed by Chris Bull and helps people understand what they are doing when they are at their best.

Theo Paphitis and loved it!

Ross is interested in being an actor because he enjoys performing, and he could see quite a lot of opportunity with that to give young people confidence.

I don't know whether Hannah and Ross will come on-board. I don't run these businesses from a management level, so they wouldn't be coming to work for mummy. It's whether they decide to and if they impress the people who run those companies. They won't be given any privileges, put it that way.

But from a very young age, they've been involved in the business, coming with me to events. We hired a Winnebago for five weeks in 2007 and they travelled through America with us, meeting members. They've done tours in Asia with us and met many members in Europe, so they have grown up understanding the importance of networking and the importance of people in business, and I think that will be reflected in them.

But equally, I've learnt a lot by watching them. I did a talk at UCL[5], which turned out quite interesting. The lecturer who invited me to give this talk really challenged me on the Hannah story and actually asked the students not to consider what I'd shared as being right. She was really forthright about it. She said it was a dog-eat-dog world out there and it wasn't about collaboration. So she wouldn't say that it was right to share your notes because you need to graduate with a competitive advantage to your peers.

I was really disappointed at the end of it. I was thinking, *God, if there are still lecturers and people in schools teaching that set of values – the Dragons' Den and the Alan Sugar style of treating people – there's still a lot of shift to occur.* A lot of young people still go into business with this '80s style, Maggie Thatcher type of indoctrination of how you make wealth. If that's the values of those organisations then the shift's going to take a long time.

But there is a *massive* surge of entrepreneurialism in this young set. In the Digital Youth Academy, we've created a set of values that are centred round twenty or so keywords to do with sharing and collaboration and love and listening and innovation. Anybody who gets involved in the Digital Youth Academy, as an employer, a delivery partner or as a youth, has to buy into the values and reflect them in the way they treat one another. My desire is that we create more demand than supply so that the young person has a choice when they go for their interviews. They can choose which company suits them because at the moment the employment situation is not weighted in favour of young people.

There's also the challenge with the current education system because teachers aren't usually entrepreneurs. So, entrepreneurship is not really taught in schools.

But there is a really healthy shift happening. There's an organisation called the Gazelle Group where five college principals have recruited another fifteen colleges to create a consortium, and it *is* all about shifting and teaching towards an entrepreneurial, enterprising mindset. They're trying to get every teacher to have some form of entrepreneurialism in their curriculum.

So there is a definite shift. It just takes a long time to steer these things.

---

5   University College, London

So what's your vision for the Digital Youth Academy?

The dream is that across the world a million young people are placed into businesses where the business respects their 'born digital' skills and listens to them and provides that innovation space for them. That's the big vision. We've already got international people approaching us because the course is essentially online, but we will also be delivering through partners who arrange events and have a lot of touch points with them as well.

We want to create lots of case studies where we can prove that this young person created an economic change to the company that they went into through innovating them.

Fantastic. And how about Ecademy, now that Daniel Priestley has become Managing Director? That's obviously going to lead to some shifts as well.

Classically, in entrepreneurial businesses, if the person who started it is still with it fourteen years on, it's not necessarily very healthy in terms of energy and innovation and ideas. Daniel is twenty-six years younger than me and a little bit younger than I was when I first started Ecademy. In a way, that means he is a new breed of entrepreneur. He's a great young guy, so he will take it to the next stage of *its* evolution.

I haven't *gone* from it. It's interesting this year because my daughter has gone to university and Ecademy has gone to that new person to run it, and both experiences feel very similar, weirdly enough. I feel like I gave birth to both, but I've had to let go. Providing they both go to somewhere that feels safe and has that same value set, then it's not hard. You miss them – there's no doubt about it – but it's time to let go of that level of control and ownership I had.

> "We usually think the best way of getting what we want out of life is by controlling – but it's not."

I think that one of the hardest things for parents is to let their babies go and make their own mistakes.

Huge grieving. Huge grieving. I watched a real paradigm shift happen once on a course with a typically corporate, closed, controlling guy. He just sat with a frown across his head the whole time. Right at the end, I said, "Ultimately, you've just got to let go," and finally he did. His body language changed, he laughed and he connected with others in the room. It was a profound shift for him. We usually think the best way of getting what we want out of life is by controlling – but it's not.

That's the ego thing, isn't it?

It is. It's assuming that we know best all the time and that we have all the answers. Actually, it's such a relief to let go.

Interestingly, feminine energy is about surrender and letting go.

Letting go *with love*.

Yes, and supporting others as you send them off with love, so your energy goes with them.

Absolutely. What would be challenging is if Daniel were a transactional businessman who was just seeking income all the time. Because with the Ecademy community, it's a bit like being mayor of a town – you can't just dominate the high street with all your own shops. You have to create an environment for success for everybody else. It's the same as being a mother – you create the environment for success and you just hope that they find their way.

I've always felt very maternal running the Ecademy community. Somebody once referred to me as their 'Internet Mummy'. They said that they go off to Facebook and Twitter and LinkedIn and these 'scary' places, but they always feel like they return to this home. That's how I want my children to feel about coming home, and it's the same for coming back to a community. You don't have to spend all your life there; you just have to know there is a safe haven where you get that sanity and reality check. When you've been pumped up with love, you go off again.

What a lovely compliment to pay you.

A load of people commented that it depended on what your own view of being a mother was. I suppose some people felt really threatened by that, probably because they had a really controlling mother. I imagine that for most people who have been on a therapy couch, it's been something to do with their mother relationship. That maternal bond can be so constructive or destructive, can't it? I love the term 'unconditional love'. Very few people can do unconditional. If you can find unconditional love in life, from a mother or in a partner or in business, then there's nothing more powerful.

> "If large companies and entrepreneurial people could start to really understand the power of the Internet, we could bring back family and all those values that we want in society."

Absolutely. It would be wonderful to have more 'positive mother' experiences in life and business.

But that's back to the power of the Internet. There are so many women who are in that corporate world and don't have that time to be a mother to their children. If large companies and entrepreneurial people could start to *really* understand the power of the Internet, we could bring back family and all those values that we want in society. It's such a *powerful* tool for us if we use it positively for change. It would be such a shame if we don't deliver something different as a result of technology.

Tim Berners-Lee, who was the founder of the Internet, made an amazing statement last week that everyone should remove their data from Facebook and Google. He is uncomfortable with the direction it's going in. It's not the shift in humanity that he foresaw. He didn't create 'www' to be a wealthy man. He created it for humanity, and it has not really created that change yet.

Again, the old underlying values have still got some influence. I suppose, as individuals, we must each do what we can.

We need to find our own path in it, which is no different to the world. I think a lot of people find relief when I speak about it because they realise that the online world just mirrors the offline world. It's about being true to yourself. But then there are all these people with a different name on Twitter, a different name on Facebook and different name on LinkedIn. That's like me living in Farnham and when I'm in Waitrose, I'm this person and when I'm in a wine bar, I'm this person, and when I'm at the swimming club, I'm this person. Nobody can connect to you and understand who you are.

What's your personal vision for the future, Penny?

[Reflecting] Personally, I can see myself being a very nomadic person. I've chosen to send my children through traditional schooling, but when we were in America, we saw a lot of people living in the most incredible RVs,[6] travelling around and educating their children on life in a different way. Thomas wrote a book called *A Friend in Every City.*[j] We've got members in 200 countries and friends all over the world. I can imagine us being quite nomadic.

I'd always want a base here. I really don't have a life plan of who or what I'm going to be when I'm older. I want to be a grand-mummy and I want to support my children. I see life being very complicated for that generation. I hope that through the adversity, the financial ups and downs that I've put the kids through, they've learnt to be very adaptable and to survive quite a lot of turbulence. I think that's very important.

What sort of financial hardships?

As often happens when you're building businesses, Thomas and I were ploughing everything into its development and ended up with no money to pay for our sons' private schooling. We didn't want to disrupt them, so I went to see the Headmaster, Mr Merrick, in tears. He suggested a solution where I paid half fees for eighteen months and worked there for free as a girl Friday, from 8.40 to 5.00 every day, covering the office, driving the minibus … and cleaning up sick in classrooms! In the evenings I'd resume my family duties of preparing tea, helping with homework and doing my Ecademy duties of answering messages, updating website content and speaking at events. It was sometimes tiring, but I treasured those times. I got to eat with my boys and sit with their friends! I learned a lot about myself. I realised that what defined me wasn't what I did but was my willingness to help others, whatever the setting.

I love a book called *Embracing Uncertainty* by Susan Jeffers. We have to all learn. Our children will learn because life is unpredictable.

When Thomas and I first got married, we used to do our life goals every year and say, "By next year, let's…." Now, it's really hard to predict. You certainly can set yourself up for disappointment if you do that. Plus, that's very targeted. Some of the most amazing things have actually happened unpredictably. Two years ago, I didn't wake up on January first thinking I was going to meet my new business partner, Darren Shirlaw, and uncover the world that he's uncovered and the confidence that he's given me to make some choices. I didn't know I was going to find investors for this youth programme and I would be stepping into that. If I had created a very rigid business plan, I wouldn't have even

> "I think the Internet has created a disconnection, and now we have to get back into the depth of connections."

---

6   Recreational vehicle; motorhome

met them. They were random things that came in, so I don't want to put a map out.

My daughter, Hannah, revealed that she was quite stressed during her first two terms of university and we talked a lot about this living with uncertainty. I realised that she feared things that hadn't even happened. I sat her down and said, "If I could say to you, you're going to die at ninety-two, you're going to have two marriages, you're going to have three children, you're going to work here, do this, would you like to carry that around? Would that give you comfort?"

She said, "No, I'd *hate* that."

I said, "Well, that's the tapestry of life. You've got to just believe that you're going to find your way through everything."

And create the world you want as well by how you feel and how you behave and live from your heart.

Exactly. And you notice the goodness in people. There are amazingly fantastic people in the world and you realise the richness of the world is inside all those people around you. It's a bit like Paulo Coelho's *The Alchemist*. People think they need to travel around to find these people, but often they're right on their doorstep if they only spent time with them to know them.

In one of the exercises I do, I ask, "If you closed your business tomorrow, who would miss it?" This question can be really emotional for a lot of people. Forget your family and friends who support you for their unconditional reasons. If you stopped blogging tomorrow, who would miss it, and you? A lot of people aren't building enough value to actually be missed and that means they've got no social capital around them or their business. This is a scary thought, as it means everybody is just sitting at a surface level. It's very sad.

In a way, I think the Internet has created a disconnection, and now we have to get back into the *depth* of connections. Once people just calm down and stop connecting just for the sake of it, we'll see the true promise of connection.

How do you see us connecting more effectively, Penny?

It's interesting, but I haven't yet articulated that vision, apart from the world just being better connected.

Maybe that's part of the feminine energy of chaos and uncertainty and potential, which seems to be getting stronger in this millennium. Women tend to be more comfortable with going with the flow than men.

Men are the natural hunters. I have many days where I wake up feeling like a hunter, looking for food; but I think women maybe do it in a different way. We're naturally more collaborative.

But I do see a massive shift in men all the time. Darren Shirlaw has a lot of female energy. Thomas, my husband, grew up with three older sisters. He's got a lot of feminine energy. I think the world is becoming more female, but it's a female energy rather than just being female. There are certainly a lot of amazing men out there.

There are indeed. I suppose it's for each person to have within them the balance of the male and female.

How would you summarise where you are in your business journey now, Penny?

The frustration I have about Ecademy and my business journey is that unless you get this huge amount of investment to create noise very quickly – which on Facebook was two and a half billion dollars – it's very hard to get attention. I get the feeling that there are more people starting to say, "I've spent a lot of time in these big places, but actually, where do I feel safe?" I just hope that we can keep Ecademy's true community values flowing and that it can grow.

We've got a lovely member called Jo Berry, who is the daughter of an MP who was killed in the Brighton bombings. She's written beautiful blogs on Ecademy because she forgave the bomber, Patrick McGee. She's an amazing lady. She says she uses Ecademy because it's the only place she feels safe to share her real, deep feelings and know that we have a set of values where people aren't allowed to harass or abuse you. This 'Mad Max' Internet possibility worries me a lot. I would disconnect from it if that ends up being the dominant energy inside it. I'm driven to ensure that there is some corner of this Internet world that feels good for people who are very values driven. Maybe that's only going to be 10 per cent, 1 per cent, whatever, of the population; but there needs to be somewhere with integrity where we can go and connect. I don't know how you verbalise that into a vision, but the Internet has to be somewhere we feel good about ourselves and know other people do as well.

> "… [Ecademy is] the only place she feels safe to share her real, deep feelings and know that we have a set of values where people aren't allowed to harass or abuse you."

What fascinating insights from Penny, who has been part of the Internet revolution since it began. As she rightly says, the online world reflects the offline world. People without scruples will behave in exactly the same way as they do elsewhere. Everything is just so much more magnified – whether for the greater good or the greater evil. What film remake will we see in the future – *Mad Max* or *It's a Wonderful Life*?

I share Penny's concerns. I have made wonderful friends and connections via the Internet, and yet I have had a few disturbing experiences too. On the positive side, both my elderly parents recently had falls and are currently recuperating in a fantastic care home in Lancashire. Although we are 100 miles apart, I have been able to communicate via Skype video calls. New technology can bridge situations, miles and generations. We need more Pennys to demonstrate the human touch in the Internet world.

Penny's husband Thomas laughed when they met because she didn't know anything about the computer products she was selling. I laughed too – because I was just the same. Penny just loved people. How many times have we heard 'people buy people'? It's as true with remote contact as face-to-face. When I was a financial adviser, I had no interest in how plans worked, but I knew how to make relationships with customers and how to help them. When I transferred from selling to training in October 1991, my biggest fear was training advisers how to use a laptop. The good news about the new-fangled equipment was that it didn't prove to be a distraction and impact negatively on sales, which was my fear. It was irrelevant to success. Those who forged strong relationships continued to be successful.

With the birth of the Internet, Penny's people-focussed perspective immediately saw the possibility of bringing about a shift in humanity. That is the gift of having a people person like Penny in a world of 'techies'. She was *of* their computer world but viewed it from her standpoint of how both she and technology could be of service to others. This is very different to the self-interested 'Old World' view of how the Internet can serve *them*.

As a mother and entrepreneur, Penny could envisage how the Internet could help families lead a more flexible, balanced life where parents could share responsibilities, work from home and avoid long commutes that end up isolating family members. Families can be part of their geographical communities as well as global communities. What a wonderful vision. This is a huge opportunity for individuals to co-create their own lifestyles and businesses wherever they like, based on what they love to do and who they attract to them. This gives so much freedom of choice. Surely this is the Brave New World.

Maybe this is the next stage of evolution from the likes of Eileen Caddy, who attracted like-minded souls to her Findhorn community in Scotland. We can each do the same, but without any of us having to up sticks unless we want to. We just need to show up in the world and see what happens.

What a great example Penny is setting as an 'Internet Mummy'. I think it's time for us to have more maternal qualities in business. In my long training career, I was fortunate to spend much of my time developing others. On a few occasions, younger team members would say to me, "I wish you were my mum." I used to reply, "I am your mum." And I really felt like I was. It is nothing to do with being a biological mother but everything to do with showing care, concern and consideration for others.

Let's follow Penny's lead and put mothering into business.

"I think it's time for us to have more maternal qualities in business."

JANE NOBLE KNIGHT

CARRY SOMERS

"I'm not interested in saying, 'I was one of the first companies twenty years ago.' It's about making changes in the industry now, setting an example and sharing everything I've learned … to push the standards higher."

Carry Somers, a pioneer in Fair Trade fashion, established Pachacuti in 1992. 'Pachacuti' means 'world upside-down' in the Quechua language and encapsulates Carry's endeavour to change the fashion industry from within to demonstrate that a company can be successful whilst benefitting both the producers and the environment. Pachacuti is recognised as one of the world's foremost ethical fashion brands: their collections of felt hats and Panama hats are shown at London, Paris and Milan Fashion Weeks and stocked around the world, while providing sustainable rural livelihoods for women in the Ecuadorian Andes. In 2009 Pachacuti became the first company in the world to be Fair Trade Certified by the WFTO and from 2009–12 piloted the EU Geo Fair Trade project to improve supply chain traceability. Carry has won numerous awards for her work and has met the Queen in recognition of her significant contribution to British business. Carry lives in Staffordshire with her daughter, Sienna, and her husband, Mark.

www.panamas.co.uk

A Conversation with
Carry Somers

Fair Trade Pioneer

It's not often that I go to a conference and am totally mesmerised by the keynote speaker. I can be wowed by great delivery and razzamatazz, but when I first came across Carry in April 2010, I was completely enthralled. Carry was the keynote speaker at the Women in Rural Enterprise (WiRE) annual conference. I was transfixed by her story and vowed that one day I would find out more. So when I came to write about pioneering female entrepreneurs, Carry was a 'must-have'.

On a sunny March morning, I set off on the hour-long journey from Shropshire through scenic countryside to Carry's shop, Pachacuti, in Dig Street, Ashbourne. I walked there from the main car park with a slight detour following misdirection by a supposed local. I had been to Ashbourne a few times before on my way to and from holidays in the Peak District, stopping to briefly wander through the streets, browsing the shops and seeking out small cafés for cream teas. But I had not come across Carry's shop.

A set of steps rose to a single door that opened into the narrow-fronted shop. Warm wooden floors created a charming, classic feel. Inside, it was like the Tardis[1] – the shop went back a long way! It reminded me of my childhood days in the fifties when I lived in Mold, North Wales. Family friends owned a small haberdashery shop on the high street, which somehow catered for an older women clientele and also served as a school outfitter. The character of the actual shop felt similar, but Carry's shop was far more fashionable and individual. There was a wall of hats on the left and rails of clothes elsewhere. I sensed a skilful designer had influenced the layout.

A smiling young woman emerged from a side door in response to the alert I'd triggered as I entered the shop. I followed her into a bright daylit space parallel to the depth of the shop, through a large area stacked with gorgeous colourful hats where packing was in progress. We went up some wooden stairs at the back to a large office area full of desks, computers and other equipment where Carry was waiting for me. Her desk faced a large window looking out

---

1   Tardis: a time machine and spacecraft in the British science fiction television programme Doctor Who, which looks small on the outside and large inside.

to trees and greenery at the back. Sunshine brightened the whole area splendidly. It was most welcoming.

Carry has a striking, stylish appearance. Her long, straight black hair hangs below her shoulders. A full fringe accentuates perfectly her colouring and features. Today she is wearing an olive green on white patterned dress with a matching shrug. Carry is slim, you might even say slight; but I sense a toughness and resilience too. She swings her chair to face me as I sit alongside. She talks about her life in her rather singsong way, with a softness of tone and an emphasis on certain words to make her points clear.

The business noises continue quietly in the background with the sounds of a radio, printers whirring and the packing; but I'm not in the least distracted as I listen, enchanted by Carry's story…

Where did your connection with South America come from, Carry?

It's strange. I've often been asked what made me interested in Latin America and the indigenous cultures of the region, and I really can't remember. Something obviously sparked it off because when I was probably about ten or eleven, I really wanted a book on the Incas. I remember getting this *thick* children's book with lots of illustrations and information all about the Incas, which I loved and treasured and kept reading. That must have helped to fire my imagination and interest.

I'd never heard of subjects like anthropology. Going to a very traditional grammar school, there were only very traditional career choices, so I ended up at university doing languages and European Studies. *Then* I discovered this Masters course in Native American Studies. I immediately knew that that was the one for me. I had a fantastic year because I was the only person on the course. (I could be incredibly self-indulgent and study whatever I wanted to.) It gave me a really fantastic chance to study all those aspects of Native American culture which were interesting to me.

That set me up for the road I took, and when I went out to Ecuador to do some research, I actually met two cooperatives. They'd both had arson attacks – one had a vehicle firebombed and the other their shop firebombed and some other threats. At the time in Ecuador, it was *just* at the beginning of the knitwear boom where everybody was starting to wear those thick Ecuadorian jumpers and the trade was all controlled by the middlemen. Obviously, having cooperatives forming posed a threat to their power.

That was it really. My idea was to help the cooperatives have another outlet. I thought in a naïve way that if I went *back* there, I could do some designs which were better than theirs. They'd be more adapted to the Western market, the sizes would be better, and this could give them some outlet for their skills and a direct link to the Western market because they didn't have any local market.

Did you have any interest in design at that time?

Not at all, really. *[Shrugging]* I guess I'd always been *slightly* interested. But I could never really afford to be interested in fashion and probably had very much my own style. I could draw some reasonable ideas and I come from quite an artistic family, but it certainly wasn't a strong point in terms of my skills. It was just really the idea that I could do something better because they were just doing lots of really plain designs.

Was it women's cooperatives or mixed groups that you were dealing with?

It was mainly women's cooperatives. One was a mixed group. I've gone more and more into women's groups over the years. A lot of the associations in Latin America are more female-based, but the first one did have some men running it as well. They do some of the knitting, but a lot of the men do the spinning.

Is that because of dexterity or tradition?

I think it is tradition – although knitting only came in with the Peace Corps in the '50s and '60s; so it's not really that traditional. I guess the men probably did spinning before for the weaving. Weaving is obviously a traditional skill. People have been weaving there for millennia.

That's interesting. I did a couple of Native American holidays in 2006 and 2007, staying on reservations in North America. Apparently, dreamcatchers weren't traditional except to the Ojibwa Nation, which surprised me. You can sometimes think things have a longer tradition than they actually do.

Absolutely. It was quite interesting. I knew one person from Otavalo in Ecuador who ended up doing an exchange between Mexico and Ecuador, organised through the government. He learned to make dreamcatchers probably about fifteen years ago, and within a year or two, *everybody* on the market was selling dreamcatchers. You go there now and there's a whole street of dreamcatchers. People have no idea that if they'd been in Ecuador fifteen years ago, they would never have seen one.

I suppose it's about adapting to the Western market.

And tourist demand, yes.

> "... I was brought up with a really clear sense of what was just and what was unjust ... something in me thought, This is wrong. This isn't fair. I thought that I could do something about it."

You described your idea for the cooperatives as maybe a bit naïve. Do you think there are some advantages to being naïve?

I do. In a way, *one* of the traits of an entrepreneur is that you act on your gut instinct. I've never been somebody to sit back and measure things, write a business plan, go out and do research, and work out if it's going to work or not. It was just that I saw the need – the really clear injustice. I *saw* individuals trying to buy wool and *saw* the people who were selling the wool *clearly* mis-setting the weight and *clearly* overcharging them.

As a child I was brought up with a really clear sense of what was just and what was unjust. When I saw that, something in me thought, *This is wrong. This isn't fair.* I thought that I could do something about it.

What did you do, Carry?

I actually had a fully funded PhD ahead of me, which was going to be fantastic. Initially, my idea was to go to South America over the summer months so I could occupy myself and earn some spending money for university and, most importantly, help the groups that I'd met. *That* was the idea. I borrowed £500 from my mother – I needed £500 for the airfare and £500 to buy the goods.

I'd already done some research into natural dyes, which they mainly used – a lot of the wool was dyed with walnut and various leaves. I created some designs based on some of the little-known cave art from the area and then brought the knitwear back and started selling it at some shows. It sold really well. Within six weeks, I'd sold out and had to get some more sent over. Hearing the impact it was making, I thought, *It's too selfish to go and do my PhD – four years of being self-indulgent when I could really be making a difference to people's lives.*

That must have been a tough decision.

Probably, but I don't remember it being that tough at the time. It seemed like a very clear decision to make because I've always had it in the back of my head that I'm going to go back and do a PhD one day. It might happen – one day.

So your heart, your intuition, told you that this was something for you to do?

Yes. After a couple of months, I really was making a difference because they didn't have a shop in town – a local outlet – although this *amazing* nun, Sister Carmella, in one group had really tried to help. She battled against arson and against the real dislike of the community who didn't seem to appreciate what she was doing at all. She was feeding hundreds of malnourished schoolchildren every day. She was this lone nun, battling against the whole community.

You must have been an answer to her prayers.

I think so because there weren't many people there who could help in that situation. She just had a few volunteers.

What benefits were you seeing that made you think *I'm just going to have to carry on with this*?

Initially, it was just those tangible trading links. It was giving them access to the market because they had the skills – they could produce – but they had nowhere to sell. The stalls in the local market were controlled by the middlemen, so they couldn't get anywhere in the central area of the market.

It was really just the *benefit* of being able to pay them a good price. Then obviously, working with Sister Carmella, I could see the impact immediately. She was training people in the local community and all this money was going back and benefitting the children and all the projects she was running. It's only as the years have gone on that you see all those other aspects of Fair Trade. So many people think Fair Trade is just about a fair price, but it's about gradually building up those relationships and investing in training.

Over the years we've supported Alcoholics Anonymous, to paying pensions, to building a grocery store. As the business grows and develops, and there's more money in the system, our support grows too.

Even in the early days when I didn't have the money, I always felt like I had the *access* to the money. Right back in the first year of the business, there was a woman making panpipes for me. She was being really badly treated by her alcoholic husband. He'd thrown her and her kids out into the street, frittered away all their money and the bank was about to repossess the house. She needed $450, which was a lot of money to me at the time, but I lent her the $450 and it paid off the bank for her house. She paid me back over the next five years in panpipes. *[Laughing]* I sold boxes and boxes of panpipes because that was her skill. So yes, I bought a house with panpipes.

That is just wonderful, Carry. There's obviously this huge philanthropic ethos as well as your enterprise.

I'm not sure they were always particularly good business decisions. There are only so many panpipes you can sell!

I'd call it a good decision, even if it wasn't a good business decision!

Where I have found business *planning* useful in decision making is with the Fair Trade system. We make three-year plans, so that's really our company's strategic review. We sit down with all the staff and ask, "What shall we do? Where do we want to be?" We look at what we need to improve but also *where* we want to be as a company and what our producers want to do. So those are our three-year goals.

Then we come up with annual plans on how to work towards that both here in the UK *and* with each producer group. Improvements might be needed with the electric system; or we might realise a lot of quality issues are down to the weavers having poor eyesight, so we set up projects to raise money for glasses.

It's really interesting that those short-term and long-term visions come both from the bottom and the top of the supply chain. We have really clear goals and everybody knows what we're working towards and how we're going to get there on an annual basis.

I really like this involvement and buy-in from everybody. It makes the vision so much more likely to happen. Now, we've really jumped ahead here... What happened when you went back and decided to not do your PhD?

I decided to set up a proper business. I borrowed £5,000 from a friend's mother and some money from the bank, and I had all my profits. At this stage, it was really hard to send money out to Ecuador – no simple electronic transfers. So I had to send money to the bank and pick it up all in one go, in cash. The largest note was a dollar bill, which was a thousand sucres. I had to collect up to ten million sucres – I'd literally have a rucksack full of money! It was quite a dangerous time in Northern Ecuador. Once, when I turned up, a couple of buyers had just been killed in the town. People knew who was there, who had money, who was buying. They obviously thought buyers from the West were a fair target.

I ended up having all of my money – absolutely everything – stolen from an apartment I rented. I thought it was pretty well hidden in the ceiling, but it obviously wasn't. Then it was Black Wednesday as well, so I had to borrow more money but the exchange rate was worse. I think I borrowed money at $2 to the pound and it went down to $1.30. Not only did I have to pay back the bank – my father had guaranteed the loan – but also a third extra on top of that. The person who stole the money sent me two different death threats if I involved the police. So I was on my own in a very vulnerable situation. I ended up spending hundreds of dollars on the police who were completely useless. I gave up in the end and lost all that money, which was a *huge* blow at that stage in the business.

I bet a lot of people would have thought, *I'm not meant to be here. What a terrible country to be in.* What made you hang in there, Carry?

I think it was probably two-fold. Firstly, my responsibility to so many people already dependent on me (so it wasn't just about my income, it was about the income of women and families and whole cooperatives); and secondly, that I was *not* going to be beaten. I was not going to let this get the better of me. I was going to work my way back again.

And that's what I did. I lived in a van for most of the year. It was absolutely freezing in November, doing craft fairs and things. Margaret Thatcher was in power and it was the time of the Criminal Justice Act. So *anywhere* I parked, the police were moving me on or people were trying to break into the vehicle in the middle of the night. The police were always really nice, but you'd always get knocks at two in the morning saying, "The woman in the house there is concerned there's going to be a hippie convoy turning up in the village. Can you move on, please?"

> "… you'd always get knocks at two in the morning saying, 'The woman in the house there is concerned there's going to be a hippie convoy turning up … Can you move on, please?'"

I read somewhere it was a Dodge van. Was it properly converted?

I didn't have heating. I had a gas stove, so I'd put the gas rings on to warm it up a little bit and it had a bed. I don't think it actually had water plumbed in. Every day, pretty much, I'd be at different universities. I'd drive from Bristol to Cardiff, park the van, set up the stand, cart round huge, heavy boxes of these thick Ecuadorian jumpers, take it down at the end of the day and drive on to the next one. It was hard physical work.

Sheer grit and determination got you through that and obviously your bigger vision and sense of responsibility to the community. You set a fabulous example. How did you develop the business? What have been the changes over the years?

Well, the first, obviously, is now we're mainly known as a hat business. That was something I've battled against the whole way through, and it's probably only in recent months that the decision has been made. It's acceptance that we really are a hat business.

This started off right back in winter '92 when I did a really big Fair Trade show in Olympia. It was quite an investment at the time. We had a buyer from The Conran Shop looking for rollable Panama hats. I only had a couple, but they placed an order. For the next few years, The Conran Shop *really* kept me going. The hats were the best-selling items in their gardening department for a long time in London, Paris and Japan.

The hats did take a while to develop. About ten years ago, the design aspect of the Panama hats really started to progress. But I've never wanted to be *just* a hat business, mainly because I've got so many people to support – people like the embroiderers I've been working with for twenty years. The last time I was out in Ecuador, it was just *heartbreaking* talking to the woman who coordinated the embroidery project who said that Pachacuti is the only company now willing to pay the price for their work. If there's no order from Pachacuti, they have to go out and pick tomatoes in the fields. It makes me realise that I *can't* just do the hats. I feel I've at least got to do some capsule ranges around it. So even if we are known as a hat business, we can have some peripheral projects and products around that.

I always wanted it to be a rounded business. I knew that if I was just doing hats, I was only benefitting one or two cooperatives rather than all the people who were dependent on me … although a lot of the work we've done in terms of training and skills *should* mean that they can stand on their own to some extent – certainly some of the groups can now. We've taken some of our alpaca groups from working off a blanket at the side of the street in the evenings to coping with proper wholesale orders. So I do feel a lot of people have progressed and can now make that transition if we do decide not to do the knitwear, for instance.

That's excellent. And you're a mother as well, Carry. How on earth have you managed being a mother with all that you've done?

Oh gosh. All I remember about the early years of having my daughter is her spending a lot of time sleeping on restaurant floors in South America and sleeping in hammocks in different places. When she was six days old, she went to a gig in London and at eleven days old, we were at our first festival where I was selling. People were looking through the rails of clothing and there was a little baby in a hammock underneath. I couldn't drop the business. I couldn't take maternity leave. There was nobody else. Her dad had his own business. He certainly wasn't going to help *me* out, and I just had to do it.

My daughter came out with me to South America and just grew up as a part of the business, which I think was very healthy. Actually, taking children with you and having children as *part* of your working life is certainly how things used to be when you look at traditional communities in South America. The children participate in the adult's lifestyle. It's only quite recently, in the last fifty to sixty years in the UK, that we've actually had the luxury and the money to be able to, as mothers, indulge our children and give up work. Life started to revolve around the children. I am in two minds as to whether that's always the most beneficial for the children. I think it can be quite an adjustment for them when they realise the world actually doesn't revolve around them.

I have to say that all my daughter's teachers have said the whole way through school that she is the most well-balanced child they have ever come across. She's always happy and contented. She certainly hasn't suffered at all from having a working mother. I mean, it was never going to be easy. She was in full-time childcare from six weeks old, which was really, really tough, and I split up from her dad when she was a year old. So really, I only got to see her on Saturdays, which was really hard because she spent a lot longer with the childminder than she did with me. She was there from eight in the morning till six at night, and I saw her before bed. But there was no other option. I tried to look after her myself for six weeks, but there was absolutely no way that I could work at the same time. It was definitely the best option for her.

She grew up with three people who she's still good friends with. So I think, actually, it was very

> "We've taken some of our alpaca groups from working off a blanket at the side of the street in the evenings to coping with proper wholesale orders."

healthy for her. It was just difficult at the time, as a mother, and even harder when she was four and five and I had to go away on business trips and leave her. I was often off for three, four, five weeks at a time. Leaving them when they're so little, for so long, is not easy.

But she's *never* minded it. I think because her dad travels a lot as well, she's just had a great attitude. She said the other day, "Mum, I don't miss you when you're away. I'm happy when you're here and I don't miss you when you're gone. I'm just happy wherever I am," which is great really.

Brilliant. Those are some really good points, Carry. I do think parents, and mothers in particular, can mollycoddle children too much.

It's certainly a lot easier now that I've got staff. I've definitely got more flexibility. Like this morning, I came in late because my daughter's granny has just died and she's off to the funeral. It's nice that I can have an hour with her in the morning. I've worked hard to win that luxury. It's a shame I couldn't do that at the beginning, but that's just how it was.

But you've obviously got a wonderful relationship with her now. As you say, the tradition was to have an extended family and community around. Being the biological mother who is 'supposed' to look after their child, you can get very hung up on it.

Exactly. Neither her father nor I had any relatives here, so she's often spent a week with friends. Friends' mothers have looked after her and she's been perfectly happy with that. It's worked out really well in the end. It's certainly brought her up to be very independent and confident. She often comes on the stand with me at London Fashion Week, and she's talked to people like the Head Buyer at Tesco's while I've been off getting a cup of tea. He doesn't know she's not a member of staff. She's very knowledgeable and doesn't get daunted by talking to older people, which I think is a good skill to have.

You were at London Fashion Week recently, Carry. How do you marry your work in Ecuador with what seems like the opposite extreme of fashion?

Mmmm, it's certainly not an easy marriage of Fair Trade and fashion – not at the top end of the fashion spectrum. With Fair Trade, we try to take the marginalised producers and give them not just the work, but also the business skills. That means training them in quality, lead times and delivery on time. To get those producers to the quality needed for London and Paris Fashion Weeks is never going to be easy, and that's probably why we are the only Fair Trade brand at London Fashion Week. We obviously are very unusual, in particular in terms of Fair Trade Certification, because we work with producers in *all* different aspects of quality. That's important for saleability of the hats. Our biggest market this season is Japan. The Japanese are very demanding. It needs to be top quality and delivered on time or they won't reorder.

I read on your website that there were some garments that you sent back because it was the wrong colour. That sounds like tough love.

Yes, it's really taken me a long time to feel comfortable sending things back. I know that the producers usually can't afford it and they need their money. But I've eventually realised that I'm not doing them any good if I keep accepting things that aren't the right colour. When you want something in a subtle pink, a natural dye, and on two or three occasions it comes in a bright fuchsia, which clearly isn't even natural, they've got to learn that they can't send this. There was one situation several years ago whilst I was in Ecuador, where I said about a couple of hats, "We can take these. There is a slight flaw, but it's not really noticeable." That then opened the floodgates and they sent us all the seconds in their storeroom over the space of the summer! I can't let that happen.

So, it's important the cooperative realise that work must be up to standard. We've had to make the president of the cooperative a bit tougher as well because she was being too soft. The weavers were turning in hats that *clearly* weren't good enough. She would point out the fault and say, "Take it back," because you can take out the darker straws and put other ones in. The weavers were like, "We've not got time for that. Just give us half price for it and we'll be happy." So she did. We were like, "No, you shouldn't do that. What are you going to do with this hat? You've got to replace it and it's your time."

We had a meeting with all the community coordinators on the last trip and did a presentation about quality control. A lot of them don't read. They've got very, very low levels of literacy. Only 37 per cent of members have finished primary education, so it's really important to give them visual training to show them "This is unacceptable." Sometimes they're quite shocked when they see the quality of the hats we have received. It's important as it makes them realise what is unacceptable.

> "We can't accept such sub-standard products. It's important for them long-term too or they risk losing the work."

This is a business, not a charity. We can't accept such sub-standard products. It's important for them long-term too or they risk losing the work.

Initially, you were selling things out of a van, but your first shop was in Exeter.

That's right. It was about two years into the business. I met somebody who invested in the business for a few years. I think he saw how hard I was working. The shop wasn't particularly profitable, but it was an awful lot easier than travelling around the country in a van.

This shop in Ashbourne isn't exactly the centre of a metropolis. I can understand people doing a little pilgrimage here because it's a gorgeous shop. Do you mainly do mail order or are you supplying retail outlets?

Most of our hats go out wholesale. We're supplying everybody from Gieves and Hawkes to Monsoon. At the moment, we're doing hats for Club Monaco (owned by Ralph Lauren). A lot of hats go to the top luxury stores in Japan. That's really good for the producers because you get the high orders. It's not as profitable as the retail side, but in terms of giving the producers work, it's very important.

Mail order is a really significant part of the business. It's suffered a bit in the last couple of years. The bad weather has probably had more of an impact than the recession. The shop is actually a really small part of the business, but it is a destination. We do get people travelling from a long way. We've got a really affordable rent here, so it doesn't make sense to move; but we're going to change it into just a bespoke hat shop in the summer, rather than offering all the clothing with designer knitwear collections and accessories as we currently do – which are designed just for this shop. It's too much to do.

In terms of staff time and profit, it's much better just to have those people who really want to buy a hat and are prepared to spend the money. So we're going to completely convert it into a hat shop. People will be able to come in and design a bespoke hat. We'll have rolls of ribbons with haberdashery counters – which is great use for all our cupboards of ribbon and trims that we've got left over. People can choose the roll, choose the ribbon and then we'll sew the hat up for them – their own bespoke hat.

So twenty years on, after your resistance to …

Exactly. We finally are hatters. There's no escaping from the tag now.

What about your current and future visions for yourself and the business, Carry?

We're just at the start of another three-year plan, so the hat shop will help our direction. We're now moving towards more fashion-forward styles. There were so many older weavers in our hat-making cooperative who found it hard to weave the fine-rolled classic hats. They can weave the brighter colours and patterns an hour faster than they can weave a plain, white, classic hat. I'm not quite sure why, but they obviously enjoy weaving the patterns and the colours, so they speed up.

The next stage is to push the quality. Over the next three years we're going to work *really* hard with our producers in terms of training, buying new equipment, buying new hat blocks, maybe doing some millinery courses ourselves, learning how to make fascinators and that kind of thing. And pushing the hat design a bit further so we can do more bespoke millinery. It's trying to establish that niche for *great quality* hats, but also something that stands up on the catwalks.

Last year we did Paul Smith's hats. It would be good to do more bespoke work collaborating with other designers. It really helps get year-round work because they want a delivery of summer hats in August/September for the following year to send to all their stockists. It means that, through those leaner autumn months, we have got some orders coming in for weavers.

What's lined up for the community?

Not much in terms of concrete projects. We've done so many in the last few years. They've built the grocery store, we've paid for Alcoholics Anonymous – there have been a lot of projects – and we still pay for the pensions for the elderly weavers. We could probably do with looking more into medical expenses. There is a fund from the sale of the hats that goes into the medical expenses. A weaver can come to the association if they need money. We have got new members joining the cooperative, which is great, and it's getting bigger. But there are a lot of elderly members. We need to make sure there's enough money to provide a safety net for those medical expenses. A lot of them can't afford a thousand dollars for an operation. It's a matter of life and death.

> "We need to make sure there's enough money to provide a safety net for those medical expenses."

We have also run a glasses project for the past three years. Local children wear glasses (sunglasses, lego glasses, anything) to school for a day and pay £1, which goes to glasses and cataract operations in Ecuador.

You're a Joseph Rowntree[2], but your community's on the other side of the world.

It is. The other exciting thing we're working on is the Geo Fair Trade Project. All of the other pilots have been commodities – vanilla, tea, coffee, cashew nuts. We're the only pilot that is involved in production as well, which makes it quite important in terms of Fair Trade and traceability.

We've mapped the GPS coordinates of each weaver's house – which is quite hard because only 40 per cent of them are accessible by road. Then we've got up to 100 different social, economic and environmental indicators. The idea is that we're going to get QR codes on our hats that can be scanned. It will take you right back to the house of the weaver who made the hat. You'll be able to see the real impact of the purchase on the weaver and on the community, such as increasing the knowledge of the members of the community. So quite diverse indicators – looking at the environment of the area, soil degradation, deforestation and that sort of thing, which obviously affects the community as well.

> "It's very important to provide traceability and transparency within the fashion supply chain."

It's very important to provide traceability and transparency within the fashion supply chain. This goes a lot further than any other traceability project because most of the ones I've seen are just a few smiling pictures of people within the supply chain, but there's no real information about whether there's any improvement, who they are, where it is. That should be happening within the next year, but we will continue to grow and push forwards as well because I think consumers *are* very mindful that there are a lot of people out there who are slightly greenwashing the whole supply chain issue.

It's fantastic that you're taking it so much further. When I've looked at information on my own ethical investments, I've thought, *Why on earth is this company one of the ethical investments*? Many criteria seem so superficial. Do you think your way is the future?

[A bit of a sigh] It depends very much on the ethical criteria. We're the only Fair Trade producers in London Fashion Week, but a lot of people do things like upcycling. That's really important because there is *so much* in terms of textiles going into landfill that that is really, really crucial as well. So I think there are multiple ways in the future.

If production is overseas, it needs to be traceable and transparent to ensure that there is no child labour, that the wages are good, that there are no sweatshop conditions and at least minimal standards are being met. We obviously go much further than that, but that does need to happen. I believe a lot of production will move closer to home. That 'Made in Britain' brand is going to become stronger, along with recycling, upcycling and the creation of new fibres – *really* good new fibres that are truly sustainable. Look at the changes in hemp over the last ten years, which went from something like sackcloth into something that can be really good fibre. There are lots of very good, new, manmade fibres. In terms of fashion, it's going to be looking at sustainability in all its guises.

---

2   Joseph Rowntree was a Victorian philanthropist and business owner of Rowntree's chocolate factory in York. He was known for his social reform skills.

I'm proud that we were the World Fair Trade Organisation's first Fairtrade Certified company. In terms of fashion, the Fairtrade Mark at the moment is only on cotton. It's just on the commodity, which is really important considering the amount of pesticides and water and that sort of thing involved in cotton. So, Fairtrade cotton is very valuable; but in terms of fashion, most of the added value is not in the commodity itself, it's in the Cut Make Trim, in the embellishment (a lot of the cases of sweatshop labour have been in children sewing on sequins and beads and that sort of thing). So it is *really* important to look at the whole supply chain and not just at the commodity.

This was the *first* certification that looks at the whole supply chain: it looks at our relationship with our staff; it looks at our packaging and our transport. We calculate all of our CO_2 emissions for our transport and travel. In the UK, we're on 100 per cent renewable electricity. We were one of the very first companies, if not *the* first, to switch to green gas. Our phones are with a phone co-op.

> "It is about making every aspect as ethical as possible... the whole supply chain."

It is about making every aspect as ethical as possible, and I think that's worked really well. It's helped a lot in terms of working with the staff because everyone feels engaged and involved in what we're doing. It obviously makes a big impact on the producers as it means that they have more of a say. In the past, I'd think, *This is what we're going to spend the money on because this is what they need,* whereas now it's also coming from the bottom up, instead of saying, "We need to get a fire extinguisher here and you need to do this." The whole glasses project came from the weavers themselves, and there are lots of instances like the lower grade fashion hats in brighter colours I mentioned. That comes from having knowledge of what the *producers* want. So, it's really helped us to strengthen the business. It's given us a much better knowledge of our supply chain and all the people involved.

It's great to be the world's first Fairtrade Certified organisation. That's been a real achievement for us.

It's absolutely fantastic. You're a real pioneer.

Yes. I was a pioneer in Fair Trade. Nobody knew what it was twenty years ago. Now I think everybody knows. Most people recognise the Fairtrade Mark and they're really aware of at least *some* of the differences that Fair Trade makes. Twenty years ago, about the only Fair Trade product you could buy was really undrinkable Nicaraguan coffee. It's really important that as one of those early pioneers, we keep on pushing the bar higher.

> "It's got to be financially sustainable. That's one of the reasons I haven't gone after a lot of funding."

I'm not interested in saying, "I was one of the first companies twenty years ago." It's about making changes in the industry *now*, setting an example and sharing everything I've learned – all that methodology, skills and knowledge – with other groups and helping to push the standards higher. People often talk about Pachacuti being quite a *rare* example of a company that has very high standards in terms of ethics and sustainability but which is also profitable.

Sadly, there are an awful lot of Fair Trade companies that aren't profitable. It's got to be financially sustainable. That's one of the reasons I haven't gone after a lot of funding. Lots of other Fair Trade companies have borrowed millions, and for me, that's not how I want to run my business. If it can't work as a sustainable business then I don't think there's any point in doing it.

Where does the name Pachacuti come from?

It means 'World Upside Down' in Quechua. So it's very much the idea of giving more back to the people on that side of the world rather than the middlemen in the West taking all the money.

Pachacuti can also mean the start of a new era, a change in time. When I set up the business in 1992, it was 500 years since the conquest of 1492. People were saying that after 500 years we want to reassert our identity as indigenous people. So it has a really good double meaning.

It has indeed. What also strikes me is how you look South American yourself.

People do comment on it often. I can be somewhere like Chelsea Flower Show, with people not knowing my business connection with South America, and I will often be asked, "Are you from South America?" I think it's the Devon side of my family, with our dark, black hair and olive skin. Some of us do look quite Latino.

Have you worked anywhere else?

I've just come back from Tunisia earlier this month. I was doing consultancy work to help them as a post-revolutionary country to discover Fair Trade. They've just got their first Fair Trade Association. There's this incredible rural poverty that people didn't realise existed before – I think it was quite hidden by the previous government. The photographs I saw were so shocking, but the people have got incredible textile skills – *really* beautiful embroidery. So it's a situation where I could make a difference. I don't want to go in and start trading with them, but to give people the skills, business knowledge and contacts. I'm sure there's a place for them in some of the luxury stores, doing beautiful embroidered bed linen for instance. Again, it's helping spread that knowledge.

You're obviously a role model to others. Who was your role model?

Definitely Anita Roddick. Without reading her autobiography, *Body and Soul,* I wouldn't have started Pachacuti. In between my Masters and setting up the business, and *in theory* starting the PhD, I went sailing for a year in the Caribbean. When I came back, probably the first thing I did was read Anita Roddick's autobiography. That was what really motivated me and started that realisation that if *she* can make such a change in the beauty industry with no knowledge, no experience, no proven market and no market research for it, then what was to stop me doing the same for the fashion industry?

Yes, I was very naïve, but so was Anita Roddick and she succeeded. She learnt along the way. She made some tough decisions, she made some mistakes, but everybody respects her for her

"… if she [Anita Roddick] can make such a change in the beauty industry with no knowledge, no experience, no proven market and no market research for it, then what was to stop me doing the same for the fashion industry?"

passion in building the company. I know lots of people who worked for the Body Shop and they still talk about it so *fondly*. Even though it probably wasn't always easy working there, you really get the feeling that everybody knew why they were there.

I was glad that before she died I had a chance to meet her and say, "Because I read your book, I'm now supporting 1,000 women in Ecuador, so thank you." I'm sure she already knew what a difference she'd made directly, but I think the indirect impact of her work and her writing is probably a lot wider than she ever realised.

We could do with more of you, Carry. The world would be a better place. Let's work towards it.

It's really important for me to encourage the younger generation. I do a lot of talks at schools. I talk to classes of Business Studies students at the local grammar school and at universities. It's *really* important for me that the next generation of fashion designers and business students actually do consider ethics. I take that very seriously. I was one of the government's first Enterprise Ambassadors when Margaret Hodge set up the scheme. I think that's a real responsibility … to show people that whatever aspect of business they're in, ethics are really important and they can bring them into any company.

That's wonderful, Carry. This is one of the reasons I am so happy you agreed to be a Pilgrim Mother Entrepreneur in my book. You are truly a changemaker entrepreneur, who I'm sure is going to make an even bigger difference than you already have.

For over twenty years I used to buy most of my beauty products at The Body Shop, but somehow it was never the same for me after it was sold to L'Oreal in 2006. I know I wasn't alone in feeling uncomfortable with the takeover. However, I still respected and followed Anita Roddick and her pioneering work.

Speaking to Carry, I see very clearly how she is continuing with Anita Roddick's legacy while adding her own spin. This is the way of legacies. They are meant to be living, not dead, and have a roll-on effect. We get inspired, incorporate new ideas and then develop our own legacies. There are many people, especially women, who have lots to thank Carry for. As well as the example she sets for other ethically-minded entrepreneurs, Carry provides a living, independence and a voice for the 1,000 plus women in her cooperatives. It reminds me of Anita Roddick's founding of *Trade Not Aid* in 1991 to help Third World communities utilise their own resources to supply their own needs.

In some circumstances, self is so important – self-belief, self-esteem, self-sufficiency, self-confidence. This is true for women *everywhere*, in our personal, community and business lives. And yet self as in 'selfish' is not the path of women wanting to fulfil their greatest potential. Carry had a higher purpose, which was to support the workers in her cooperatives that kept her going. This mission drove her business. Despite hostility and challenge in several situations (like Sister Carmella who was also misunderstood), Carry displayed incredible courage and perseverance. She withstood death threats, theft of all her investment cash and freezing conditions living in a van, and she still managed to run an international business as a single parent.

I have great respect for Carry surviving in a way that seemed to bring her even closer to the communities she was supporting. She was one of them. In a minor way I can identify with living in freezing conditions in a van. On my first night of sleeping in my motor home in November 2010, I slept fully clothed in an Arctic sleeping bag because I couldn't remember how to turn the gas heating on. Yet this was luxury in comparison with Carry's experience.

One thing that strikes me strongly about Carry is how she looks as if she could fit equally easily into high fashion and traditional indigenous cultures – which of course she does. She is the bridge between the two worlds. But more than that, she is a changemaker, a catalyst, between the two. She brings commercial skills to her cooperatives and ethical considerations to high fashion. What a gift. She has brokered a successful marriage between two most unlikely partners.

There's so much more I could write that resonates with me about Carry – her sense of justice and fairness; her concern that it's not always healthy for life to revolve round your children so much… but for now, I'll let Carry's story speak for itself.

"In some circumstances, self is so important – self-belief, self-esteem, self-sufficiency, self-confidence… Yet self as in 'selfish' is not the path of women wanting to fulfil their greatest potential."

JANE NOBLE KNIGHT

MARIE-CLAIRE CARLYLE

"Find your heaven
and don't settle for
anything less."

Marie-Claire Carlyle is a top Business and Success coach, inspirational speaker, Feng Shui consultant and Author of the Hay House bestsellers *How to Become a Money Magnet* and *Money Magnet Mindset*. Marie-Claire left the corporate sales world at the age of forty, following her intuition, to travel and immerse herself in spirituality and personal development. She is passionate about helping people to make the most of their lives. Marie-Claire currently lives in Chester, UK.

www.marieclairecarlyle.com

A Conversation with
Marie-Claire Carlyle

Ms Money Magnet

That's what friends are for — making helpful suggestions. When I first started my quest in March 2010 to interview modern Pilgrim Mothers, my friend Sue Hall immediately enthused, "You really need to speak to Marie-Claire Carlyle." Consequently, I looked at Marie-Claire's website and absolutely agreed. Marie-Claire certainly radiated the energy of a Pilgrim Mother.

I arranged to meet Marie-Claire shortly afterwards. After I pulled into the driveway of an impressive detached Victorian house near Chester, Marie-Claire greeted me at the door. She exuded energy and sunshine, from her dazzling smile to her brightly coloured red dress and dark, curly, free-flowing hair. On this occasion I recorded a video interview – or so I thought.

Marie-Claire showed me into the lounge, with a large bay window, at the front of the house. I was a few weeks into my first round of Pilgrim Mother video interviews, so I was building up my experience in finding the best place for the interviewee to sit, with something of interest in the background and natural light but no direct sunlight. Marie-Claire co-operated fully with my stage directions and made some suggestions of her own. When we were both satisfied, Marie-Claire settled down in the chair, attaching a tie-clip mic to her dress. I felt really pleased with myself, *Perfect! I'm getting the hang of this….*

But as it happened, the camcorder mysteriously switched itself off a few times without warning. Damn! I still managed to get some great clips, but many sequences, as I was to discover later, were curtailed. The camcorder was exchanged soon afterwards!

I naturally followed Marie-Claire's progress after our first meeting and was thrilled to be invited to her book launch of *How to Become a Money Magnet* in Waterstones, Chester in September 2010. I was honoured to join the many guests who gathered to celebrate Marie-Claire's success. It certainly gave me a taste for what it would be like being a published author!

So I am excited, two years later, to catch up with Marie-Claire, synchronistically the same day the first

copy of her second book Money Magnet Mindset arrived in the post for approval. This time I have a voice recorder rather than a camcorder to master. Thankfully, there are to be no hiccups this time.

Join me in a colourful conversation with the vibrant Marie-Claire…

You're a successful author, Marie-Claire. What's your story?

I grew up, the daughter of two entrepreneurs, so I really got the value of hard work and the idea that whatever you want, if you work hard enough, you can get. So I had lots of part-time jobs whilst still at school and I went on to get two business degrees. My motto was always to 'work hard, play hard'. Then I ended up working in sales, where I had the experience of being the worst salesperson *ever*.

How did you manage that because you seem such a natural salesperson?

That's a really good question. I think I was trying too hard. Too much yang.[1] Too much pushing. I was coming from a place of 'how do I do this?' rather than allowing myself to just do it. I was with the Xerox Corporation. I had the best training in the world and I was in the best business to be in. I had a great team and I had great support. I studied hard and I worked hard.

I was so intent on being successful I would just walk down the whole length of the office and get on with work. Somebody said to me, "Marie-Claire, why don't you say good morning to people?"

And I was like, "I haven't got time to say good morning to people. I would never get to my desk. I would never get any work done. I'd never get any results."

I was very much 'work equals results', not people. It was a real pattern in my life for that period. Results were more important than people. It was only when I learnt to stop and listen to people and effectively network that everything started to open up for me.

So what happened?

First of all, I was the worst salesperson ever for twelve very, very long soul-destroying weeks. If you can imagine, fifty-seven guys and three women all looking at you every Monday morning when you had to call out that you hadn't sold anything, but you were ever hopeful of getting one the next week. Sales is the worst job in the world if you're no good at it because you end up at the bottom of the league table.

Then I had the breakthrough. I realised I had a limiting belief about sales. When I got that out of the way, I got clear on what I wanted. I left Xerox after about ten years and became a successful sales director in software. By then, I was achieving a million pounds every month. That was my period of yang. Work hard, play hard.

Then started my period of complete surrender; I just let go.

What brought that about?

Back in January 2003 two key things happened. I was invited to an Aurora Women's Network event. They had a panel including two mediums talking about using your intuition in business. One

---

1   In Chinese philosophy and religion, there are two universal principles, one negative, dark and feminine (yin), and one positive, bright and masculine (yang), whose interaction influences the destinies of creatures and things.

did a couple of exercises where you had to guess what she had hidden from the audience. I got them both spot on. I realised I'd always been successful at recruiting people, based on my gut feeling.

As my two girlfriends and I were leaving, we were talking to one of the mediums. I had never done any spiritual work or anything spiritual. Suddenly, I felt really strange – I couldn't speak or move for what seemed like ages before I could actually say, "I'm struggling. Why am I struggling?"

Quite nonchalantly, the medium said, "We've just had a spirit join us and it affects people in different ways."

I was *seriously* unimpressed with that answer. It just didn't mean a thing to me. I managed to turn round, walk ten paces and then burst into tears. I couldn't stop weeping. One girlfriend said, "Close your chakras down," and I thought, *What on earth is she talking about?* Hard to imagine, but I had no idea *at all* about energy then. Then I suddenly realised I felt absolutely amazing. I didn't want to stop crying. It felt fantastic.

> "When she put her hands on my head, the tears just flowed and flowed. I couldn't stop weeping all day."

It reminded me of five years earlier when I had gone for a Reiki treatment. The lady had explained that spirits would come and heal whatever needed healing. When she put her hands on my head, the tears just flowed and flowed. I couldn't stop weeping all day. It was really *embarrassing* for the beauty salon. They had to hide me in a room at the side because they had all these people waiting for treatment and I couldn't stop crying. Eventually they had to almost smuggle me out. *[Laughing]* It was hilarious, really.

I remember shopping in the local supermarket with my sunglasses on whilst still quietly weeping. It was amazingly cathartic. But then the Reiki lady vanished and that was it for another five years.

After that networking event, the plug had been pulled again. I remember getting on the train at Waterloo, going to my Wandsworth flat. I couldn't have described it in words *then* but I was in a state of bliss where I felt connected to every single stranger on that carriage. Like I *loved* them all – deeply. *[Laughing]* Fortunately, I didn't try to kiss them or anything! It was a different type of love – like a connection. It was like I'd tapped into the other side – the consciousness of love. It was just unbelievable. Very moving and I couldn't stop weeping – gently. It was surrender.

I woke up the next morning, put on my make-up, put on my suit to go to work thinking I could just put the mask back on and carry on with life. Within two hours, I'd burst into tears again with a member of my staff. Incidentally, she came into my office most upset because she said she kept getting up in the middle of the night, going into the kitchen and crying her eyes out by the washing machine and she couldn't understand why. The flat where she lived was a former psychiatric hospital. Then *I* started crying and I thought, *This is not on. I need to sort this.* Still very yang.

I made my excuses, saying someone had died in the family, and left the office. I followed up *two clues* from the previous evening. I booked an appointment with a recommended Reiki Master and a reading at the College of Psychic Studies that day. I remember crying my eyes out as I drove down to London and feeling very clear that my best friend, who had committed suicide ten years earlier, was sitting in the passenger seat of the car, guiding my hand. On the radio came the song,

'Heaven Must Be Missing an Angel Because You're Right Here By My Side,' by Tavares. It was just amazing. At the time, I felt, *What on earth is going on?*

I've still got the reading from the College of Psychic Studies. It said 'your career is going to do a 180 degrees turn. You'll end up working with a group of people, globally, where you get as much out as you put in and there's no real leader. You're very equal. And you'll be more successful than you have ever dreamt of.' I thought, *What a joke. I can't possibly be more successful than I am now.*

As I walked out, there was a flyer on the wall saying, 'Sun, Sea, Spirit in Barbados. Two-Week Holiday.' I thought, *That looks great.* I booked for May and I never went back to work from that holiday. My intuition had been awakened – the female yin. There was an opening. I remember being in the supermarket and picking up *Spirit & Destiny* magazine and seeing an article about 'Free the Inner Voice'. Aha. Singing lessons. Fabulous. I couldn't sing. Can *you* sing?

Yes. But I can't whistle.

Well, not being able to sing is awful. One time I was part of a rugby singsong in the pub and a guy asked, "Why aren't you singing along?"

I said, "I can't sing."

He said, "Don't be daft, we're in a group. Join in. Nobody will notice."

I started singing and he turned round and said, "You're right, you *can't* sing."

I'm sure it was a joke, but it didn't feel like a joke at the time. Remember, you're talking to a super-achiever here. Part of me thought, *You're either born with a voice or not,* and the other part – the massive yang – was like, *I'm not having this. I'm going to find out how to sing.*

I arrived in my sports car, all suited and booted and really thinking, *I'm above everyone and I'm going to learn to sing.* It's unbelievable. Everyone was in socks and tracksuit trousers and I thought, *Hold on a minute. This is supposed to be a singing lesson.* Nobody could really explain to me what went on, which was even more disconcerting. And then things got worse when somebody said, "You can borrow my tracksuit trousers." I thought, *Beam me up, Scotty.*

Anyway, I ended up putting on the tracksuit trousers and my bottom and thighs were hanging out and it was like, "Oh, my God." They were the perfect garments because it meant as soon as I walked through the door, I was forced to leave my ego outside because I just looked horrendous. The first thing we had to do was sing our name in a circle. I remember thinking, *I've come here to learn to sing.* The session was with Nikki Slade from *Free the Inner Voice* and she very cleverly sold you two sessions. You couldn't come for just one. You had to buy two. I spent the whole first session thinking, *What on earth is going on here?* At the second one, I could get into it.

Nikki's work is incredibly powerful. It's about expressing your True Self. I worked with her for six years. It really helped me work through all my stuff. What I distinguished was that as a young child, it hadn't felt safe for me to express myself. I had a very powerful mother. When I was seven, I picked all the bluebells in the woods and came in with them. My mother went berserk and I was sent to my room. My best friend was sent home, which was very humiliating and I remember my mother saying, "Don't you look at me with those eyes of yours." My eyes wanted to say, "This isn't fair, I didn't mean any harm," but there was no space for me to speak. That was it, and I was a good girl for the rest of my life. I did what I was *meant* to do which was – work hard, play hard, earn lots of money and then you'll be loved.

In May 2003, I left work and went travelling. I hung out in London for a while and then I started my Feng Shui business back here in October 2005.[2]

What attracted you to Feng Shui?

I've always been interested in people and houses, and I'm really nosey. As you walk into somebody's house, you get to know the person almost immediately. The house says something about them. It's quite interesting because I'm cheating by being interviewed here because this is effectively our family house. I don't invite anybody to my house in Chester. It's quite interesting because it's not my chosen house – it's a house that happened. I just fell into it.

I was at Nikki Slade's fiftieth birthday party last week and it was an amazing transformative group of women. Gosia and Davina Mackail were there. I overheard Davina saying something about number 41 being a transformative number. I think it's linked to the fact that it is 4+1=5 and 5 in Feng Shui is coming back to Self. The number of my house in Chester is 41.

I can understand that. I feel as if I'm living in a temporary base. It's not my home, but it's fulfilling an important role as a cocoon while I write, incubate my work and birth it into the world. This is my period of hermitude.

Yes. You know it's not permanent – it's a place for transformation. I never committed to this house. I bought it as an investment to rent out. I never spent any money on it more than I had to. In fact, nearly everything in that house I got for free. It's incredible. I furnished it for nothing and I could walk away from it tomorrow. Apart from my paintings, there's nothing of value in there– except for very, very decent beds.

You could almost be talking about me.

It shows what's important to us, doesn't it? My television and my stereo, I got from a neighbour. And I've got a good quality bookcase a librarian friend gave me. And yeah, I could walk away. Minimal possessions, and it's like there's a huge clearing out going on. I'm seeing it with so many people. A lot are going bankrupt. Everything is just clearing out, clearing out, clearing out, and so they create anew and afresh. It's really exciting.

That feels like me too. I've spent the last seven years with virtually no income, but still investing in myself and developing deeper into who I really am. I know this is a springboard. It's been very liberating.

Well done. A lot of people are very fearful because they spend their money and can't see any more coming in immediately. They get scared and either blame themselves or other people. A lot of fear comes up to be processed. I love your clarity. I agree with you, but it challenges people.

It's challenged me. Then you get to a stage where you just let go and trust.

So how did you come to Feng Shui?

---

2   The Chinese practice of creating a living and working environment in harmony with nature and the flow of energy.

I really can't remember. I love learning and I was at a loose end. I must have just read somewhere about Robert Gray's Feng Shui Academy in Buxton. The course was over 3–6 months at weekends – which suited me. I got to meet people and it was a change of scenery.

It's fascinating. Houses say so much about people. For example, I grew up in this detached house with no neighbours. There's a riding school next door, but that's all derelict now. This is a big house – significant. It sends a certain message. That's how I grew up. During college I lived all over the place. Then I found myself in a little cottage before I moved into a penthouse in London. So again, I'm above everyone. Isolated but above everyone.

Then I went travelling before coming back home briefly. I soon manifested another penthouse in Chester. Stunning. The top of a Victorian house in the turrets. Talk about Princess in the Tower! People had to walk up thirty-nine steps to reach me! I had views over the River Dee and the meadows. If that's not wanting power, I don't know what is! I was still being significant. Still being, 'I'm above people and protected and nobody can hurt me.' Very interesting.

Then, by default, I end up in a terraced house, à la Coronation Street[3], which was my idea of hell. Talk about change! I was in with the people. It was amazing and absolutely perfect. I could start to get related to people rather than holding myself aloof. It was the perfect house that I would never have chosen myself.

How did you come by it?

That was amazing. I went to sell the property in London, did some Feng Shui space clearing on it and got that I shouldn't be selling it. So I carried on renting it out. I did another space clearing a short while afterwards and got, "Yes, now is the time to sell. Right now." I asked the estate agent, "Have you had any disappointed buyers in some of the flats?"

He said, "Funny you should mention that. Two weeks ago, we sold the flat opposite yours and we did have one disappointed buyer."

To cut a long story short, I sold the flat two weeks later to that buyer for *£20,000* more than the almost identical one opposite.

I had spare cash from the sale. I know what I'm like with spare cash, so I thought, *Quick, I need to sink it into property.* I was just looking for an investment – a nice little terraced house that I could rent out to a young, professional couple or students, close to the station in Chester and an easy buy. I had an ex-boyfriend who was good with doing places up. He needed to get on the property ladder, so I thought that would support him. I ended up living there.

It all works out, doesn't it? What else was happening in your life as you were transforming?

I went back to the College of Psychic Studies where I learnt to do tarot readings and mediumship. I even did stage mediumship. I thought I was hopeless at it but anyway, I've done it. I met a Reiki Master – Jake – black as the ace of spades. He looked like he'd just walked off a Brixton street corner as far as I was concerned. He had one of these stocking things on his head and was the complete opposite to anybody I would normally choose to bring into my penthouse – and he was like an angel. He was my spiritual teacher for a number of years. He would come for an hour's Reiki where

---

3   A long-running British soap set amongst a working class community.

THE INSPIRING JOURNEYS OF WOMEN ENTREPRENEURS

he could sometimes stay for five hours. We had amazing experiences.

There were always spirits that would come to join us and he would always describe them. Sometimes my friend who committed suicide ten years earlier was there. One time, he was giving me Reiki and he said, "We've got a live spirit."

"What? You mean someone who is living has come and joined us?"

He went, "Yes."

We worked out it was my sister. I phoned her and asked, "What were you doing last night about 10 o'clock?"

She said, "I think I dozed off in front of the telly – very embarrassing."

I said, "What were you wearing?"

She said, "Dark green trousers and dark green top."

And that was exactly how he described her. I said, "Well, we think you popped in on our Reiki session."

She said, "Claire, that's really funny because just before I dozed off, I was thinking, *I wonder what this Reiki thing is that Claire's up to. Must check it out.*"

Isn't that amazing? We had lots of experiences like that, and then Jake came across Diana Cooper. He said, "Marie-Claire, you need to go on Diana Cooper's month-long retreat at Buckland Hall. It's about £2,000. I can't afford to go, but my gut feeling is you must go."

I said, "Well, I'll tell you what, if I find £2,000, I'll go on it."

As I was going through my accounts, I found £3,000. So I booked and then I found someone to rent my house as well. It was perfect. The course was interesting, but it was just a bit too angel-y for me – at the time, anyway. I didn't think angels were my thing. But Diana taught me something. I remember sitting down with her and saying, "How do you manage to speak about angels when so many people don't believe you?" She said, "When you really believe in something, you just stick with it and then people listen to you."

That's what I got from that course. She taught me how to be a leader, I think. It's trusting yourself. Sticking with what you believe irrespective of what other people think. A while after that, someone from Diana Cooper's school contacted me about Transform Your Life teacher training. That was far more up my street than angels.

> "Most people want to be happy ...loved ... fulfilled. But try being happy, loved and fulfilled if you haven't got any money to pay the bills."

From that course I took a lot of the principles and the way they facilitated and then created Money Magnet. Literally, I looked around and thought, *What do most people need and want?* Most people want to be happy, they want to be loved, they want to be fulfilled. But try being happy, loved and fulfilled if you haven't got any money to pay the bills. So I thought, *What most people want is money, even if they're not saying so.* They want to feel secure. It's the bottom level, isn't it? It's pretty difficult to be spiritual if you're not grounded. You've got to put the roots down before you can reach up. So that's where I was coming from. I thought, *Okay, that's one thing I've done all my life – help people create more money. Let's take everything I've learnt from Law of Attraction – working with Bob Proctor and Richard Bandler and Diana Cooper and all that stuff – and combine it with what I know*

88   JANE NOBLE KNIGHT

from the business world and put it all together in a one-day workshop.

We did it at a friend's lovely place in Overton-on-Dee. I met her originally at Diana Cooper's retreat. She was the complete opposite to me. I was the yang-yang businesswoman and she was the mother and wife, blonde and blue-eyed, very airy-fairy, into the angels. We were complete opposites that came together and created this workshop. She had the premises and I was the main facilitator. We charged £50 for the day, and it was a lovely day out in the countryside. We quite often walked out to the river and stuff. And it worked!

It's something I say to audiences a lot. The question to ask is, "What do people want and need? How can I help people and how can I reach as many people as possible with what I have, to make a difference?" I'd worked out a way to help people with the workshop. The next thing was 'How can I get it to more people because this works?' The obvious thing was to write a book. I used to be a 50-a-day smoker till I read Allen Carr's, *The Easy Way to Give up Smoking.* I had a shift in my mindset so complete that I couldn't wait to give up smoking. *That* is a miracle. Unbelievable. So I wrote with the intention that *my* book could shift people's mindset around money.

The next stage has got to be the training of Money Magnet coaches. Only this morning I suddenly remembered that when Diana Cooper started her teaching school, she handed it over to a group of people to do it. I remember finding it quite strange that she literally handed it over to them and said, "Here is the Diana Cooper School. Go and run it for me." I think that's what I need to do with the Money Magnet.

How did Hay House come to publish your book?

When I wrote the book, I self-published. My website designer put me in contact with a guy who designed the book, and he knew how to load it on Amazon. It didn't cost me an awful lot and it all just happened quite easily.

I was having a conversation with my girlfriend in Australia. She was one of only two people to read the book before I published it. I thought she was so far away that if it didn't work then I could cope with the rejection. In fact, it worked really well for her. She's recently sold her business for an incredible $350,000. She told me, "People don't buy books from Amazon in Sydney. The shipping costs are too much. If you want the book to be available over here, you really need to get a publisher."

I'm not quite sure why I thought of Hay House, but they had offices in Australia. Funnily enough, it had nothing to do with, *"I want to be a Hay House author. I want to go worldwide."* It was purely so that I had an excuse to visit my friend in Australia. I still haven't managed to see her.

Many people buy into this notion that they have to go to lots of publishers and write lots of letters to get published, but if you believe in Law of Attraction and you get a good feeling about something, for whatever reason, you just approach *one.* I posted my book to them and they phoned me up straight away and said 'give us six weeks.' Then they said, "Yes, come and see us." I'll never forget it because I got off the tube. I had a PA at the time and she'd emailed me the directions. I was walking down the street on this sunny day and I had this gut feeling I was going in completely the wrong direction. This felt like the most important meeting in my life. They were either going to take the book or not.

A guy comes past on a bike wearing a hoodie and I stop him and say, "Am I going the right way for Hay House?"

He said, "No, you're going in completely the wrong direction."

I remember thinking, and in fact I said it out loud, "I've got to trust you now, haven't I?" I was so aware that I was now talking to a complete stranger who had given me the opposite information to somebody that worked for me. I was left with a choice of whether I trusted him or not. He said, "Yes, I'll tell you what – I'll come with you," and with that, he got off his bike and pulled down his hoodie. He was the most *gorgeous*-looking young man. Dark, curly hair with blue eyes, late twenties. Honestly, you could call him an angel.

As we walked along, I told him about the book and about helping The Monastery in Manchester raise a million pounds. He said, "The Monastery? You see that church over there? We call that the Monastery. I know I may look like a hoodie, but I'm actually a personal trainer. My father and I have a boxing gym in that church. We pull in all the kids off the streets and teach them self-respect through boxing. The problem is we need £600,000 to keep the gym going." He looked me straight in the eyes and said, "Can you help us?"

I said, "Yes, I think I can." I went all goosebumpy. We swapped business cards and gave each other a big hug. I remember thinking, *This is a complete stranger I'm hugging and he trusts me.* And I trusted *him*. It was just incredible.

I got to Hay House on time. When the Editorial Director turned round and said, "Why do you want to publish this book," I literally told her the story of this guy. I said, "I want to publish this book because there are so many people out there doing good work who need money and I want to make a difference for them. If I can contribute in any way I can to create more money for good causes like his then that would make my day."

She said, "Yes, you're a Hay House author. We'll take you on board." And that was that.

Excellent … What's it like for an independent, self-published author like you to be part of a big organisation like Hay House?

I'm starting to fully embrace it. At the beginning, I was still coming from a place of almost 'me against the world'. If you're used to handling everything yourself, it's quite difficult to let go.

There's a funny story. A few years ago, my friend Rachel said, "Why don't you speak at Millionaire Bootcamp?" Brilliant idea. I emailed Stephanie Hale saying, "Can I be one of your speakers?" She said, "Yes, what are your percentage sales per blah, blah and what's your experience and what products have you got to £10,000?"

I was just like, "Oh my gosh, I'm not ready for this." And then I looked at her website and I saw all these multi-millionaires on it and I thought, *No. Duck. I'm not ready. I'm playing above my station, here.* I didn't even respond to her email. I was so scared and thought, *I can't do it.* Then she came back ten days before the event and said, "Okay, we've got you a slot on the Friday morning," and went through all the details of needing products of £10,000 and don't wear black and all the basics. I was like, "Yes, yes, yes." Got off the phone and went, "Aaaarrrggh, quick. Got to create some products."

I charged into motion and it was incredible. In ten days, we created an audio CD set which ultimately became this *(indicating a set)* read by me with a really sore throat in one hit on a Sunday in a radio station. A team videoed the Money Magnet workshop and I already had a CD of Money

Magnet Tips. So we created three products just in time for the bootcamp.

Amazing! Then I was having lunch with the Editing Director of Hay House, literally the day before the Millionaire Bootcamp, and I was sharing the story with her and saying, "Wow, I can't believe it. I'm so proud of us. We were a team and we all came together and it was amazing." And then I looked at her face and she said, "Marie-Claire, I don't think you can do that." I was puzzled, *"What?"*

Suddenly, I realised what she meant. I had a contract with Hay House which meant *they* published my material, not me. And it was like, "Oh, my God." The concept of being in partnership with them hadn't really sunk into my conscience. That was my wake-up call.

I never did sell any of those products. I threw them in as part of a package. I kept to my word.

So what's next, looking into the future?

It's really interesting. In Feng Shui's 9 Star Ki[4], I am now in my No. 1 Year, which is hibernation. It's the seed that's in the earth. All the seed needs to do is nurture itself and keep itself safe.

So I'm in a real place of trust. Normally, I could say to you, "Well, I have this strict plan and this is what I'm going to be doing." But, actually, lots of things are coming to the fore that are slightly crazy. But what I see is that my work on this earth is about being with people. It's absolutely speaking from stage. There's no question about that. It's natural. It's what I'm meant to do. And it's connecting people. Running the business is *not* for me to do.

So I seem to be creating new money-making opportunities where I don't need to do an awful lot. All I need to do is to connect with people or speak and have fun, and that's what's been missing. Personal development is a very intensive business and sometimes you can suffer from analysis paralysis – it's exhausting. But I feel like I'm waking up and remembering who I am – the real essence of who I am. I'm somebody who likes fun and I like to laugh and I like to be free and I like to be with people. That's my priority and whatever comes out of that is what comes out of that.

"We can make money and have fun, and I'm finding ways of making money that are fun."

I spoke at this gig on Saturday morning. It was so funny because I was offering the two-hour breakthrough session. I put it up on the screen. My PA had done the PowerPoints the night before – I'm really bad at detail. I just do my thing.

At the end, I got off the stage, but I'd forgotten the last click of the button to put the price up there. And what was ostensibly a gross error actually worked perfectly because I had this long line of people all queuing up to find out what the price was. They didn't even think to ask each other. It was hilarious.

[Laughing] So how do you put fun into your work?

It's really interesting. I come from a Catholic background where you say 'Lord, I'm not worthy to receive' every week as an affirmation in mass. Yet there is something about creating a business that

---

4   Star Ki is a system based on complex and Oriental thoughts about the Universe and time. To learn more, check out the 9 Star Ki app created by Marie-Claire and company.

celebrates the fun and the joy. There is this view that all of this personal development is such hard work and making money is such hard work too. It's really not. So can we just lighten up? I want to have fun. I want to do something trivial that's not heavy and meaningful. So that's what I choose for myself. That's what I focus on.

I've learnt that I don't have to do everything. So my role is literally bringing people to the pot. I've got a Managing Director, I've got a Finance Director, I've got people to do it. So that's in the space.

And then my dream is to have my own TV show. Lots of people say that. I manifested it – we filmed three series for Sky TV and then it got stopped.

A friend of mine recently asked me, "Marie-Claire, what do you really, really want?"

I said, "I really want my own TV show." It just came to me very easily. I'm fascinated by people and it was very easy for me to do.

And he then replied, "Oh, the person whose house I'm moving into is a BBC TV producer."

That might come to something and it might not. And the most important thing is having fun. That's my major thing. Life doesn't have to be hard work. I think that's been my biggest breakthrough. We can make money and have fun, and I'm finding ways of making money that *are* fun.

> "... the easiest way of getting in touch with what you want is looking at what makes you happy."

A classic example recently … I'm invited to go on a boat for drinks, not networking, literally just going on a boat with some friends for drinks and meeting new friends. I meet a lady. She's totally inspiring. She's re-launched a members' club in London that's been going for years and years. Ideally, she needs premises for the club. She tells me where the original premises were and I said, *"Wow, wouldn't it be amazing if you could get back into your original premises?"* and she says, "Oh, that would be our dream."

Then I remember a few months earlier somebody telling me that they were selling literally the building that she was talking about. I realised that if I connect the two of them and take a broker's commission, I've just made myself a lot of money doing what I do best – having fun and connecting people. So I get that it doesn't need to be hard work to make money. You just get in your flow.

I'm also very committed to there being a hundred Money Magnet coaches worldwide and making a difference to global poverty. My new business managing team will set it up so that we can spread the word. I'm also looking at the next books that I want to write, which include one on how everybody can become a philanthropist. My creativity knows no bounds, so it's exciting. And more time off, more holidays.

Fantastic. What especially have you learned on your journey?

The biggest lesson is definitely that you get in touch with what *you* want. But it's not as easy as it sounds because we're so conditioned. To me the easiest way of getting in touch with what you want is looking at what makes you happy. When was the last time you giggled and felt happy with life? For me there is nothing better than sitting at the table in the sunshine and having some good food with a bunch of interesting, gorgeous, loving, fun friends – heaven. Other people climb mountains and do marathons and God knows what, but that is my idea of heaven. So find your heaven and don't settle for anything less.

People often think that's selfish, but actually, if you imagine a daffodil trying to be a rose, it would really *mess* up the universe. It would really mess up the harmony of nature. All the daffodil needs to do is be the best daffodil it can be. All you need to do is be the best you *you* can be. It's that simple. And give yourself permission to do what you want to do.

I had this conversation with my sister this week and she said, "Yes, but Claire, isn't that selfish? We've got to think of other people. We can't always have what we want."

I said, "Give me an example."

She said, "Well, you know, if Mum wants to do this but I want to do that, wouldn't it be nice if I did that for Mum?"

I said, "Well, it sounds like what you want is to please Mum, so *that is* what you want."

She went, "Oh yes, I see what you mean."

So, you can still do the something else. It's just do what you want to do and *trust* that intuition. It's the balance of yin and yang. When I left Xerox, I got that inkling that I was going to leave with money in my pocket. I followed a series of purely intuitive actions that led to me leaving with a big lump sum of money. That had never, ever happened before at Xerox. People didn't get made redundant, voluntarily or not. It was a job for life. I couldn't believe some of the stuff I did, but I was in the zone of trusting my intuition and being very clear on the outcome.

> "So, trust your intuition, and … take action."

When I left the corporate world, again, walking away from a job that I didn't even have to work hard at that paid me a quarter of a million pounds – it appears to be crazy. But if I hadn't walked away from that job, I wouldn't be a Hay House author speaking alongside Louise Hay and Wayne Dyer.

So, *trust your intuition*, and the last thing is to *take action*. I have people – very few, fortunately – who say, "I'm doing all this Law of Attraction and I'm not getting any more money." They're doing the meditations and the affirmations, but they're not taking any action. The more they say, "I'm not getting any more money," the more they're not getting any more money. So, you have to do something that you haven't done before, and it takes guts. It takes courage, and it takes trust. It's an amazing journey – amazing.

And it's worth it, isn't it?

Well, it's funny, because I spent most of my life chasing goals, like I've got to achieve something. I remember that when I published the book, I didn't really get it then. The highlight for me came at the book launch in Chester that you attended. I just remember feeling immense love. My goal was never really to be an author. My goal was always to be loved. So I think that was the *biggest* thing I have got in my life to date. Most of us search for love, but the love is within, it's not without. I now know that love is within. I attract love because I accept the love within.

> "I now know that love is within. I attract love because I accept the love within."

I never really got present to being an author. It's only now that people are phoning me and saying, "I've just seen you're speaking at a Hay House conference," and I'm thinking, *Okay, I need to get this. I need to own it.*

It's interesting. Only this morning, a friend of mine asked me, "Right, what are you going to achieve this morning?"

I thanked him for the question and told him two things that I was planning to get done that morning. He said, "Right, we'll speak again at midday and you tell me that you have achieved them."

> **"If you start with the base of love, anything is possible. That's what it's all about really."**

That's what we did, and it felt great having that accountability and I said, "Yes, tick, tick, I've achieved them and all this other stuff as well."

He said, "And are you feeling joy and happiness and delight that you've achieved this?"

I was horrified because I recognised that a bit of me was going, "Yes, but I've got to go and do that … but that email has just come in and so and so doesn't think well of me ..."

Actually, my focus wasn't on pure delight and joy at what I had achieved. He made me really stop and get present to it. And then he said, "How are you going to celebrate what you have achieved this morning?"

"Wow, that's a really good question. I'm celebrating by allowing myself the delight of having a conversation with you."

Which is gorgeous.

It is.

There's definitely something about pausing long enough to receive. As I said, I'm in hibernation. It's about pausing to receive. It's absolutely gorgeous. After years and years of pushing, it's nice to just go, *Okay. [with a deep breath out]*

It's time, isn't it?

Yes. All of us represent a possibility. We're not things, we're not people. We create ourselves each day to be who we want to be. My identity is Marie-Claire Carlyle and my Self is the possibility of love. That's who I am. And from love comes miracles. If you start with the base of love, anything is possible. That's what it's all about really. It's the whole thing.

Very true. Thank you very much for all you've shared, Marie-Claire.

Turn me on and I'm off.

When Marie-Claire said her biggest lesson was to get in touch with what you want, that really resonated with me. When I first began my personal pilgrimage to find out who I was in 1999, I hadn't a clue. I think many women are probably similar. I always seemed to be thinking of other people instead of myself. I was an "I don't mind. What do you want to do?" person. Boring!

It may sound silly, but my daughters nudged me into who I am now when they gifted me a massage that Christmas. It was the first proper indulgence I can remember. It started me allowing myself to be pampered and to do things that I wanted to do – for me. I am now a big fan of regular treats!

Interestingly, I found clues to all my greatest loves in my first seven years of childhood. For example, I was mesmerised by pantomimes. I love going now to a wide variety of live shows and events – concerts, theatre, musicals, conferences, talks, agricultural shows. I had a brilliant time volunteering at the International Eisteddfod in Llangollen in 2011.

I was also always fascinated by stories of other cultures such as the Native American and Egyptian. I loved to see the gypsies and their dogs in their horse-drawn caravans by the roadside in North Wales. I have enjoyed many holidays on reservations and in Egypt since I allowed myself to indulge in my passions. I even have rescued lurchers – the traditional gypsy dog. And, of course, in 2011 my two lurchers joined me for seven months travelling round the UK in my motorhome, though my beloved companion, Sammy, is now chasing rabbits in heaven.

I loved wandering – I would go out for hours with my childhood friends, making dens in the sandpits and borrowing ponies to roam round the Welsh lanes. I'm still a wanderer – a pilgrim through life.

I adored books, stories and learning. My dad would share information about what we saw round us – the Romans in Chester, Liverpool in the war, the wonders of nature – and my mum would tell funny stories about herself and her family. Now here am I learning about the stories of Pilgrim Mothers, sharing my own and writing this book.

How about you? Do you know what you want, what you would love to do? Perhaps the clues can be found in your childhood too. Have a look and then, as Marie-Claire says, find your heaven and don't settle for anything less.

"Allow yourself to be pampered and do the things you want to do. …
What would you love to do?"

JANE NOBLE KNIGHT

DAWN GIBBINS MBE

"…I believe that we women are going to change the world…"

Secret Millionaire, spiritual coach, philanthropreneur, keynote speaker and dream catcher, helping people to live the life of which they dream. Dawn has received multiple awards including Veuve Clicquot Businesswoman of the Year 2004, Most Influential Person in British Manufacturing 2006 and an MBE for Services to UK industry in 1993. Dawn founded the world leading seamless flooring company Flowcrete Group Ltd in 1982 with her father, Peter Gibbins. In 2004 Dawn was made a Pioneer to the Life of Our Nation by Her Majesty the Queen. She added The Legend of Industry Award from The Variety Club of Great Britain to her achievements. Dawn still lives where she grew up in Congleton, Cheshire, which she has successfully turned into Beartown!

www.dawngibbins.com

A Conversation with Dawn Gibbins

The Yin Crowd-Puller

When was the last time that someone you had never met before flung their arms round you and lifted you off your feet? For me it was the day I met Dawn Gibbins. With my SatNav's help, I had easily found Dawn's home up a narrow lane in Congleton, Cheshire. I parked by her car, chuckling at her personalised number plate which broadcasts for all to see that she is very happy being 'WOO WOO'. I had only exchanged emails with Dawn till now, though I felt I knew her from her *Secret Millionaire* appearance. I could see Dawn chatting on her mobile beneath a tasteful round gazebo situated on a patio area next to the house. Six solid cane chairs with bright, comfy cushions were placed round a central table. Dawn and her two friends, Alison and Richard, looked up and smiled while Dawn gave me a big wave as she finished her phone call.

She made her way down to greet me with open arms. "I feel like picking you up," she said… and promptly did, swinging me round for good measure as we both laughed. I'm no lightweight, even though I'm small, and Dawn is definitely a strong woman in more ways than one!

Yes, with Dawn Gibbins expect the unexpected.

I first emailed Dawn in March to invite her to be one of my Pilgrim Mother Entrepreneurs. She sent me the most exuberant email I have ever had the pleasure to receive. It was full of joy and enthusiasm and energy. It reinforced my impression of Dawn as a generous, free spirit.

I had first come across Dawn's name in 2008 when I read *Making It: Women Entrepreneurs Reveal Their Secrets of Success* by Lou Gimson and Allison Mitchell [Capstone Publishing, 2008]. I had bought a copy after meeting Lou because my younger daughter happened to feature briefly in it.

Then in 2010 I watched Dawn in Channel 4's *The Secret Millionaire*, which you now know I absolutely love. I got hooked with the very first episode when a gentle, young man in his twenties revealed he was a millionaire.

Out of all the moving and inspiring encounters, Dawn's spell in Bristol is in my top three. She was so natural and honest. No airs and graces with Dawn – just love, empathy and compassion in bucket loads. The fact that Dawn is the second highest donor from about sixty episodes says it all.

Dawn took me on a guided tour of her garden outbuildings – her peace pods and 'shed' ("I must call it a barn!") with its large windows and patio doors overlooking the Cheshire countryside. From this lofty vantage point on this beautiful sunny day, I enjoyed the same stunning views as Dawn's colourful bear on the lawn – a reminder of Dawn's successful venture to rebrand her hometown of Congleton as Beartown. The spaces inside and out were immaculate, exuding harmony, as you would expect from a Feng Shui ambassador.

As the gardener mows the grass in the background, we settle down on the comfortable sofas. Dawn uses her full vocal range to express herself. Sometimes she speaks in conspiratorial whispers as she leans towards me to share secrets and at other times she shouts out excitedly with extravagant gestures to share her passions. Balanced – yes. Monotone – never. Come and be entertained…

I love your asymmetrical haircut, Dawn. How did you come by it?

When I was about twenty-two, I had a bit of a bohemian lifestyle. I travelled with a guy who was a hairdresser. He originally cut my hair. He shaved one side and I had the rest permed very long and curly. I've always had this golden brown hair, long on one side, since then.

When my two beautiful daughters hit about sixteen, they thought Mum was a bit Afro and wild, so they asked me to calm down a bit. That's when I became straight. The only time I had it all cut off was when I was about forty, but then I missed my asymmetrical style and went back to it.

Also, I'm a Gemini – like two people. So my hair has one side very feminine and the other side quite masculine. My friend, Alison Levesley, believes my spirituality has come from Feng Shui. It's that balance – the yin and the yang. I basically look that way as well.

It reminds me of how Vidal Sassoon created Mary Quant's signature haircut, and she has retained the 'bob' style. It obviously captures who she is – like your own cut!

As you say, balance is really important. Were you always balanced growing up, Dawn?

I think my dad wanted a little boy, so maybe that's a factor. I'm the only child of two beautiful people – Vera Banks and Peter Gibbins. The daughter of a great British inventor! From the age of five, I lived a life outdoors. I used to go fishing with him and *[dropping to a deeper voice] shooting with him* – killing animals – which I wouldn't go anywhere near now. When we used to go fishing off Anglesey on a little boat, the locals, in typical Welsh fashion, would call me 'Dawn the Fish' because I would win all the fishing competitions down there.

When Mum and Dad went into the bar of the hotel, I would stay on the beach, selling all the mackerel.

I don't go fishing or shooting now. But as part of my role in the business – because it was the construction and manufacturing industry – I loved taking all the contractors and floor layers out sea fishing. My job was to gut the fish and throw all the innards to the seagulls. All the guys were like "Eewww, how can you do that?"

So … my childhood …

Childhood was basically council house, no money. Mum used to make all my clothes, and then she taught *me* how to sew. I used to make my clothes as a teenager. My dolls were the best-dressed, most fashionable dolls because I *love* fashion design. Yeah, we had no money. I always had to get up and make the coal fire that heated the water because we didn't have central heating.

I just lived in the great outdoors, bicycling everywhere. For one of my first jobs I used to cycle to the pub to serve behind the bar and cycle back home in the dark. I'd sing and scream when I was going past woodland and things – quite scary! For me and everyone else!

I went to this little teeny village school with only thirty children. There was one quite rich girl who had this swimming pool and really prestigious house, but of course *we* didn't. But my dad, the little darling, he used to think, *I want to try and give that to my daughter.* So he dug a hole in the garden and lined it with 8 by 4s. Then he covered it with fibreglass and made a swimming pool in our council house garden. We used it for a summer and then, basically, it went green and slimy and got frogs. *[Laughing]* My childhood was very, very happy.

Dad had a big heart. He was a beautiful man. He was also quite a naughty man. I think he had lots of relationships with secretaries and so on, but my mother *loved* him so much. She always had him back, which I'm thinking, *Well, you were a crazy woman,* you know.

Part of that generation, though, do you agree?

Yeah, but anyway he came back. My mum was always a 'stay at home'. She was very stable – rock solid. You can't move my mother – whereas I'm very excitable and passionate, like my dad. But I've got Mum's 'stickability' to make things happen, which is nice.

My mum was always the one to say "No, you can't do that." My dad was always "Come on, you *can* do that." I really wanted a horse. Other people had horses. We couldn't really afford one, but, anyway, my dad made it possible. I had this real cheap, bony mare when I was about nine or ten. Cindy-Lou, her name was. Beautiful. My dad got her in the field down the road. I had some friends with ponies. So my dad got a few more 8 by 4s and oil drums and we made jumps. It was very practical. My bunny rabbit had the best run because I'm good with my hands. I'm quite artistic.

Dad helped us start a horse show – which eventually became a 3-day gymkhana and horse show. My friends and I were quite enterprising and active – *with* my dad's help. So Dad and I did get on very well together when I was younger. Then he disappeared when I was about 18.

School wise, I did great early on. I got ten O-levels. Then I went to college and just lost the plot – socialising, enjoying myself with all the different students – Chinese, Iranians – it was like a new world. I'd been to a girls' school, so of course college was great. But … I *failed* my A-levels.

Anyway, I loved animals. I really wanted to be a vet, but my head teacher at grammar school told me that I wasn't clever enough. I actually think, looking back, one of the reasons I haven't written a book yet is that there's this subconscious, limiting belief within me that I'm not intelligent

> "… one of the reasons I haven't written a book yet is that there's this subconscious, limiting belief within me that I'm not intelligent enough. But now … I think, Bollocks to that."

enough. But now, with all the self-chat, I think, *Bollocks to that.*

At the time it affected me. But I loved art – portraits and murals. While I was doing A-levels, I did my O-level Art – my only A in O-levels. I thought about fashion design, but I didn't do anything about it.

Instead, I got a job similar to my dad's in a laboratory – which was *not* my cup of tea because I'm not numerical. I'm not a scientist. It was an aluminium-smelting place and I was doing all the quality control. I got on with all the guys on the shop floor. *But* there was this miserable, grumpy man in that laboratory and I just kept looking out of the window thinking, *I need to escape.* I worked there for a year. Then I decided to go hitchhiking around France, Spain and Portugal and ended up actually staying there for three years.

In Bordeaux I met up with that hairdresser I mentioned. We picked peaches and apples in a place near Perpignan in that first summer. The farmer suggested we come back to do the vendange – the grape harvest. So we did. Then he said, "Come back in February. You can do pruning and plant salads and I can employ you all year." So we went back two years on the trot. We lived in a tent for the first year and a house for two years, which was phenomenal.

I think that was what got me into Feng Shui in the end – living with nature, seeing how the French in the little villages lived, working on the land and eating what you were growing. Aaahh. The energy and the connection with nature were just sensational – beautiful.

Of course, what was also freely available over there was alcohol. Unfortunately, my friend turned into a bit of an alcoholic, so we had to come home and we split up. *[Quietly]* What was very sad, Jane, was he died last year. His family found me to come to his funeral. We were together for three years and at his funeral the vicar read out that the happiest days of his life were spent in France with a girlfriend. That made me cry. And the music was all Van Morrison, *Brown Eyed Girl*, which was our song, and I'm thinking, *He never found himself.* He got into drugs and, in fact, the alcohol and drugs killed him at the age of fifty. It was so sad.

However, he kept the beauty that we'd got together; but where I moved on and found beauty, he didn't. But we did have something special there, that really connected me with nature, and that was gorgeous.

So back to France …

I came back from France and started to work with my dad. I've mentioned to you before about him being a 'Great British Inventor' – passionate inventor, mad inventor, very generous inventor – gave away everything. That's why my mother and I never had anything as a family – because he did everything for everybody else. Even in his love affairs, he gave – we never had anything, so we lived in a council house. But in one of the love affairs he had, he'd bought this woman a house. He had a son with this woman. So I've got a stepbrother down in Birmingham. When he was on his deathbed, Dad said, "Dawn, will you help me? Would you sort these other people out?"

So you didn't know until then?

Not until he was almost dying. He'd got this guilt. I believe cancer is very much an emotional issue. A lot of people deny it, but you have got something in your past that's eating you. Okay, you've been exposing yourself to toxins and you might be living on geopathic stress, you might be being hit with radio waves and eating foods that aren't right for you, but you've got something emotional that has basically triggered those nasty gremlins to come and attack you.

With my dad, it was all that emotional stress of how he had lived his life. He was guilt-ridden. He had myeloma that ate his bones. When I looked into the leukaemia research, it suggested that myeloma was prolonged exposure to hydrocarbons.

In fact, this week I did a speech and one of the ladies in the audience came over. She had myeloma as well. I'd never really connected with anybody with myeloma before. Her mum used to use paraffin – she had tropical fish. It was that volatile organic compound that killed her mum and my dad. All the solvents that we had in the flooring industry, the tar extended resins that we were using, killed him. *Well – as well as* the guilt, which we talked about – and the smoking.

But also – I couldn't believe this when I got into Feng Shui – I went to dowse his house and found he was sleeping across a geopathic stress line … right under his neck. He actually lost a vertebra in his neck – one of the first ones he lost – that then paralysed him. Those crossing stress lines … I lost a dog to leukaemia too and his basket was on crossing lines.

So, one of my big 'raison d'êtres' in life is to bring the consciousness of geopathic stress into the UK – the consciousness of the invisible hazards in homes. Yes, I'm going to get ridiculed and I'm going to get called 'woo woo'. But in Germany, Scandinavia and Austria, architects and doctors have gone through all that and they basically, now, advise clients – patients – to look at their environment. Look at what they're eating. It's lifestyle. I believe that's one of my callings – to really make a mass awareness.

> "I believe that we women are going to change the world."

So I've got to get a language – *change* the language – about the invisible hazards. Otherwise, people will think I'm just a 'woo woo' woman.

There are three core areas of my purpose. One is my *spiritual* purpose, which is basically to transform the lives of women and children – give them techniques and confidence. I believe that we women are going to change the world. It's this *Yin*, feminine energy, that's going to actually make a real difference to the consciousness of this planet. Women don't mind the spirituality of 'woo woo'.

The second is my *physical* purpose. We need to change the way that doctors work – that *we* work with doctors. I believe we've got to *challenge* the NHS – not in an aggressive, warlike way, but work together with them for change. So when someone goes to the doctor, the doctor *refers* that patient to a health coach, a lifestyle coach. Then the coaches work with the doctors to heal. So it's like a natural healing.

Doctors look at whether patients need operations and sometimes drugs. *But* mostly, if you've got blood pressure, watch your salt. Look at your water intake. The simple things that you should be looking at that they don't.

[With passion] Then there's my *emotional* purpose. The emotions of the corporate world really need a *big* challenging. I've got this brand – The Yin Crowd. We all gather together. *[Singing]* "We're in with the Yin crowd. I know where the Yin crowd goes." Business brings a lot of stress into people's lives – at all levels – the executives too.

We need to harmonise business through storytelling and bringing more love and compassion. It's all about people living their truth. So Yin stands for 'Your Inner Nature' – Y. I. N. We've got to look at the inner nature of businesses and the inner nature of the individuals working in those businesses. *Everybody* has got to look within to find out who they are.

So we look at the purpose, the passion and the pride of the individuals *and* the businesses. The purpose is why you are here; the meaning of your life and the life of your business. The passion is, hey, what talents have you got? And then using those talents … now, this is the big one… *for the greater good of humanity.* Why the hell do you exist? Why does that business exist? I believe that *every* business exists to help and support humanity and the community, but they don't realise that – yet. And that's our calling as well.

"I believe that every business exists to help and support humanity and the community, but they don't realise that – yet."

One thing that is on my cards – and I'm not there yet – is getting white papers of evidence together that look at businesses allowing their employees to work in the community, to work with charities, to put back. That's what I did in my business. My business was successful because my staff felt good. They had spirit because they knew that we were doing things for the greater good of the community and humanity. That brings *pride.*

My dad influenced me a lot in my life. He had a passion that he wanted to change the world. That's where I got my passion from. He wanted to make people's lives better. In the flooring industry I was campaigning to ban the builders' bottom, but, really, my dad got it right. He saw there were a lot of back and knee problems, so he was developing all these self-levelling, self-smoothing flooring products that you just pumped onto the floor. So the operatives didn't have to bend over, which was *great.* And… we didn't see the bottom cleavage!

My dad was really a Feng Shui Master because he saw how you could transform the environment by bringing beautiful, healing floors – easy to clean floors – but also floors that didn't grow mould and disintegrate. I learned from him.

We used to put silver into the floors that killed bugs. We had these anti-microbial floors that killed E. Coli, salmonella and MRSA instantly. One of the other scientists, who I thought was fantastic, said that if you look back into medieval times to King Arthur and the like, they used to drink from silver goblets and use silver utensils. Silver has always been used as an anti-microbe to kill bugs. We never realised this at the time, but my dad, the scientist, did.

"We should be lobbying governments to look at the performance of business on that triple bottom line [People, Planet, Profit] – not just the bottom line."

Once I had experienced my dad dying of cancer, I set about getting rid of solvents and toxins from *all* aspects of my life. We've got a big job on our hands. I was doing it in the flooring trade, but *now* I find out a lot of cosmetics and food packaging have these 'nasties' that are affecting us. We've got a *mass toxin alert* to get out there to the general public to stop us actually absorbing them into our bodies.

Since my dad died, lots of people with cancer started to arrive on my doorstep. That made me very passionate about getting toxins out of the industry.

So … Purpose, Passion and Pride.

I believe that a lot of businesses need to take a look at how they're giving back. The money that I made came from giving back, from looking after my people. That triple bottom line – People, Planet, Profit.[1]

We should be lobbying governments to look at the performance of *business* on that *triple* bottom line – not just the bottom line. This entire credit crisis has come from looking at the bottom line too much. We should be looking at the softer elements, how we're saving the planet and the nurturing of people, the nurturing of sustainability and the eco side that basically the bottom line comes from.

I think once businesses realise that they can actually give back in a way that their staff *love*, where they inject the 'feel good factor' into their staff, they'll *then* be so successful.

I'm in that place at the moment where I'm just getting ready to go, *[Roaring loudly]* **"Raaaaaa."** Watch out, World. Dawn is about to come out.

The great thing with you, Dawn, is that you've been very successful in the business world. You have gravitas – even if some people might think you're a bit wacky.

I think it's about learning communication skills – how to communicate very clearly with different types of audiences. My world was a very male world. *Men love* straight lines. *Men love* black and white. Look at all the sports. Men love aiming for a goal. Look at golf – put the ball in the hole. Look at football, rugby … you name it. You've got a very clear goal that you're aiming at. You need that in business, very much so.

Then you look at women: women love stories, they love mystery, they love to be seduced, they love the nurturing mother. I learned *a lot* from men – I learned the hard way by being a woman and being laughed at with all my 'woo woo'. So when my business became very successful, I switched the 'woo woo' off, basically. Well, I *used* 'woo woo' but I didn't *call* it 'woo woo'. In 2004 we were turning over 20 million and it was the first year Flowcrete lost half a million pounds. I said to myself, "What are we going to do? Come on, you've got the answers, you're the boss."

So I *turned* to Feng Shui. I'd just been out in Bali in 2003. I'd also done Karen Kingston's course, 'Clear your Clutter with Feng Shui,' and learned all about space clearing and understanding energy.

I've got Karen's book too.

Actually, after that course, I bought *200* of her books and gave them to everybody. They all thought, *Oh, Dawn's on her 'woo woo' planet here.* But then I discovered this organisation called The Manufacturing Advisory Service – now I was a big manufacturer.[2] In the MAS they spoke about something called '*Lean* Manufacturing', using what was like another language. It was as if I was speaking Chinese (Feng Shui), and they were speaking Japanese. They used things like Taizan and Six Sigma and the 5S Method. 5S was based on five Japanese words. So we translated them into English words: Strip, Sort, Shine, Standardise, Sustain.

It was actually Feng Shui clutter clearing. So what I did – which was the clever bit – was say,

---

1   The 'people, planet, profit' phrase was coined by John Elkington in 1995 while at SustainAbility.

2   MAS is a support agency designed to help manufacturers streamline their processes, reduce waste, become more energy efficient and generally improve and grow their business.

let's leave the Feng Shui for the women in the home and let's bring in this corporate de-toxing – 5S. We cleared the clutter, simplified the business – the IT, the brand, the structure.

I learned to speak male. To be successful, you've got to learn the language of your customers. I brought in this term, 'TLC'. We know it as Tender Loving Care, us girlies. We love to cuddle each other and hug each other and kiss each other, right? TLC in business stands for:

Think Like a Customer

Talk Like a Customer (their language)

Text Like a Customer.

So you communicate in the written word, on your website, in your letters, emails – everything – like them. *But* I learned from one of my salesmen that there was one more – you *Tailor Like a Customer* as well. When we were aiming at the manufacturing world, we could see all our customers (these engineers and manufacturing directors) wore a uniform – t-shirts with their logo on. Basically, we did the same with our boys. When they went to see manufacturers, they wore a Flowcrete t-shirt. And it worked.

> "To be successful, you've got to learn the language of your customers ... Think like a customer, talk like a customer, text like a customer ... and tailor like a customer."

But then, again, the other side of the business was aiming at big, commercial buildings: big airports, hospitals, retail parks. We were aiming at architects; *[putting on a posh voice]* architects are much more into detail, specification, British Standards, CPD. So we had to speak their language.

I learned that from a lovely guy who was my Midlands area manager. One day he came in to see me and he looked *beautiful* – really lovely and sexy. He had a gorgeous suit on. I hadn't noticed how attractive he was before. He had bright blue eyes. I said, "Are they real?"

He said, "No. I've got bright blue contact lenses in."

I asked, "What are you doing?"

He replied, "I had three lady architects to see today. Dawn, I suss out who I'm going to see and I dress accordingly. If I've got women, I put my blue contact lenses in. They look into my eyes and they connect with me better."

I'm thinking, *You're smart.*

I knew nothing about what this was until after I'd sold Flowcrete and I did a diploma in NLP about rapport. Everything I was doing was all about rapport. *[Loud and animated]* The language, the style – it was NLP. Rapport, connection, mirroring. I was doing it but didn't realise what I was doing. I'd learnt it naturally from being very aware and listening.

Success came from this TLC – really focussing and communicating with the customers. But not only with customers; it's also with all your *staff* – because you've got to connect with them too and get this rapport.

You talk about being aware and listening in business, Dawn. When did you become aware of being on a spiritual path?

I did my first Feng Shui practitioner's course in 2000 when I was about forty. I think women go through a change in their mid-40s – actually women *and* men, maybe. That's when it started. *Meeting people*. It was learning about energy. Earth energies and meditating. Spiritual energy. Talking to trees and hugging trees and learning about nature spirits and thinking, *What world is this we live in?* Woo woo world.

What was it about Feng Shui that attracted you?

In the late '90s, we had a factory in Malaysia where we were *forced* by staff to have a Feng Shui survey because we'd got bad luck going on. *[Dramatically] Oh this building, this building, bad Feng Shui.* It was £2,000 for a Feng Shui consultation. This consultant basically said, *[Low and knowingly]* "Oh yeah, you've got bad Feng Shui."

Our factory was on a T-junction at the end of a very long road. It had this shar chi, this negative energy, hitting it. So the consultants made us build a wall. Then we were told we had 'death' next door – cars wrecked in accidents – so we had to put cacti along the edge to ward away the negative spirits. We had to block one door because we had two doors to get into the building … All sorts of things. And I just thought, *What a load of cobblers. What the hell is this?* But we did it and it worked, and we started to become successful.

Something else happened back in the late '90s. My husband and I moved into a house and I lost all my energy. I used to run a lot and I stopped running because my energy went. *Then* my husband had to have an operation on his shoulder and I thought, *"What's going on with this house and the energy?" That's* when I thought of the Feng Shui. I did a two-day foundation course in Buxton with a most beautiful guy called Robert Gray of the Feng Shui Academy. I was instantly hooked. *Instantly hooked.*

He taught us about astrology, dowsing, colours, energy, clutter. Oh my… it just opened my mind to a beautiful world that I didn't know existed. So I taught my two children, who were ten and twelve, to dowse. We got Mark – Dad – to put something under one of ten cups in the centre of the kitchen. Then we would come in with one dowsing rod and point to the correct cup *each* time. You can find *anything* with dowsing rods – earth energies, streams, pipes… After that, if we lost a school blazer or the car keys, we could just find it like magic.

My husband was like, *[sing-song-y] "What is this? Oh, this is just too much for me,"* and he dismissed it. I think Feng Shui is the reason why I had a divorce. I was on this spiritual path and my husband, who is the most beautiful man on this planet, just didn't understand my spirituality. He was *laughing* at me about dowsing, about feeling energies and this space clearing – not in a nasty way, but he didn't understand this adventure.

That Feng Shui course *then* led me to Bali in 2003 to do space clearing … feeling energies … even feeling colours when you've got your eyes closed or blindfolded. **Wow.** *[Loud and extra animated]* You can walk into buildings and feel depressed, you can feel atmospheres where they've had arguments in them; you can feel if that house has got geopathic stress in it. You can *feel* it. And yeah, I think that really kicked me off. Bali, *Bali [low]* is my spiritual home.

Bali – I've been back there six times. Every year, I'm going back to the Bali Spirit Festival. The temples in Bali, I can feel them. I just feel at home there. Balinese people live half in this world and half in the spirit world. They will not eat anything or do anything without blessing their food. I've taken my children out there. My children love Bali – Bali and Buddhism. The Bs. Both my daughters love the Buddhist energy and Bali energy … and ceremony.

I love the Balinese ceremony – like the ceremony of the five key things they bless. First, they thank the Universe for who we are – all our family, all our friends. Second, they thank the Sun God for coming every day to feed us energy and help all the plants grow. Third, they thank the Universe for being all one and connecting us all together. Fourth, they thank the spirit of place – the energy and the spirits that live where they are. And fifth, ultimately, they *connect* with the Universe to communicate and harmonise with the divine for what they want to happen, and to help them as individuals and as the community. *You can just feel it.* There is harmony in that land.

We need that harmony. Coming back to *business,* I wanted that harmony. I wanted my sales teams to have joint incentive schemes where they benefitted from working together. But, oh, could I try and get that with all the male egos? But hold on, not just male egos. There were female egos – women with a lot of male inside them.

Absolutely – because many have had to succeed by taking on male qualities.

How did you meet Mark and come to work together, Dawn?

I met my husband through having a relationship with a man who was manically jealous. My husband was one of my *first ever* employees back in 1983 while he was a Medieval English student at Bristol. We got on brilliant. We were like brother and sister. We used to go drinking together after work. He told me his inner secrets – even his love secrets.

One night we went to the King's Arms in Congleton. This guy I was going out with was standing there in the corner, just watching us. I thought, *What the hell are you doing? That's ridiculous.* He was jealous of my relationship with Mark because we got on so well.

Anyway, this guy started taking me to church, thinking I was a wayward woman, and I wasn't. I didn't even *fancy* Mark. But with that guy being like that, I started to think about Mark. It was true we had this *bond.* Mark had gone back to university and I thought, *Bloody hell, let's get together.'*

I organised a fishing trip to Anglesey and got both families there. I thought, *Mmmm. If it works out, I can make my approach on Mark and we could have a relationship because he's so beautiful.* So … I did. All the family had gone to bed. We were in this pub and I made my move. I went to kiss Mark. He was very shocked and knocked the table over with all the glasses because he was like, *"Oh my God."* I was in business with my dad, but I'd also recruited Mark's father. His father's boss was about to kiss him!

Anyway, we had this secret relationship and I fell in love with Mark. We eventually married and had two beautiful children; but I also had a miscarriage at six months with a second child. At the time Mark went into the office for me, little darling, to interview some people and have some business meetings. Mark was like my mentor. At the time he was doing a Masters degree at business school. So I was learning what he was learning and I was using it in my business.

When Mark left business school, he went to Shell. We'd moved in together by then. Shell wanted him to move to Thailand, so he was chatting me up to move to Thailand. But I said, "I'm sorry, Mark. I can't." I was pregnant for the third time, with April. "Why don't you join me?" He halved his salary and joined me at Flowcrete. He is *amazing. He* has been my *rock* all my life. He is the grounding influence. In Feng Shui astrology, he is pure earth. He's a 2-8-8. He is an absolute rock. He's a mountain man. Solid.

You obviously have a lot of respect for Mark, as I'm sure he has for you too.

Now you've sold the business, Dawn, does that give you more time to focus on your personal path?

Definitely. I've got a spiritual mission. In fact, Jane, I've decided I'm going back to study to become an Interfaith Minister, like Alison. I was down in Glastonbury and I kept seeing this sign about One Spirit Interfaith Foundation. I was thinking, *I really want to bring spirituality into the workplace. If I learn about the different religions, I can pick beautiful elements and develop a way to get it into the business world in their language.* It's going to be magical.

You're perfect for being an Interfaith Minister.

You are also the absolute epitome of a Pilgrim Mother. You are indeed Dawn the Fish, a 'fisherwoman'. You cast your net far and wide. You draw people in.

I'm on a never-ending journey. On that journey, I meet people. In Feng Shui terms, I'm a mother on the inside and I'm a *fire woman* on the outside. So this *mother* meets people, connects them with others. I support them, I feed them, I nurture them to grow into magnificent human beings. My new job title is 'Dreamcatcher'. That's what I'm doing with everyone I meet. I'm helping them catch their dreams.

I also believe that I'm married to the divine, the Universe. I am somehow married to this *divine spirit* that is just leading me – as a mother, a divine mother – to actually help this planet.

I totally get that.

This Yin Crowd is driven by women. I meet some very powerful women. We'll get a big database of women, strong women, and then, as an army – a gathering – of women, we can move in on the corporate world, speak the corporate language, bring love and spirituality, and transform it.

Actually, it may include female-men as well… So a group of us who are very balanced inside can bring this female energy to balance the male corporate world.

It reminds me of the Knights Templar. I read that they were actually spiritual leaders and ambassadors who only went into battle as a last resort. Maybe it's the time of female knights.

That's an interesting thought.

In recent years I've considered my name 'Noble Knight' as a cosmic joke. It took me a while to step into my name.

I'm just stepping into my *'Dawn'*. Nina Simone.[k] *[Singing]* 'It's a new Dawn. It's a new day. It's a new life. And I'm feeling … good.'

But also, if you look where I've been, I've lived my middle name – Heather – most of my life. Heather is a colourful flower on a wild, savage landscape. I've been living in that construction/manufacturing environment, but I haven't lost my colour. I've stepped out of it, but I'm going to go back in. I'm going to go back in *more* colourful. I'm going to make it colourful. I'm going to *bloom* in there – in that wild, savage landscape.

Then there's my Gibbins – monkey. A bit of a cheeky monkey. I've got a bit of naughtiness. I'll probably get away with it. I'll do it by being a bit naughty. Names are amazing.

They are indeed.

Before we move on, tell me about your experience on The Secret Millionaire. I loved your episode.

The producers sorted out about ten charities that I could have gone into. I was attracted to three that were all run by women. The first was The Wild Goose Café – though actually it wasn't run by women – but there was a strong woman in there, Lisa Mannion, who basically ran the show. She was only in her thirties, but she was a powerful woman.

That whole Bristol experience was enlightening to me. In fact, it was a bit like the impact of Rhonda Burns' *The Secret* on me.[3] The first night I worked at the Wild Goose Café, we all stood round in a circle with the volunteers. It was basically like – what did I call it? – a step of faith. The volunteers said a little prayer. "Please keep us safe so that we can rescue people off the streets." It was like having a positive vision for the night. Amazing. That was religion and *The Secret*, all in one.

The second charity was Teenage Parents. Deana Stone is the most beautiful person. In fact, she's going to do the interfaith ministry course with me. I went to her marriage a couple of weeks ago. She's been living with this guy for five years. You can feel the love between them. On her wedding day, I said, "Deana, today has made me decide that I'm going to be an interfaith minister."

She said, "I've wanted to do something like that for years."

I showed her the stuff and she's going to sign up too.

Anyway, that project was just phenomenal, but it was very upsetting as well. When I went back again and again, I found out that out of all the 250 girls that have had babies, not one of them breastfed – to give the antibodies and things like that. I was told they didn't because they were teenagers and didn't like authority. So they rebelled against the midwives and the NHS and did the opposite. Now they want to make films and education courses to teach young mothers about good parenting. I want to make it happen for them.

Then there was One25, supporting street sex workers. I didn't know that happened in this world. I thought it was glamorous. I thought it was in nice hotels. I didn't know that women would sell themselves for £20 for full penetrative sex. £10 for a blow job. It was disgusting … in people's cars, under motorway bridges. 250 sex workers on the streets of Bristol. It was heart-breaking for me; particularly when we went out in these vans and sixteen year olds, twenty-one year olds, came in. They could be my daughters. And learning that 70 per cent of them come from abused family backgrounds or homes where they'd been sexually abused … it was horrible. And 99 per cent of them were on drugs. Again, that taught me about self-worth. They didn't value themselves. Horrible.

So that was *The Secret Millionaire*. I was under very clear instructions from my whole family that I would only give forty grand. So when I got back, my kids said, "Well, did you give away £40,000?"

I said, "Yes, I did."

---

3   Best-selling book and film based on the universal Law of Attraction.

It wasn't until it was in the press that I'd given away a quarter of a million that my kids found out. "MUM!!" But my kids are so proud of me. They don't mind if I have no money. In fact, see this bracelet – my daughter's just gone away on a Buddhist retreat for a month, all by herself – and this came in the post. She said, "Mum, the little dragonfly is our spiritual connection and the hand is the hand that you've always got there for me to support me." And she said, "You can forget any material wealth, you can forget any money. It's that spiritual connection that we've got that's the most precious to me."

How beautiful is that?

How wonderful that they're so supportive of you in return. They're not thinking, *Oh God, my inheritance is going*, or anything like that. They are their mother's daughters, aren't they?

Well, they've got their dad making loads of money and they've got their mum who's sharing it.

My future is about being a money conduit, a magnet. It's going to flow through me to charities. My key thing in the future with all the businesses that I'm involved in now is for them to contribute 5 per cent of their earnings to charity. That's going to raise millions.

I think money is a great energy and we've got to make lots of it to do good with. That's the key. This is all about entrepreneurs. It's the 'do good' entrepreneurs.

> "I think money is a great energy and we've got to make lots of it to do good with. That's the key … 'do good' entrepreneurs."

We need entrepreneurs.

And *philanthropreneurs. And* – what was it Richard said earlier? – 'Entrepreneuses'. Come on, women!

What an exhilarating experience it was to spend time with Dawn. She is so full of life – Chi, I suppose, in her Feng Shui language. Dawn's observation that her Gemini nature makes her like two people strikes me as being incredibly accurate. And yet more than just two people – two *contrasting* people. A woman with a foot in two very different worlds – bringing extremes together in harmony.

After meeting Dawn, it is hard to imagine that she would ever suffer from any form of limiting beliefs, let alone that she had not yet written a book herself because she 'wasn't intelligent enough'. How many of us hold these limiting beliefs, I wonder, that hold us back even in just one area?

The great thing about Dawn is that she takes positive action and that one little belief hasn't held her back elsewhere. I shared my own story with her. I had always loved books and reading, but at grammar school when it came to writing essays, I was always near the bottom of the class. Miss Sumner, my English teacher, told my dad at a parents' evening that she found my style too whimsical, a bit like Lewis Carroll! (Apparently, to her that was a bad thing!) Despite this 'compliment' and gaining top grades in my O-level exams, I carried with me the belief I couldn't write stories – until now that is!

"Right," Dawn instructed me, "let's go back there now. Mine was called Miss Wilkie. She had tight permed hair. She wore 10-inch foundation – brown and horrible – which left a line round her chin. She smoked like a chimney, had about three cats in her office and the office stank. She would be the worst role model that you would ever, *ever* think of, and so I look back now and say, "Thank God I didn't turn out like her." What was yours like?

I described an old-fashioned, Margaret Rutherford-Miss Marple type. Nice enough. Doubtless, she had no idea of how she had injured my impressionable mind. Dawn and I then immediately cleared ourselves of these negative memories through a small meditation and celebrated all our positive attributes. That's typical of Dawn. She takes action.

Sometimes immediately.

Sometimes after reflection.

Again the contrast ... She makes choices.

We all make choices, all the time. We can choose which opinions we take note of and which we discard. After all, they are only opinions and we know what's best for us if we listen to our inner guidance.

I'm choosing to heed the dazzling Dawn. We can each be a new Dawn shining light on each day ... a bright force for the greater good.

I definitely want to be in with the Yin Crowd!

Count me 'Yin', Dawn!

"... we know what's best for us if we listen to our inner guidance."

JANE NOBLE KNIGHT

STEPHANIE J HALE

"Nowadays, I come from the place of what can I give to others and putting myself in other people's shoes. It's more about fulfilling other people's needs rather than just doing it for yourself."

Now a publishing expert and writers' coach, this former newsreader, reporter, editor and freelancer for UK radio and TV, and Assistant Director of Oxford University's world-famous creative writing programme, Stephanie is the founder of The Millionaire Bootcamp for Authors and co-founder of The Millionaire Bootcamp for Women. Stephanie is an award-winning author of books including *Millionaire Women, Millionaire You* and has helped hundreds of authors get their books noticed by top publishers and literary agents through her programmes and her Oxford Literacy Consultancy. Stephanie lives in, of course, Oxford, UK.

www.stephaniejhale.com

A Conversation with
Stephanie J Hale

Publishing Pundit

How many times do you get invited to a LinkedIn or Facebook event and you inwardly groan or tut or sigh? It must be a 90 per cent reaction for me. But this time I was excited. This time I *knew* without any doubt whatsoever I *had* to be there. Stephanie Hale had sent me a complimentary ticket for myself and a guest to attend her Millionaire Bootcamp for Authors in London. I had a quick look at the speakers. Wow! Just what I needed. Yes please!

I had not met Stephanie before, but she had been on my radar for a while. I can no longer remember when our connection began, but we have hundreds of shared connections, so we obviously have mutual interests.

My excitement mounted as two months passed by prior to the bootcamp. I wasn't disappointed. They were three brilliant days – all the better for sharing them with my great friend, stand-up comic Shelley Bridgman. Just as when I had first met Shelley, I immediately warmed to Stephanie.

I didn't need any persuading to join more than a hundred other would-be writers on Stephanie's 'How to Finish a Book in 30 Days' workshop in Oxford a month later. What struck me strongly was the wonderful warmth in the packed venue that seemed to touch everyone. Indeed, at the end a participant stood up. She declared that she had taken it upon herself to thank Stephanie for the day and for her gentle, encouraging and supportive manner. Her minute-long appreciative speech was followed by at least the same length of applause. Stephanie is much loved by her followers – that's for sure.

From the four days I have spent so far on Stephanie's events, I feel relaxed as I wait for my laptop clock to move to the appointed time for our conversation. I feel as if I'll be talking with a supportive friend. However, I am intrigued to know more about Stephanie's life as I know from her introduction to Millionaire Women, Millionaire You that she has experienced some challenging times in her life. As I make the Skype call, I wonder what secrets she will share about her journey to success…

When you were growing up, Stephanie, did you always love books and writing?

Yes, I usually had my head buried in a book. My parents separated when I was quite young. I have one sister whom I'm close to. My mother, who was a single parent for quite a long time, had me when she was seventeen. She started all over again. She took her A-levels at college and then went on to university and studied English Literature. As there were always lots of books on the shelf, I started reading those she was studying when I was quite young. It just seemed like a normal thing to do. Everyone thinks that what their family does or what their home life is like is normal; so it's just what you become accustomed to, really.

Also, because I had quite an unhappy childhood in various ways – I won't bore you with the details – I think that reading books and writing were fantastic forms of escapism for me at that time.

Who were your favourite writers?

I loved Enid Blyton. Of course, she's gone out of favour now. They say her books are not very PC, but I loved them – and all the fairy stories – anything that was escapism and fantasy. They would have been mixed in with something like Flaubert's *Madame Bovary* or Henry James. All the love and sex elements were completely lost on me as a ten year old. I would have read it on a very different level than an adult. It's just that when you are unhappy, seeing other people's lives, which are either more miserable or happier than yours, allows you windows into those lives. It allows you to step into those shoes and you briefly inhabit that world while you're reading. I think that's why I loved Enid Blyton so much, because of the wonderful, magical fairy tales. Also *The Little Princess* by Frances Hodgson Burnett – the idea of a little girl who was really a princess. I mean, who didn't want to be that princess? And no one realised she was. She was stuck in an environment she didn't really want to be in.

I felt the same way about books. I loved Enid Blyton too. And Madame Bovary. Great stories.

Who were your role models as you were growing up?

I wouldn't say I consciously had a role model for a very long time. My mother became editor of a newspaper, but I didn't really have an awareness of wanting to be anything other than a mother and a wife. I was brought up in a very traditional way. My grandparents had a very strong role in my upbringing because my mother was so young when she had me. I spent a lot of time living at my grandparents after my parents separated. My mother is quite traditional too. Probably I would say till my early thirties, all I ever thought I wanted was to be a wife and mother because that was my primary role. And if I had a secondary role, it was having a job. Initially, I followed the same path as my mother. I became a journalist and a newsreader, but I never really saw that as a primary role in my life. I had academic success at school and with reading books and writing as forms of escapism. I suppose, it evolved very naturally into my career path. I saw it more as a means of making money or helping to support the household. I didn't really see the job as my main role.

I don't think I even thought about my own needs and desires for my life actually. It was always, 'What does my husband want or what do my children want?' I felt that my needs somehow were secondary and I think that's probably the same with many women. Not *all* women but many women are probably conditioned in that way.

I went to church a lot when I was younger, so that secondary role of women was something that I was reading about from the Bible. I don't go to church anymore. I would say I'm still quite spiritual, but I wouldn't say I'm religious. But that's certainly something that was very influential in my early formative years.

At what point did you start aspiring to be more than a wife and mother, Stephanie?

Well, *[laughing]* the marriage that was supposed to fix all my problems and last forever broke down. I lived temporarily in a refuge. I went from a lovely five star lifestyle, living in a big house with a Jag on the drive, nice holidays, to a *not* such a nice lifestyle. Things changed very dramatically from that point.

I had probably five years of very, very tough times. We were living in a red light district. We had a house – I say house, but initially my son and I were living in a room in a shared house. He was four at the time. We moved into a whole series of homes that were not very desirable – two with water pouring in through the ceiling and mould on most of the furniture. We had prostitutes outside the house, local winos howling into the night, people getting beaten up, my car getting smashed in … you name it … my neighbours stealing my handbag while I was bringing in the shopping. I couldn't hang out my washing on the line without it getting stolen.

The final turning point came when there was a child of four who was raped on a playing field a very short distance from our home. We had no proper garden so this was where my son would have been playing. I used to take him kite flying on the field where it happened. That, for me, was the absolute turning point where I thought, *Oh my God, I don't want to be bringing up my son here forever. This is ridiculous.* I'd been so well trained – academically trained. I had two master's degrees and one bachelor's degree at that time. I had loads of training as a journalist and as a newsreader, but I didn't want to go back into that because the hours were horrendous. And I just thought, *I have all this training and I don't know how to make money.* Well, not enough money to support myself and a child in better circumstances than we were living in.

It was just so grim and such a struggle that I thought, *I've got to work out how I can get myself out of this.* And also, to be absolutely honest, I wasn't happy working as a newsreader because I found the environment very cynical. It was very negative and it wasn't in line with *me*. Every day I went to work, I felt I was being someone that wasn't true to me … I was assuming a mask.

So, although times were very tough, it was also a brilliant time in a way because otherwise I would never have stepped outside of that. I was sleepwalking up to that point. I wasn't fully living my life and I wasn't doing anything to help anyone else. Not a single thing, apart from my family. I felt like I wasn't giving anything at all – I was taking. As a journalist, you're going out, getting stories and collecting stories, and you're taking, in a way, rather than giving.

That's a really interesting perspective on it. How old were you when you thought 'Enough.'

I was probably in my early thirties, so quite late compared to some people, actually.

It's quite young in respect of others though! *[Both laughing]* So what happened next? What did you actually do, Stephanie, to turn your life around?

I did two things. One was I handed in my notice at my job, which shocked everyone. It was quite a dramatic thing to do because at the time I was working as Assistant Director at Oxford University. It sounds very grand – and on the outside it *looks* very grand – but you don't get paid very much for it at all. I was one of the very few women doing it, as well as one of the youngest. People were saying, "You're one of the first dons that has ever handed in their notice." Pretty much you stay in that position till you die *[laughing]*, but I just thought, *Why am I doing a job that doesn't pay very much?* At the time I wasn't getting maternity leave, sickness benefit or pension, or anything like that, and, also, I felt I wasn't being true to myself. I think in every job I've ever had working for somebody else, I felt like I wasn't really being me. I was having to live by other people's rules and I didn't have any control over my life.

Also, when you're a mother, you want to be able to have time with your children. And I wanted to be able to give to other people on my *own* terms rather than living by somebody else's rules, especially when those rules didn't feel aligned with my own values. That was really important to me.

Initially, I went to the library and I just brought loads of books home with me. I didn't even know what I was looking for. Basically, I looked for anything with 'money' and 'wealth' in the title.

Then I set up a business, Oxford Literary Consultancy, which helps authors. It seemed a natural progression for me to go to that from teaching creative writing, which is what I was doing at the university. I'd also worked for the Arts Council. So I was helping authors to write their books with editing services and helping them to find literary agents. And in addition to that, I learned how to trade commodities and became a trading coach – but that took three or four years to learn. So I was doing the two, side by side, in the early years.

How did your business develop? Who were your major influences?

The number one influence was Robert Kiyosaki with *Rich Dad, Poor Dad*, like so many people. That book prompted me to leave my job and just say, "Right, I'm going to go for it." The next big influence was when I became very ill. I spent about a year in and out of hospital and I started losing the sight in my right eye. I was told I might have a brain tumour. So that was a big shock at the time.

I *didn't* actually have a brain tumour, but a part of my brain is missing. *[Laughing]* That *really* made me *reassess* my life *massively*. I felt I'd always been on a journey, particularly when I started getting successful. I was always doing something *today* for something that was going to happen tomorrow. I realised I wasn't actually living in the here and now – I had plans to write my book at some indefinite point in the future. And I just thought, *I've got to get on and do what I want to do, rather than it being next year and next year* – this rolling next year that kept happening.

> "I didn't actually have a brain tumour, but a part of my brain is missing. That really made me reassess my life massively."

Off the back of that, I wrote *Millionaire Women, Millionaire You,* which was about twelve women entrepreneurs and how they went from welfare to millionaire. In addition to that, I organised a seminar – or what I *thought* was going to be a seminar – but it ended up as a massive conference, The Millionaire Bootcamp for Women. That was just an unexpected success. I didn't expect more than about 200 women and we had about 3,000 register for it. It was a runaway success.

Really, I stumbled into that. Then suddenly, out of nowhere, I realised that I could hold big events in London and hundreds of people wanted to come to them. I had 100,000 people sign up on my different social media sites, 40,000 people on my newsletters, and it just completely blew me away. I also realised, at that time, that I was making a massive difference, as you will with your book, to people's lives. I was getting so many emails every day from people whose lives I had no idea that I had changed – in the same way that I felt towards Robert Kiyosaki, who I've never met and never spoken to in person. He completely changed my life and now people were writing *me* letters like that. I felt, *Wow, I've never met this person and they feel like I've really helped them.* That was really exciting.

The other thing for me was that having been in that desperate position of having nothing and feeling like I'd hit the bottom of the barrel, I wouldn't want anyone else to go through that, especially when they've got children. I think this applies to so many women because women try and do things for other people. One of the differences I notice, anyway, with a lot of women entrepreneurs, is when women learn something, they want to help their community or they want to help their children or they want to help their families. So you know when you're helping a woman, you're helping hundreds of other people, not just *that* person. You know she won't just keep that to herself. She's going to spread it … spread the word.

Then it seemed natural, off the back of The Millionaire Bootcamp for Women, to hold The Millionaire Bootcamp for Authors. So basically that's how it evolved.

> "So you know when you're helping a woman, you're helping hundreds of other people, not just that person. You know she won't just keep that to herself. She's going to spread it … spread the word."

Wonderful. I was moving house when you held The Millionaire Bootcamp for Women, so I wasn't able to attend. But I thought The Millionaire Bootcamp for Authors was terrific. Was that when you felt you were really helping people, by writing the book and running the bootcamps? That you had tapped into something important?

I'd say yes. I think anyone understands who's had one of those near-death experiences such as when you've had a critical illness. I mean I've had various life-threatening illnesses over the years, but never one that shaved quite so close. Also, it was the thought of leaving the earth and leaving my children behind, and having not left anything to guide them. By that stage, having built up a wealth of knowledge from other people, I knew I could radically change people's lives. Yet, I hadn't left the blueprint behind to show anyone how to do it. I'd verbally spoken to people and I'd held seminars, but I hadn't left anything on the page, as it were. So that was probably a defining moment for me.

How did you choose your women millionaires in your book and at your bootcamp?

I looked at loads of other entrepreneurial conferences and women's events and I basically looked for women who had gone from nothing to millionaire or multi-millionaire. I didn't want there to be anyone that you could say, "Oh, they were born with a silver spoon in their mouth," or,

"Their husband helped them," or anything like that. I wanted it to be people who had been there and either lost everything or they had gone from nothing. I wanted to show everyone, not just women, that they've got no excuse.

For the longest time I was living in not very nice circumstances in the red light district and I would think, *God, how am I ever going to get out of here? I can't do it.*

I'm not clever enough.

I don't know enough.

I'm not connected enough.

I haven't spent enough years learning about business.

I haven't got an MBA.

It was all negatives, but I wanted to show people positives and deconstruct what these women had done and just show that they were ordinary people. It wasn't anyone that was super-intelligent or super-clever or super-qualified. It was just ordinary people who were really determined and just didn't give up.

If you've made a mistake, I think there's a tendency to give up and try something else, whereas actually you should see it in a positive way and move forward. Whenever I fluff up, *[laughing]* and believe me, it happens a lot of times – whether it's in parenting or business or investing or whatever – I just think, *What can I learn from this?* Usually, when you come back, you come back much stronger.

I so agree with that. Perseverance. Also people can have a tendency to look at successful people and say, "Oh, it's all right for them." It's so important to know the stories behind the success and all the struggles.

What are you focussing on at present, Stephanie?

What I love at the moment is helping other people to lead lives of what I think of as 'freedom' and 'fulfilment'. I think we're all conditioned from a very young age to work really hard at school, get our qualifications and then go out and work and work and work until we drop. And yet, people are so busy working they don't have enough time for their children necessarily, or as much time for their families, or for their hobbies and all the things that actually give them pleasure. In fact, they might not even think about what gives them pleasure or what their real heart purpose is.

So what I love doing is working particularly with entrepreneurs and coaches and consultants and helping them to set their ideas down on paper and to turn those into books, so they can share their ideas and get their message out to other people. It's a corny phrase that 'the pen is mightier than the sword', but it's so true – a book survives you beyond the grave, and it's there forever. Anything you write down is there to help and inspire other people through the generations, for your children and children's children. That's what gives me pleasure.

> "… a book survives you beyond the grave, and it's there forever. Anything you write down is there to help and inspire other people through the generations."

Fantastic. Are there any people in particular you have helped who stand out for you?

There are so many. It's hard to single out individuals. I've had children come to my seminars and then go away and write books. That, I think, is amazing, that someone at age twelve has gone away and been inspired to write a book that will then inspire other children.

Equally, I've had people who are in their eighties who I've helped to get best-selling books. They thought they would never get published because in their head they were too old. They thought they weren't going to accomplish anything. They didn't think anyone was going to read their book and suddenly… they've got people all over the world buying literally thousands of their books.

Those are the things that *really* inspire me. I work with people who are already celebrities, millionaires, well-known writers, award-winning writers, best-selling authors … but the thing is you expect them to do well. You know they're going to achieve amazing results. What I find really exciting is when I have someone come to me and they've been rejected by 100 publishers or by 200 literary agents, and then I get them a top literary agent and a deal with a top publisher.

They've gone from absolutely nothing and desperation and being at their wits' end and thinking, *Shall I barbecue this manuscript? [Laughing]* They'll come and say, "Is this any good? Shall I forget about writing and go back to the day job and just not think about it ever again?" And then they go on to achieve wonderful things. And especially in this age where we've got the Internet to reach thousands and thousands of people all over the world.

There are so many stories of people who have sold thousands of books or changed people's lives with their books, and that's what really excites me.

You mention the Internet. The world of books and publishing is changing beyond all recognition. What are the main changes that you have seen and what do you foresee for the future?

Well, the changes have been phenomenal. I worked for the Arts Council of England as a literature advisor for quite a long time and at the beginning people were a bit snooty about self-publishing. Self-publishing was considered to be vanity publishing, as though, somehow, a self-published book wasn't a worthy book. There was an idea that mainstream publishers were the only way to get published and that was the only way to make lots of money.

In the last 10–15 years there have been massive, radical changes. I'd say now that self-publishing, to me, is the most likely way that any author is going to make huge sums of money. If money is what you want to make and you want to reach a huge audience, and you want to have control over your book, then self-publishing is the very, very best way to do it, whether via Kindle or eBooks or print-on-demand publishing or all three.

In the past, you would have launched a book in a small bookshop or at a literary festival or in a library and you would have perhaps spoken to fifty people or, if you were lucky, 100 people or more. Nowadays, you're reaching thousands of people or *tens* of thousands of people or

"If money is what you want to make and you want to reach a huge audience, and you want to have control over your book, then self-publishing is the very, very best way to do it …"

hundreds of thousands of people via the Internet. You're leveraging your time enormously by doing that because there are only so many hours in the week that you can actually spend promoting your book. And of course promoting your book is probably 70 per cent of your job. 30 per cent or even less than that is the writing of it. So those are the biggest changes.

And Kindle is a big change. eBooks are a big change. Vast numbers of people are buying Kindles and Kindle books. At the moment the demand for Kindle books is way outstripping the supply. Not all authors have cottoned on to the fact that Kindle is a very good place to get published, and also how easy it is to do it. I think there's a lot of mystique about eBooks and Kindle that somehow you have to be very technically savvy to be able to do it – and believe me, *I am not. [Laughing]*

That's refreshing to hear.

I struggle with the remote control to the TV a lot of the time, but I do know how to publish a Kindle book! So if I can do it, I think probably most of the population can.

It's fascinating to hear your take on this because you've been involved in the book and publishing world while the changes have been happening. Are men or women more likely to be seeking out your help?

It's probably 50/50 – which is interesting because you would think that with the women's events, I would get more women. Some I help with writing, some with promoting their books and some with making money.

What's interesting to me is that my client base has changed. It has gone from being perhaps more academic, fiction-based and poetry-based when I was, say, working at Oxford University to being more non-fiction now, with mainly entrepreneurs and coaches and consultants and business people. I find that quite exciting because, largely speaking, a lot of entrepreneurs have had a very similar journey. They're also willing to think outside of the box. They're not held back by so many limitations and they tend to say, "I *can* do it," rather than, "I can't do that. How am I going to do that?" They don't see the obstacles. They see the challenges and they think, *Right, I'm going to go for that. I know it seems impossible, but I'm going to take the leap of faith and I'm going to go for it.* And I love that. I love working with people who are prepared to do everything it takes to make their book a bestseller, to make it a massive success and to get it out to millions of people.

That's thought-provoking. I can see that in the past writing a book might have been seen as a more intellectual exercise. But now, the message coming across is that you have to be able to market your book. So in a way, writers need to be entrepreneurs.

Definitely. When I first started writing, I wrote novels and fiction. My first master's degree was in Creative Writing, so I very much believed a lot of those traditional beliefs and I wanted to win literary prizes. Somehow, if I wanted to make money, it was a bit crass or vulgar. It wasn't my job to do the PR or market the book. It was the publisher's job. Those beliefs were very limiting and disempowering because they were about being passive and letting somebody else do the work. Also, they were quite self-indulgent because it was about the book and my needs – it wasn't about the reader.

Nowadays, I come from the place of what can I give to others and putting myself in other people's shoes. It's more about fulfilling other people's needs than just doing it for yourself. And of course, if you're doing it for yourself, you're only ever going to be your own biggest fan. A lot of authors write for themselves and for their own needs, rather than writing for their reader and seeing it from the reader's perspective, or indeed, from the publisher's and the literary agent's perspective.

It's important that authors look at it from a different viewpoint. And of course, a book is one of the most valuable calling cards or business cards. If you *do* work for yourself, it's one of the best business cards you could have. Also, for giving to friends and family members … it's a good way of getting people on side and persuading people to your way of seeing things or challenging their beliefs. If you want to change the world, you literally can *change* the world.

Absolutely. You've mentioned your family a few times, Stephanie. What are the benefits of the way you work now as opposed to when you were employed?

Massive benefits. I've got three children. I'm a single parent still. My youngest two are six and seven and my eldest is coming up to sixteen. I'm working from an office based at home, so I'm always here. If there's a sports day to go to or holidays or something unexpected like an illness, I'm always here. I've got a flexibility that I certainly wouldn't have had when I was working for anyone else. I would have had to pull sickies. *[Laughing]* With your children, it's like a relay, isn't it? One gets chickenpox and the next and the next. *[Laughing]* So that's a massive benefit. If it's sunny, we can go to the beach. And I hardly ever work weekends or evenings anymore.

Also there's the longer-term benefit that my oldest son, for example, has had quite an entrepreneurial streak from about the age of ten. He was selling chocolate bars to his friends at school (although that has stopped now). He saw both myself and his father as entrepreneurs and, to him, it's normal. We certainly haven't pushed it on him. It's just he has an entrepreneurial mindset.

It's nice being in your own home environment and fitting things around your children. When I occasionally work weekends, we have a nanny who comes in. I feel as though I'm actually *living* now whereas in the past I was sleepwalking. I wasn't living to my utmost potential by any stretch.

Excellent.

That's a brilliant story about your son. Was it the school that stopped his enterprise?

My son was very driven. He would get up early and we would have to go to the cash and carry and get stock for him. So he knew about balance sheets and profit and loss, and things like that, from an early age. He's known the difference between what's going in and what's coming out and what the profit is and what are called loss leaders in supermarkets, where you sell something at a loss to make people buy other things. So he's quite well-versed in all of that without perhaps knowing the technical terms for them.

He's done that quite naturally, certainly without any pushing. It's given him a sense of identity as being the 'go to' person for chocolate and drinks, but the school didn't like it because, obviously, he's not at school to be an entrepreneur. He's at school to learn academic things. So perhaps it wasn't the right environment to be doing that. And, of course, there are new obesity rules within schools, so they don't really want anyone going to school and selling loads of chocolate and fizzy drinks.

That sounds like an excuse to me. I've been speaking to other women about how to get that entrepreneurial spirit within schools. It seems a shame that your son was stopped because that's the sort of spirit that we need for the economy.

It is. This summer, for example, he's spent the last two weeks in Derby on his own, working on a film set as a runner. He's working from 4 pm to 4 am and sometimes 4 pm to 7 am because he wants to be a film director. I know I'm his mum and I'm bound to sing his praises, but he's got a much stronger sense of who he wants to be and what he wants to do at fifteen than I had for years.

I think that's because he sees my clients, he hears about the people I work with and his dad works with, and that it's not their school qualifications, or anything that they would have traditionally learned, that has necessarily equipped them to be where they are today. No matter what setbacks they've faced, they've gone on to success because they've been determined, they've been persistent, and they've learned the skills as they've gone along. My son can see the value in that.

That's fantastic. He deserves every success. He has great role models in his parents.

In the same vein, can I ask you about your mentors, Stephanie? What have they given to you and how do you choose them?

Oh my God, I wouldn't be remotely where I am without any mentors. I've had so many of them. I must have had nearly 100 mentors and probably fifty over the last ten years. *[Jane laughing]* I'm not kidding you. I was very academically bright, but anything beyond that I was completely lacking in.

My mentors ranged from Robert Kiyosaki and his book that I'd read, to people that I'd paid for one-to-one mentoring. As I got more success, I was able to invest in seminars or workshops and have full-time mentoring. My early mentors taught me to trade equities or Forex or commodities. I was very fortunate because I was a woman in a very male-dominated profession. So I had a lot of people prepared to mentor me for free early on.

Then I had people teaching me about internet marketing and business. Literally, as you acquire one skill, you look for another. For example, when I held my very first seminar, the thought of paying £20,000 (which was once a year's salary for me) or even £50,000 (which is what I spent hosting my most recent event in London) … the thought of doing that without somebody there, saying, "It's okay, you can do it. This will be a success as long as you do this, this and this," *[laughing]* it would have been terrifying. In fact, it would have been madness. And in some ways, it felt a bit like madness, but you get to the stage where once you've done something outside your comfort zone a few times, you get used to feeling uncomfortable. You think *It's okay that I feel uncomfortable. It doesn't mean I have to stop. It just means I have to keep pushing through it and keep going.*

At the moment I've got a mentor who I speak to once a week, every week. Some things we discuss are psychological. Some are business such as hitting targets. You can make a certain amount of money or you've grown your business to a certain level like £1 million and then you want to go to the next stage. So we might talk about that.

Perhaps the harder thing that I've found actually is psychological where you want to be available to people. But as your success grows, you find that there are *lots* of people wanting your time. You want to give more and more of your time to help people, but there's not enough of you to go round.

It's coping with psychological things like that, as your business becomes more successful, which you wouldn't imagine. If someone had said to me, "You're going to make a million pounds and have all these people signing up for your seminars and it's going to be amazing," I'd have thought, *Oh my God, how can there be anything at all that I can find fault with in that?* I wouldn't have dreamt in a million years that you'd find anything, but of course there's always another level you've got to learn about. You've got to grow all the time and next year there'll be something else to grow into and learn about.

Usually, I choose mentors through word of mouth. I listen to what other people are saying about them. My mentor at the moment is somebody very, very successful in the north of England. I heard a lot of other internet marketers saying, "Wow, this guy is getting amazing results." So I knew he had a lot of respect from his peers. I had a shortlist of about fifteen people. I probably will still go back to some of them. Maybe one will be my mentor for next year when I have a new challenge. This year I'm focussing on automating my business and using video to do that.

You're certainly a great advocate for mentoring.

The thing with mentors is you gulp initially, when you think, *Oh my God, do I really have to pay them that much money?* But ultimately, you know you're going to get ten times that back in financial rewards and in growth. It's going to take you absolute quantum leaps because they've done it before you and it saves you ten years. It saves you all those painful mistakes – so it's exciting.

It is exciting. You mentioned earlier how important it is that you do good in the world, Stephanie. Has that always been important to you?

Integrity and having very strong values are really, really important to me. A lot of that is rooted in my childhood. I went to a Church of England school and I spent a lot of time in church. Although I'm not religious anymore, it gave me a very strong sense of right and wrong. I probably notice it more nowadays because I see with my children that they perhaps don't have that. I don't go to church and they're not at a Church of England school. So they are not exposed to those values. I grew up with a very strong sense of wanting to help others and thinking that doing things for the wider good, to me, was just a normal, natural thing.

Even now, if I saw an old lady by the side of the road, I would stop and check that she was okay. In fact, yesterday I was in the Peak District. The Russian Olympic squad is based up there. Some of them were staying at the same hotel as us in Sheffield. There was a woman coming down in the lift looking really distressed. I asked if she was okay. I was ready to give her a hug. I can't *not* do it. I can't. For me, it's part of being human. I find the 'me, me, me' culture very hard to relate to. If I had to pinpoint where it comes from, I would say it probably comes from having it ingrained in me from a young age.

> "I have a strong sense of commitment. If I say I'm going to do something, I do it. As far as I'm concerned, I'd rather die than not go through with my promise."

I have a strong sense of commitment. If I say I'm going to do something, I do it. As far as I'm concerned, I'd rather die than not go through with my promise. *[Laughing]* As I said, I was brought up by my grandparents for quite a while, so that 'olde worlde' sense of old-fashioned values of 'my word is my bond' and having a sense of honour was instilled in me. People respect you simply because you are who you say you are, and you do what you say you're going to do. You don't need a signed piece of paper. I have to dig deep to find where this comes from, but that's where I root it. I wouldn't say it's something I consciously think about until I find other people who are not doing it. *[Laughing]* I think, *What's going on? Why don't you think like that?* I suppose then it makes you realise.

Do you notice any differences between large and small enterprises?

At the moment, entrepreneurs or solopreneurs or solo businesses have a *huge* advantage over corporations, especially in the times we're at now. This is something I find day to day. They're so much nimbler and able to change, whereas if you go through a big corporation, they're slower. They're held back by that. You ask them for a decision and they have to go to a committee … then some sub-committee … then they've got to ask the MD … and then they've got to ask different tiers of the organisation.

Whereas with a solopreneur, if you see some change that you need to adapt to within the marketplace, you can change overnight. You don't have to wait six weeks or even six months to go through all that process about whether you're going to change the colour of your front door to red or orange or change the logo on your website.

These are really exciting times for entrepreneurs. A lot of big businesses are folding and going under, but entrepreneurs who are focussed and know what they're doing, and learn and adapt, can do really, really well in these times. Of course, many big companies have formed during times of depression or times where the economy is not doing so well. So this is the time to get in there. If anyone is thinking about starting a business or even struggling with their business and thinking, *Gosh, why isn't it happening for me?*, rather than get out and give up, I'd say, "Go for it and get more training. You just probably need more learning and mentoring to help you get to the next level."

I absolutely agree with you there. Are there any other changes you've observed over the year; for example, since your days in the media? At the moment, we're in the midst of the Olympics with some great female role models coming to the fore.

I think the danger with it – if there is one – is that there are successful women in the media. There are people that you look up to, but they tend to have male characteristics. They're being applauded for characteristics that aren't necessarily female. Although it's fantastic to see women achieving so much in the Olympics, at the same time I wonder slightly whether it's still part of that same value system.

Qualities that are important to me as a woman are being nurturing, empathetic, sharing, community-minded, giving, caring; being less competitive and more cooperative. Those are the values that I see in women *outside* of the media, but *within* the media, those aren't necessarily the values that we're seeing. There are still those values of being more competitive, more challenging and slightly more aggressive, and *less* cooperative and *less*

> "Qualities that are important to me as a woman are being nurturing, empathetic, sharing, community-minded, giving, caring; being less competitive and more cooperative."

giving and *less* empathetic. It's still slightly more male.

It's fantastic to see women achieving and it's important for girls to see that, but not at the expense of all those values that I think you need as a mother and a carer. It's not to say that all women should *only* be empathetic and *only* be nurturing and *only* be sharing. But it's important to me to value these qualities as well.

I think that separation of roles is bad for women. When I was a newsreader, I certainly felt like I was assuming a mask when I went to work. I had to be one person there and another completely different person at home. I felt like I was split in two. That's not healthy for anyone.

Yet if you feel like your work is effortless and it's not like work because you're enjoying it, and you're passionate about it and you love it, you're still giving all those values in your work as well. Obviously, it's difficult in something like athletics because you've got to be competitive. In other roles within the media, it would just be nice to see more of those feminine values there.

For example, coming at it from my newsreader perspective, the news tends to focus on war or negative things or politics. But there's a huge amount of news that comes in every day that is positive, and it's ignored. It's given less priority than other aspects. Every time you watch the news, you're absorbing that into your psyche and that's giving you a perspective of the world that isn't necessarily reflecting the balance of good and bad in the world. It might be that 10 per cent of things that happen in the world are bad things and 90 per cent are good, but we focus on the 10 per cent. I think the balance needs to be redressed. But that's just me. That's just my perspective.

I agree with you. It's vital that we redress the balance and celebrate positive, feminine and mothering values too. What I took from the Olympics athletes was that they had to love what they did in order to train with such dedication as they did. Those are qualities needed by entrepreneurs. And we often saw them as part of a team too. There were some touching moments between athlete, coaches and commentators. I read an Olympics article criticising some of the male commentators for being a bit emotional – a feminine characteristic I value. I actually applaud the men's compassion. So maybe that's a small step towards us all embracing our feminine and mothering qualities.

Thank you for all your insights, Stephanie.

It's my pleasure.

There are several parallels between Stephanie's story and my own. I too attended a Church of England School for three years. My own parents didn't go to church, but I used to attend church every Sunday evening with a friend and her parents for a few years, until we joined other youngsters going to communion at the parish hall on Sunday mornings and then to church in the evenings. Then we'd go back to the parish hall a mile away for the coffee evening. There was youth club on Mondays, so my teenage social life revolved round the church-related activities. It only stopped when I went off to university.

Until I listened to Stephanie, I hadn't thought about the impact that church and religion had had on me and my values. I actually taught Religious Education part-time for two years in the mid-1980s when I worked as a temporary teacher in a rural comprehensive school in Staffordshire. The Head of RE prepared the lessons for her own classes and I just had to deliver them to my two classes. It was very different from Scripture during my school years, with the total emphasis on Christianity and all the wonderful bible stories and parables. I had to learn about other religions before I could lead lessons myself. I missed the stories, but the information was fascinating. It was a great gift to expand my horizons. Each religion provides a set of values, a foundation, even if humans do sometimes corrupt them. Today, like Stephanie, I class myself as spiritual, not religious.

I was moved to hear that Stephanie wrote her book *Millionaire Women, Millionaire You* as a legacy for her children after she became very ill and was told she might have a brain tumour. Thankfully, she didn't. I can't imagine what it would be like to have a life-threatening condition when you have three young children. The closest I got was after I had my first daughter in 1978. I took her to the GP for her six-month check-up. While I was there, he said to me, "By the way, your smear test's come back positive." I went into total shock. To me that meant I had cancer. I asked for more information, but he just dismissed me with, "Oh, there's no point worrying yet."

Yet?

But there *was* cause for worry? I spent about six weeks, hardly sleeping, waiting for my hospital appointment, thinking I was going to die. When I got in front of the consultant, I asked him what it would mean at best and what at worst. I would then know what I was dealing with. That was okay – I could handle that. It was the not knowing that was worse. As it happened, the scenario was the 'at best' one and I spent a day in hospital having a minor operation.

What the experience taught me was gratitude. Just thinking for a short while that I was going to die soon led me to look at my life and what was truly important. It was a big wake up call. That feeling of gratitude for everything in my life has never left me. At that time, it didn't lead me to leave the legacy of a book, as it did with Stephanie. But here I am over thirty years later … writing. Now I feel I have got something to write about. Everywhere I go, the women I meet are amazing. The entrepreneurs in this book are incredible. I feel honoured to hear their stories. I am excited about sharing these stories and inspiring other women to be all that they are.

It is time to celebrate women for all our feminine qualities. As Stephanie says, now is the time to redress the balance.

"Each religion provides a set of values, a foundation, even if humans do sometimes corrupt them … I class myself as *spiritual,* not religious."

JANE NOBLE KNIGHT

GINA
LAZENBY

"I want to see a validation of feminine values, an acceptance, an embracing. We want the greater participation of women bringing their feminine values."

CEO and Founder of the 'Women Gathering Project', creator of world's first professional training school in Feng Shui and co-founder of the Feng Shui Society in the UK, Gina is a multi-award-winning businesswoman whose stand is to 'bring feminine wisdom to the fore in the world'. She is a best-selling author of over half a million books: *The Feng Shui House Book, Simple Feng Shui* and *The Healthy Home* and is co-author of *The Wealth Garden — Catching Butterflies Without a Net*. Gina's life is a testament as to how to live with grace, ease and flow. She has appeared regularly on TV and travels widely from home bases in Yorkshire and London, UK.

www.ginalazenby.wordpress.com

A Conversation with
Gina Lazenby

Space Holder

Have you ever come across someone a few times, quite unexpectedly, within a short space of time? When that happens to me, it triggers a little 'ding' in my awareness and I take note. Gina was one of those people.

Since 2010 I had been aware of 'Women are Gathering' events in London. The network was too far from Shropshire to warrant a special trip, but fortuitously an opportunity arose for me to attend in June 2012 when I was staying with my good friend, Shelley Bridgman, near London. As a regular member, Shelley invited me along.

The meeting was at Gina's mews house. There had been torrential rain for several hours, so the evening felt more like autumn than June. Gina's front door was unlocked as we shouted hello and entered. We hung up our wet coats, deposited our umbrellas and shoes in the hall, and walked through the door at the end of the short corridor into a warm, bright living space. Inside were comfy sofas and an oval table with unlit candles set out for supper. Mmmm … wonderful aromas were wafting across.

From the kitchen area in the far corner Gina called us over and introduced herself. Wearing a pinafore to protect her summer dress, she gave us both a warm smile and a friendly hug. We were invited to join the earlier arrivals in various food preparation tasks. None of us seemed to be a particularly confident cook as we were all asking questions. Gina made the event into an informal cookery lesson. Amongst other delights, we were shown how to cut tomatoes and fennel properly. On the stove was a large pan full of a bubbling stew into which Gina chucked various ingredients, offering us spoonfuls and asking whether we thought the dish was spicy enough.

Cosseted in this warm virtual embrace, by and by we gathered round the table, savouring our food and sharing our stories and insights. It was a precious, particularly feminine get-together, where I felt as if I'd spent time with a close sisterhood, although I had never met most of the women before.

I was therefore delighted to meet Gina and Kay, another guest from that evening, on my next visit to London a few weeks later for a small, informal Sunday event. My antenna rose, but I was still not yet sure what the connection was. A week later I was…

Until then I had believed that my complement of nine Pilgrim Mothers for this book was complete, but out of the blue my inner guidance suggested that one of the entrepreneurs actually belonged in *another* book, still to be written; so there was space for one more entrepreneur. But who?

So I meditated and asked for guidance on my final woman. Shortly afterwards, as I browsed Facebook, I spotted a link to Gina's blog post called *The Power of the Feminine Mind is Needed to Serve a World in Crisis*. I read the article and found it totally mirrored my own thoughts.

As I explored Gina's website presence, I thanked the Universe for providing me with my ninth Pilgrim Mother – if she agreed. And she did …

After a few delays with laptop malfunctions and Gina's travels to America and Canada, I connect with Gina on Skype. Warm memories of the delicious foods and communion of spirit I experienced on my first 'Women Are Gathering' event stir within me as I see Gina sitting at her oval table in the now familiar living room of her London home …

Your focus seems to be increasingly on women and leadership, Gina. What is your current thinking on the subject?

Women need to work side by side with men. Feminine wisdom is a huge force on the planet: we need to tap into this in a new way.

I was guided to read *Striking a Light* by Louise Raw about a women's strike in London's East End at the Bryant and May match factory in 1888. History reported that the London Dock Strike of 1889 started the modern trade union movement, but it was the matchwomen's strike success that had inspired the men to take large-scale action. Prior to that, unionism was more about friendly societies and collecting money to cover times of illness.

> "Feminine wisdom is a huge force on the planet: we need to tap into this in a new way."

Yet these women were written out of history – dismissed as girls who were the pawns of reformists. In fact, they were mainly women in their thirties and older, who did the unthinkable when they went on strike. These matchwomen were self-directed, but the men didn't want to recognise that women were capable of this.

The writer recorded three archetypes for women in the 1800s: (1) Angel of the Home; (2) Celibate Spinster; (3) Promiscuous Prostitute.

Nowadays, there still aren't many archetypal roles that describe the female worker. What is the archetype for women handling work/life balance and a family with ease? For most, it's always a division, a challenge. So for me, it's an interesting area to explore.

It's no coincidence that I found this book because I do operate my life – at least for the last twenty years – guided and blessed by synchronicity. Since I first came across Feng Shui in 1992, I've understood how the Universe might be speaking to me, how to interpret those messages and signs and, as time has gone by, to give more importance to them.

For example, in the late '90s, I was doing interesting work in the field of ancient wisdom and Feng Shui. So it was much more of a mission and less about the money – although for me work's never been simply about money. Yet my approach to work was still a challenge. It was a source of stress.

My office was in London's West End. I was really struggling with this question of what's next for me in life. One day I walked round, probably in tears, with some degree of anxiety. I followed my feet round Marylebone, Manchester Square, behind Selfridges and all the way back to the top of Marylebone High Street straight into Daunt Books, a fantastic bookstore. My feet took me up some stairs at the back of the store. Unusually for bookstores, it has a big glass atrium and gangway where you can walk up to the top. I walked along and my hand reached out. I picked up a book, waiting for this great wisdom and instruction to fall out from the sky through this book ...

... It was on mountain biking.

What the heck?

Almost on the first page was a photo of a man on a mountain bike, just the back of his head. I thought, *That's Simon. That's my ex-flame.*

I didn't *definitely* know, but I felt sure it was. Simon used to do rides for a friend who had a mountain biking editorial business. *It has to be him. What's the message?*

Simon was the same age, from Yorkshire, like I was. He'd gone to live in the Cotswolds from London for a better quality of life. That was the defining part of him. I thought, *Maybe it's time to leave London.* That galvanised me towards creating a life in Yorkshire.

Then again, around 2009, I was completely following my inner voice. I was feeling a bit lost in terms of *explaining* to others what I was doing, but I knew I was going 'somewhere'. I wasn't lost – I'd just been silent and quiet, mainly in my house in North Yorkshire. I'd been slow and really understanding the concept of 'slow'. It had been more about 'being' than 'doing'. So there I was, a decade after the Simon message, wandering into Daunt Books and I thought, *I'll see if there's another message.* I went to the same section and pulled out at random a guidebook entitled *Slow in North Yorkshire.*

Are you having a joke? On the cover was a picture, an amalgam, of what looked like my cottage, Yorkshire stone walls, sheep, exactly what I look out at from my window. I thought, *How amazing!*

Then, in May this year, I woke up wondering if spirit had a message for me. I went into the store and as I walked up the stairs, I got a message, *fourth row along, fifth shelf.* I walked along, counting, and reached out my hand. It was that book I mentioned *Striking a Light.* It was definitely the book for me – the only book that wasn't about bikes and tourist London. It was about the history of women and London and how women have been written out of history – like your Pilgrim Mothers.

So I follow instructions and the trail of breadcrumbs. It's really amazing where it has taken me and guided my life.

There comes a point in life where you start to have an understanding of the inner world. I used to have these hunches, but I didn't know what they were. When I ran my marketing consultancy business, I used to get a feeling for what the problem was in various projects. Then I would have to spend a long time coming up with some logic for it. Even when I wasn't involved in a project, other consultants would come to me for the 'Gina touch' – for me to tune in and say, "You need to do this, this and this," and they would go, "That's brilliant." I could have trained them to do what I was doing, but I didn't understand what was happening.

In business, I was very intuitive. I didn't always realise that other people didn't get the same strong messages.

If you're working in a traditional corporate environment that's masculine, logical and rational, you've only got to get shouted down a few times or told you're odd when you have these subtle feelings and nuances, or not have them recognised, and you quieten the voice inside. You still think or feel it, but you don't necessarily express it. It becomes unsafe to do so because you're going to be ridiculed. In an environment where intuition's encouraged it gradually comes out.

I've been in a situation where I say, "I'm now going to talk about something in a more feminine way, more heart-centred," but I've felt the atmosphere, even with women, was a bit too judging. Knowing that, I've had to change the atmosphere. "Let's have a break. Let's put some music on and have a dance. Let's change the room. Let's change the energy. Let's put some fresh flowers out. Let's clear out what is not needed and create a shift." I change the space first. Then I make a sacred space, one where the harsh vibrations have been shifted so I can speak about softer, emotional issues.

I talk about myself as a space holder. My business partner is one too. We hold a space for something to happen by setting an intention and working with the emotional atmosphere. It's a completely invisible skill. We create the food, the energy, the atmosphere, in which transformative conversation happens. So it's a nicer party, a better gathering, a more productive meeting. If it's a challenging meeting, you use a great deal of energy just absorbing stress in a charged atmosphere, and that is before you have done anything tangible in terms of what other people can see as effort or work!

In fact, 'space holder' could be an archetype. I interviewed a Professor of Aboriginal Studies in Australia. She talked about the 'emotional labour' that the Aboriginal women do in their communities – a wonderful way to take pride in what we do, expressing those feelings, having a language around emotion that men often shut off from. For so long, 'I hope you are not going to get all emotional on me' would be a judgment against a woman in business. That kind of comment would really close us down.

That's why you and I are seeing so many women leaving the corporate world because it is impossible for them to be authentic in their professional life. Of course, there's been a shift in the last 15–20 years; it may not be safe to express feelings in most corporate environments, but we know that we can do it outside that environment. It then starts to become a way of being for us.

That's fascinating. I too create a sacred space before a workshop or meeting, or a coaching session or phone conversation (particularly if I envision it will be difficult) or even an email. It's a moment of getting in the zone and asking for the greatest good to come out of the interaction. It's like creating a nurturing womb. Of course, the feminine is the void, the chaos, the allowing. So it makes absolutely perfect sense that we should create the space and allow whatever transpires to happen.

'The void' and 'allowing' are key feminine words because the masculine is so much about certainty. There's a place for certainty – it is really important. But often you need the allowing nature of doubt to create a subtle space, a womb in which to birth the invisible into a new idea, a new direction, a new way of being or thinking or feeling or action.

You have to do that in a predominantly feminine environment. Men might think it's too 'woo

woo' or odd, or why don't we get on with things. But a group of individuals can each bring a piece to the conversation where no one knew the answer on their own. Together we allow a solution to emerge. Then we go "Wow, we've arrived there."

That's the journey a lot of women are on. They leave corporate life; they go into this 'don't know' period. It's often scary. They're following this individually guided path, whether or not they really understand the role of intuition. Sometimes there'll be periods of excitement where they'll be drawn to take up a new skill, start a new venture, which then doesn't succeed financially. But they say "Never mind"… They learn from it and then they're drawn to something else.

When I'm hosting women's gatherings, I'm acknowledging that they've come to this space with that diverse range of skills that the new way of working will need, will draw on – even if that is not yet obvious. The women have been through that journey of allowing themselves to develop. It's not a known career path, but they've emerged as a new woman. They will draw on all that valuable experience, even though they may not see it now. The world will need that. A new name will be given to the kind of role that they have created from their unique experience, skills, gifts and talents.

> "… often you need the allowing nature of doubt to create a subtle space, a womb in which to birth the invisible into a new idea, a new direction…"

Interesting. It's a slowing down and allowing state.

I was at a health spa in Queensland, telling my friend about how I came upon the *Slow in North Yorkshire* book. I turned round and there on the coffee table was a magazine called *Slow Food*!

I have certainly been a speedy woman. Speed's been a big part of my persona – like coming in the kitchen and ten minutes later, there's dinner. Mum did that. I'm still fast and efficient, but I have long periods of slowness in my life. I let things emerge. At the same time, I have this voice saying, "What are you missing out on by living at this pace? Are you sure it's okay? Don't you think you should get on with things?"

I was brought up with the Protestant work ethic and I sometimes struggle with doing nothing.

I've got the same thing. My mother never let up. In fact, I'd walk in the room where she might be having a cup of tea and she used to say, "I've only just sat down." As if she had to justify having a moment of quiet! But I have worked on that in myself. That's why I travel and seemingly do nothing in places. I read patterns; I bring different ideas together from different cultures or diverse situations. This gives me insights and I can see what's happening in the world. I can only observe these from slowness.

My study of Feng Shui has helped me enormously with life in general. I know what happens to the seed, unseen below the surface in the ground. If I didn't, I would be asking, "What's going on? I'm watching it and nothing's happening." The seedling comes out and it's like, "Wow, at last! A result." But because I understand the nature of winter, I can recognise the seemingly still fallow phase of life. I know that can actually be a very productive time. I can go, "Okay, while I'm having time out, Universe, this is what I need. I need to meet this person. I want this solution."

I'll go and enjoy myself, and then I'll come back and bump into that very person. And I'll have an idea that resolves a problem rather than fretting or churning over it. I don't have to work at it. It comes to me.

I was on a nine-week trip with my mum about three years ago. She wanted to revisit Cairns and the Great Barrier Reef – so we did. And I was quite clear that for the next few days I wasn't going to be writing, even though I really did need to get something published.

So we were out on this boat and I asked for some wisdom. I was scuba diving for the first time with a shoal of fish following me and I started to get insights. I thought, *Thank you.* I wrote them down quickly when I got back. I'm always gleaning something. It was all very effortless. I feel I have had my fill of hard work and stress, so I requested a life of joy, grace and ease. Along the way I'm given what I need. I don't feel guilty for not working hard because I'm always, in a sense, showing up and making myself open and available to insights, ideas, connections and resources that are going to be useful to me.

> "I read patterns; I bring different ideas together from different cultures or diverse situations. This gives me insights and I can see what's happening in the world. I can only observe these from slowness."

That's fantastic. It's almost like you're a pilgrim who's drawing your own community to you.

What I do see is a theme that emerges from each overseas trip I make. I go with very little agenda. I show up, I meet the right people, I'm extremely blessed, and I usually have a women's gathering wherever I go in the world. I just have an amazing time.

One of the things I have witnessed across the globe is how many women have left corporate life because of suffering major stress. A few weeks ago in a Brahma Kumaris gathering in London[1], Sister Jayanti called it 'a crisis of values'. Some of us really aren't living our values in business. If you're a woman in an environment where you have to work by a different creed or code to your own values, it's very unsettling.

Somehow, I think it can be easier for men. They do tend to compartmentalise things. I had a partner years ago who really did not get on with his boss. They had lots of arguments. Then he went out for a drink with him. I asked "How can you go out and socialise with somebody you don't like?" He just replied, "That's work. It's different."

I couldn't get over that. If women have an issue with someone, I don't think we can just go and have a drink with them. We need to resolve tensions. Or if we've got a challenge where we can't express ourselves, we're holding it in and letting it eat away at us. There comes a point where if we suppress enough unresolved stuff, it can actually be killing us. What I'm seeing is women leaving business because they can't live by a code that's not authentic for them. Their way of resolving a situation that they cannot easily confront is to step away from it.

This problem of a values clash does not just affect women. On the last trip I met a man very much in contact with his feminine side, who was very good at business development and building

---

1   The Brahma Kumaris World Spiritual University (BKWSU) is an international non-governmental organisation with spiritual headquarters in Mt. Abu, Rajasthan, India with over 10,000 centres in 130 countries, territories and islands.

relationships; but he was being pressured to deliver sales by very tight deadlines. It was interesting to hear a *man* speak about his difficulty and challenge in trying to survive in a very uncompassionate system.

We do have to change the system. It's not simply about bringing more women onto boards. We actually want a system where we can really be a woman and use our feminine qualities so that we can influence the whole organisation. We need to make the workplace a more generative, compassionate environment that is not dominated by greed; somewhere that we can live by our values and is a safe, nurturing place for everybody to work. HR research has identified the huge financial loss of women leaving for whatever reason. There is a massive loss of talent. So, organisations are actually looking at ways to retain women by making workplaces woman-friendly.

In doing so, many corporations are making themselves more attractive places for men to work. So a man can be both the corporate employee and the father who can go home early to lead his son's scout group – and he can feel it's okay because women are doing the same thing. Men can bring their family needs into work and live more as a whole man. That's what we need – a more balanced life-and-family-friendly work structure.

Reinvention of work is really what it's about. Corporations were invented by men for men. We're stepping into a system that wasn't designed by women or for women, so we can't fit in easily without changing ourselves. We tried. We masculinised ourselves and made ourselves ill. So it *is* a pilgrim movement to go and create a new world of work from within.

Neither of us is using a strident feminist language. The feminist movement was often portrayed as anti-men. Some of it was, but it was hijacked by the masculine media filter. Who would want to be a feminist by the time they've written about it? Feminism wasn't allowed to mature into its next phase. When we hear about the values and goals of the feminist movement – equality for women and equal pay – who wouldn't want to be a feminist? But we wouldn't want to now in the 21st Century, or any time onwards from the '80s, because feminists were treated like witches who were metaphorically burned. In a sense, their character and identity were burned.

I'm now involved in seeding a new movement to bring in feminine values and wisdom so that we change the world of work. We need to learn to work together in teams and develop better collaboration.

I've learned so much from the Brahma Kumaris about how they make things work. I was truly thrilled to hear Dadi Janki, their ninety-six year old female leader, express that it's not about our ability to get on with other people. It's our ability to be so connected to our soul, to our spirit guidance, to God, that in that connection we know who we are; we know what our value is; we know what it is that we're here to deliver; and we are able to see that in others. This transcends the need to be liked.

When you know what your role is – that you're here to serve, to bring in your special talent – and how it fits with other people and you all become a connected team, it overrides personalities. You're here for the service that you're jointly doing, and we are not doing it by ourselves. So we have to work

> "Each one of us can bring our own genius to enable somebody else to bring their genius out in the world. Without each other, we wouldn't flower."

together because we have that soul connection. It transcends personal idiosyncrasies. It's not about having to get on with everybody. It's about bringing forth what we're here to do. The more inner journeying you do, the more you connect with your purpose and you know that you're going to be of service.

Just over a year ago, Kevin Kelly, who founded Wired magazine, talked about how technology evolves just like humans evolve. Although it might look like chaos, there is an order, an evolution, to this journey of technology. For example, he said that Mozart was a genius with the music he created, *but* without the genius of the invention of the harpsichord, Mozart would not have been able to bring his genius into the world.

Each one of us can bring our own genius to enable somebody else to bring their genius out in the world. Without each other, we wouldn't flower. We actually are what I call a 'soul family', unlocking each other's soul keys. I think that's why there are so many older women opening their own businesses; they're more in contact with their soul wisdom. We've had to journey through to that awakening to our wisdom years. Youth and beauty change into a different kind of beauty – an inner beauty.

Where we bring that wisdom to the world, not just for ourselves but in that inquiry of 'how can I make life better', we are, as Dr David Paul explains, changing the conversation and moving on from, 'Okay, we got the vote.' But when have we come together since then? We haven't, really, not in any organised way. So now there is something for us to come together for – conscious conversations – in a time where it's easier to connect. Imagine if we were trying to get the vote now, how much more quickly we could do that; it was hard without the level of communication and technology we have now.

"We are aiming to support, empower and accelerate existing women's networks."

We're definitely here to create the change in the world – to lead that change, to lead in relationships and to lead in emotional connection. Last night I was at the Brahma Kumaris' Inner Olympics event to celebrate the Olympic values. Geoff Thompson, a five-times Karate world champion, said how you win the Olympics is 99 per cent in the head. It's that focus. It's those inner capacities. He pointed out that in the 2012 Olympics it was the first time women have been represented in every single sport.

Dadi Janki said that in the spiritual Olympics, women are already leading. We're doing our inner exploration. I believe that's what we'll bring to change the world of work.

I really want to explore bringing in more feminine words and language to business, rather than a 'killer app'. Even 'leader' is seen as military. As Dadi Janki said, "I don't see myself as a leader." She calls herself an 'instrument' of spirit.

But language about sport and military campaigns peppers business. I'm looking to see how we can create a more feminine language, such as 'cooking up new ideas', 'bringing all the ingredients together'. There are cooking terms, but I'd love to highlight more.

Tell me about what else you're working on at the moment.

I've got a new business called the Women Gathering Project, which is a technology platform, to support collaboration, and also a consultancy. My business partner and I are working with new technology that will change the way we use the web. At the moment everything you share about yourself is not private. With this technology you can choose what you share, but all the information you input is used, privately, to search to match you with exactly the right resources and contacts.

You can structure your profile around your needs such as, 'I've got a water project in Africa and I need investment.' You can also list what you have expertise in. Our technology finds suitable matches for you in a way that you currently could not easily find people. We are aiming to support, empower and accelerate existing women's networks. It's almost like adding baking powder to a women's movement, amplifying connections and supporting women entrepreneurs and changemakers.

When will it come to fruition?

Hopefully soon. We're a divinely guided business. We're patiently waiting for investment money from a particular source. When we start, it will be the right time.

We're a women-owned, women-financed, women-led business, learning and supporting a new way of working. We have men in the team, but business is done in a much more feminine, collaborative way. We walk what we talk.

I'm personally passionate about supporting the rise of the feminine on the planet. I feel that technology will help us do that. I want to see a validation of feminine values, an acceptance, an embracing. We want the greater participation of women bringing their feminine values.

Dr Riane Eisler wrote the book *The Real Wealth of Nations* about caring economics. She illustrates how feminine values – nurturing, caring, volunteering, community building, mothering – are not currently counted and measured. Therefore, we don't value them. They are the underpinning on which everything in government, business – the whole economy – is run. The economic world could not exist without this parallel world, this unpaid economy, led by women. Yet it's not valued in any way. I deeply resonated with that language after all my years of experience working with women, communicating about the healthy home, cooking and leading my life from the home.

My last twenty years have been about homemaking. I started out in my teens learning Housecraft and Domestic Science. Then I went to hotel school. I was cooking in care environments before I shifted into the office environment in the hotel industry. So I've always been involved in some kind of service. I've been serving meals since the age of nine, working in my parents' hotel, so hospitality runs through me. Party-throwing, making people feel at home, providing nourishing food has been the continuum in my life and now I'm using it as the complete foundation of my business.

When I started a new wellness business from my home in the 1990s, I invited friends and contacts round, made them soup and gave a presentation. For me feeding people symbolises feeding them new ideas. When I look back, I see that I love to make people feel at home. I don't particularly have any airs and graces. There's me out in the world doing business and there's me who will cook your dinner, invite you to stay the night and bring you a cup of tea in the morning. It's the same me.

I didn't set out to be known for that, but I am now. For years I've thought, *I'm valued, but how can I use it in business?* When I lived with my former partner in Yorkshire, his business associates would visit. Even though I had my own business and busy schedule, I would often drop everything and look after these people, be the 'corporate wife', creating our home, pouring love into it, which I think people could feel. The quality of the business discussion and transaction was completely different because it was in a very sacred environment that we consciously created. They would therefore want to know what I did. They found out I wrote books on healthy living – half a million books have been sold actually. I'd send them away with food and water for their journey and maybe some fresh insight about their life, which hopefully added value to their life's journey.

So it's like I've been running this hostelry for people on their path. Innkeeping has been an internal metaphor for me. I've been nourishing people. Now I can bring some language to how I do that in business for people, to see that it has a value. It is often invisible. So it has been hard to bring those qualities to the world of business and have them recognised, but it's important now.

It absolutely is. It's as if you're creating a home wherever you go – almost like the snail that carries the home with it – but you're sharing your home, this safe environment.

Long ago, I'd taken up the image of the Bedouin and the tents and the blankets, just wrapping everything up. I have often been away for three months, living out of a suitcase, travelling to many cities.

I learned that I could be at home anywhere. Outside order in a space helps me to have internal order. I change a room, maybe put the ornaments away, move this here, put that there, do this, do that … I take time for peace and acclimatise myself, recognising I often have an interim period when I don't like things. I used to get upset and find it hard to settle in a new place. Now I realise that's just my 'changeover day' where I am adjusting to the new energies and new routine. I give myself permission to honour that so I can get over it faster. The next day, I feel at home.

I have my criteria when I'm flicking through places to book. I know what works for me. I like to find a swimming pool nearby and yoga classes. I really must have a big view or fantastic vista. I am clear that I must have light, nowhere dark.

So I have some way to understand where I'm going and how to work with my inner guidance. Rather than 'What shall I do now?' I ask myself questions like 'What am I being called to do today? Who am I needing to meet?'

I then find I meet people. I get insights. I've learnt to live my life by being in the power of the question and being in the enquiry. When I was consulting years ago, I lived in certainty and I knew all the answers. I was paid to know. So I had to go through a period of time where I had to re-form my relationship with the inner world and with the spirit. From around 2006, I've been training myself to say, "I don't know." It took me a while.

A senior business executive in Brisbane asked, "What are you doing?"

I answered, "I'm travelling."

"Are you working or on holiday?"

"I'm doing both at the same time. Along the way, I meet people who become pearls or jewels that I put into a necklace. A gathering of people, showing up."

If I had known years ago what I know now about faith, I wouldn't have been so riddled with anxiety about whether I was doing the right thing. I got depressed and had real dark nights of the soul. I didn't go with my trusting and knowing. I always felt I had a different future from the norm, but I didn't know how to express it and go counter-culture.

> "If I had known years ago what I know now about faith, I wouldn't have been so riddled with anxiety about whether I was doing the right thing."

When were your darkest nights?

I had two main periods. The first one was the break-up of my marriage. I got married at twenty-three to my teenage sweetheart of seven years. We seemed perfect for each other. And within two years, it was over.

I was ill before the wedding, so it was brought forward. My illness was probably about me not getting married, but instead we brought the wedding forward! There was no confidence in me to try something else – to go and find myself.

So I stayed with it. It's like that moment when Princess Diana had that doubt and was told, "You can't back out now. Your face is on the tea towels." I was thinking, *All that money we spent on flowers and food and the dress.* The moment of doubt was so fleeting, it was like *Keep it to yourself and don't tell anyone.* Looking back, I was so young.

At that time I was very much supported by my parents. From the age of about twenty-three, my mother had run a small hotel for twenty-five guests and cooked three meals a day for the summer season in Scarborough – the Queen of the Yorkshire coast! There was me and my brother who was five years younger. My dad worked as a printer and helped in the hotel. Until I was ten, I waited at tables and grew up in this environment. Then my parents changed it into holiday apartments. So every Saturday, the changeover day, I had to help clean.

Naturally I went to hotel school. I didn't allow myself to think of other possibilities, although I could have done. So I had a career ahead of me, whereas my boyfriend failed his A-levels. Then he flunked his polytechnic Business Studies. So his parents got him an apprenticeship in insurance broking.

By this time, I was Assistant Manager of the Playboy Club in Manchester. It was great – glamorous. I worked so hard, the General Manager didn't come in till 5 o'clock instead of 9. They had confidence in me to let me run the day operation. I'd been there less than a year when my husband came home and said, "We're moving to Northampton. I've got a new position."

I just went, "Okay."

There was no discussion, no choice. We both just assumed we would go and I would leave my executive job. Off I went and became unemployed in Northampton. I got rather depressed and to cut a long story short, one of my job interviews was for a motorway service station on the M1. They really wanted me, so they gave me my choice of shifts. One of the roles was – this is the killer line – I would be motivating the table clearers. *[Jane laughing]* This is where I'd got to. Shoot me now!

Around the same time, my ex-boss from Manchester rang me and said, "I need you." I went back to work for him for a couple of months, travelling five hours a day on a train. Then I got a great management job in London, which was only an hour away. By taking smaller steps, I was able to make the shift. I would never have looked for a job in London. I know now that I was taking my Chi, my energy, away from the marriage.

I built myself a wonderful life in London. It was a means to get me out of my marriage, to engineer my husband to break it up, a passive way of leaving. It was very painful and I didn't know how to talk to anybody about it. If only I'd said "Look, my ambition is being thwarted. I can't see what my role is."

So I was out on my own in the world, in London, cut adrift from what I'd known. I forged my way and bought my own apartment in Wimbledon but always felt I needed a man or somebody more senior to me to guide me, support me. I was content to be their No. 2 and be shepherded along. I never saw myself as a No. 1 or a leader. I often earned more than my man but felt financially secure when I had a man. Looking back, it's ridiculous. I had financial security in myself because I ran a very successful business, mentored by a man. He gave me the head start, so I'm deeply appreciative. In no way do I mean this to be anti-men. I am very appreciative of the support I had from the men in my life, but I don't think I had the right balance in my relationships.

But then my big emergence came in 1990 when my key relationship, which was effectively a marriage, broke down. After five years he said that he was questioning things, effectively ending the relationship. That was cataclysmic for me. Catastrophic. I was deeply hurt. I was settled into that relationship in my mid-thirties. He said, "I'm releasing you so you can have a family with somebody else." It's very hard to start again at thirty-five with the then ambition of having a family.

So I was out on my own again. Two years later, I got a really deep, clinical depression. This is my second dark period. I absolutely had to stop work. My ex-partner ran my business while I went to a private psychiatric hospital for a month for help and to start exploring my inner world.

During that time, lots of synchronicities happened. I got a day pass and went to a Mind, Body, Spirit festival. William Bloom's book, *The New Age: An Anthology of Essential Writings*, fell into my hand. For the first time, I learned all these concepts about reincarnation, consciousness, about soul. It opened up a whole new world. I read *A Road Less Travelled* [M. Scott Peck] in two days. Oh my goodness me, it so deeply affected me that I couldn't get out of bed. I underlined every page. It was like I'd been run over by a steamroller. All my mental and psychic energy had been used up in processing everything I had been reading. I realised how an idea can have a profound effect. I had a similar experience when I read Tony Robbins' book, *Awaken the Giant Within*. It helped me see life and myself in a new way.

I had an appetite for learning. Via a friend I'd received a mailing from Brian Tracy. It went completely over my head at the time, but when I went into hospital, I took it with me for some reason. When I started reading it, I thought, *Oh my God, that's me.* It talked about, do you lack confidence, do you lack this, do you lack that and do you feel this way? It was describing me in a positive, productive, proactive way rather than treating me as an illness and with pills, which is what the psychiatric route was. By a stroke of luck, there was a course within reach the next week. So the hospital took me off medication and gave me permission to go out on day release. I arrived there as colourful me, just like this, and I eventually shared that I was in a psychiatric hospital being treated for stress and depression. They were like, *"What?" [Both laughing]*

I went back to the hospital with this book and set of tapes and it was like, having been starving, suddenly being given a banquet of food. I'd discuss the ideas with others and most people thought I was an employee of the hospital rather than a patient! *[Both laughing]* When I wasn't well, I had my down moments in my room, in private.

Anyway, I recovered and left hospital. I had a marketing consultancy for hotels at that time. When the Bank of Credit and Commerce International went bust, two of my key clients with whom I'd won prestigious awards from the English Tourist Board, the Caterer & Hotelkeeper Magazine and the Institute of Marketing, suddenly went bankrupt too, through no fault of their tradings.

That was all part of everything falling down around me. I still had a thriving business, but I had six or seven full-time employees, offices in Cavendish Square, lots of expenses. I'd created a monster that needed feeding and I didn't know how. I just knew how to do what I did. I'd started with one client from synchronicity. Then all the other clients said, "You've got magic. We want what you did for him." So I didn't have to market myself. But now I wondered, *Do I actually want to do this business?*

So there was this major life transition in 1992 where I had to reinvent myself.

I tried to make a breakthrough in sharing my vulnerability. It's a stigma to have a breakdown or mental illness, yet it is really a spiritual crisis. When you change the language, it becomes something completely different. And people showed up along the way as guides. My next-door-neighbour in London was a photographer. All we ever said was hello, in all the years I was there. One day that neighbour knocked on my door – which he never did usually – and I answered in quite an emotional state. I could have hidden away, but I didn't. He could tell that I was upset, so he asked, "Are you okay?"

> "It's a stigma to have a breakdown or mental illness, yet it is really a spiritual crisis."

"Yes ... no, not really."

How do you tell your neighbour, a stranger, you're depressed when you don't know how to put it into language? Anyway, he came in and kind of reached out to me. He said, "I think there's something that might be interesting for you," and he gave me a leaflet on psychoneuroimmunology [2](PNI). I'd never heard about it before, but inside I had that click of recognition.

At the time I'd been working for two years with an iridologist/nutritionist on terrible PMT I'd been having. My three days of depression a month had over time become thirty days, but I didn't realise because it was just PMT getting longer each month. We were treating the physical side by excluding gluten, wheat, dairy, sugar, caffeine, meat ... everything. At Christmas she sent me to have colonic irrigation saying, "Don't let him talk you into having more than one."

He talked me into having seven! One every day.

In the middle of winter, I was having a lot of cold and damp put into my body when really your inner system needs fire. So it was the wrong time of year to do it; though maybe the right thing. I'd gone into a deep cleansing and was getting really depressed by witnessing all of this negative coming out, and I didn't have anybody to supervise or handle it with me. When my neighbour gave me this article on PNI, it was a trigger point and felt meant to be.

From there I reached out and got help. I went to see the right psychotherapist for treatment and that started me on my path of personal transformation. I then thought, *You know what? I got this from stress, and other people are going to have it. I'm not the first and I'm not going to be the last.* So I opened a Personal Development Centre to share all my teachers with others.

It was part of my transition to share everything I'd learnt. At the same time, I came across Feng Shui and I knew that it had a huge inner calling for me. Eventually, I started a school with my mentor and teacher. I co-founded the Feng Shui Society and decided from 1992 that I was going to put Feng Shui on the map with all my marketing expertise and PR skills. I won an award from the Institute of Public Relations for that.

That whole journey started my deep connection with my inner wisdom after having had

---

2   Study of the interaction of human behaviour, mind, body and immune system.

depression for four years on and off. But I think my connection with the Brahma Kumaris has been my biggest growth and saving grace. They're a spiritual organisation led by women, deeply connected with the feminine way of being. Dadi Janki was eighty-seven when I first met her. What a woman, now aged ninety-six, leading this global organisation. How amazing and professional it is – and nobody pays anything. It's all by donation; they call it a Gift Economy! And it's all done with complete grace and ease and no stress. My spiritual journey has been really strengthened and amplified by studying with them.

Recently, I came across Christian Pankhurst's work on Heart Intelligence. Until he expressed his ideas, I didn't know what I already understood unconsciously. I now realise I have unconscious competence in a lot of things to do with wisdom and spirituality, but I only recognise it within me when I hear it through somebody out there who is teaching it, or I see it's an issue for someone.

For a long time during my life transition period, I felt I was a nobody who didn't know anything or have anything to offer. It seemed as if entrepreneurship was all about young people with energy and I haven't got the energy to do what I did years ago in the early days. I didn't realise there was a way I could do it that could be graceful, through wisdom, through spiritual connection. I began to realise that of course I was needed. So I reinvented myself. And I did go through that phase of being this older, invisible woman. I deeply know that,

> "I didn't realise there was a way I could [be an entrepreneur] that could be graceful, through wisdom, through spiritual connection."

and it's been painful because my key relationship of ten years ended when I was just over fifty. So I felt very abandoned. He's since gone on to have relationships with much younger women, many years younger than me, and my other partner did that too. So I've had to face being the older woman who's not wanted and not seen to now really finding what my contribution is and making myself visible.

I've also been through a physical transformation. It just happened. I spent virtually one whole summer – my menopausal summer – in bed for three months. I haemorrhaged and got anaemia. I couldn't do anything. I couldn't read. I couldn't take any information in. But I knew my brain was being reprogrammed. Sometimes I had to sleep for a week while I was taking downloads. My mind was changing. I lost use of language. I used to say, "I need that white thing, the circle that you eat from." My business partner's husband had a stroke and he had a similar language from his stroke.

So it was quite weird. I knew I'd had a brain change. I was thinking differently. I was becoming a different person. My hair grew longer and blonder. I lost weight. My style changed and I changed. People who I had not seen for a few years could hardly recognise me.

It was a makeover from spirit, acknowledging the work I had done on the inside. It's interesting. I've found my way as a powerful, older woman in touch with my wisdom. So I really do feel I can help women of any age go through a process, just as I have been – other than childbirth and mothering – although I've mothered projects, like my books and I started the Feng Shui movement. I co-created many movements, started things and brought new ideas, although my name hasn't always necessarily been there. But that's the thing about birthing and the female role of not being seen.

I've now got to the stage where it's okay. It doesn't matter. I don't need to be seen. There was a time where I'd be hurt and my ego would feel injured. Now I can handle it, and now I could also handle the fame. In the past I almost landed a TV contract. Then a whole set of circumstances stopped it. If I'd had that fame then, I don't feel I could have handled it well. Now, I would be fine. I have deep inner resources to draw on. I don't need large audiences, but I do want the effect of what I do to be large in the world.

I know that I've developed the capacity to hold a global business, to hold a global movement, to hold global change. I didn't have the inner capacity to do it before, whereas now I do… So thank God I've had that journey.

I echo Gina's words. Thank God I've had that journey!

I was one of the women Gina described, leaving corporate life suddenly on my fifty-fourth birthday in October 2005. It was a huge contrast from long, exhausting, often combative days to spending most of my time without routine or structure at home. I relished the opportunity to visit places I'd been drawn to since early childhood – Egypt, Native American reservations plus many places closer to home. I immersed myself in an eclectic mix of learning, from hypnotherapy to ancient wisdom to various healing modalities and shamanic teachings. I loved it. I also often, like Gina, recognised that I somehow knew the truth of what I was hearing, as if it was already within me and being awakened through hearing it from a teacher. Like a candle wick, just waiting for somebody to gently set it alight.

One of my lasting memories involved a weekend with a friend in October 2007 at the Brahma Kumaris Global Retreat Centre near Oxford. It is a large country house surrounded by 55 acres of grounds, bordering the Thames. We stayed in a room on the top floor with a distinctive round window. It was a deeply nourishing weekend. The talks, meditations and drishti-giving sessions were incredibly powerful.[3] On the Saturday afternoon we were invited to experience silence for about four hours while we ate, wandered round the grounds, spent time in our rooms or did whatever we chose. It felt strange at first, yet liberating, as we smiled and gestured our communications. Part of me wanted to stay quiet for longer. However, I noted how uncomfortable some people were with silence and could not cope. I observed them talking while strolling, some seemingly not making any attempt to be silent. Interesting.

Like Gina, I have total respect for the Brahma Kumaris and how they operate. They live by their values. From my outsider's view they certainly appear to embody a new, feminine way of operating – a way I am also embracing.

I have not always been in this tranquil space. I would often get panic attacks as I searched for a new means of income. Many times I knocked at, and sometimes walked through, possible business and financial doors but always seemed to find myself in a wardrobe rather than Narnia. A few years ago, I decided to take life one day at a time and see what happened, letting my inner guidance

---

3   Drishti-giving is spiritual power donated soul to soul via the third eye.

lead me. I have experienced highs and lows, the life of a hostess, the life of a hermit. At times I have felt confused, lost, isolated, abandoned; at others exhilarated, ecstatic, jumping up and down excited. I'm still travelling, at peace, but with a spark of anticipation to see what new learning and adventures await me, a bit like that moment before Gina would walk to Daunt Books and put her hand out to see what's coming next…

"I'm still travelling, at peace, but with a spark of anticipation to see what new learning and adventures await me…"

JANE NOBLE KNIGHT

Final Words

The Pilgrim Mother – Jane Noble Knight

What inspiring journeys these women entrepreneurs have undertaken!

What an inspiring journey *I* have experienced through hearing, absorbing and sharing their stories.

What strikes me the most is that these women have truly answered their calling.

In *The Law of Divine Compensation – On Work, Money and Miracles (2012)*, Marianne Williamson talks about one's calling:

> "One of the most positive transitions you can make is from viewing your work as a job to viewing it as a calling. A job is an exchange of energy in which you do a material task and someone provides money in exchange. A calling, however, is an organic field of energy that emerges from the deepest aspects of who you are.
>
> … You have a calling because you're on this earth with a divine purpose: to rise to the level of your highest creative possibility, expressing all that you are intellectually, emotionally, psychologically, and physically in order to make the universe a more beautiful place.
>
> … Your calling is what you would do if you were paid to do it or not. Your calling is what you have to do in order to be happy. Your calling is what connects you to your deepest self, and to the rest of life around you."

I believe that each one of us has a calling – the voice, the tug, the magnetic force that beckons. Life changes when we take heed and follow.

How do we follow our calling?

We sit in stillness.

We become slower and less busy.

We listen to our intuition.

We become aware of synchronicities.

We act upon 'signs' – pointers to our next step.

We release our attachment to outcomes.

We follow our hearts and do what we love – the clues can often be found in childhood.

We persevere – no matter what.

We hold out for our biggest dream – no settling for anything less.

We trust that we live in a world full of love where we are constantly supported, however the outward situation may appear.

Each one of us has our own unique calling. We are born with it. Sometimes we follow that calling immediately. Usually we get on with our lives till we become aware of the call and take action – only to discover that our lives up to that point have been perfect for the road ahead.

As Steve Jobs famously said in his June 2005 Stanford commencement address, "You can't connect the dots looking forward; you can only connect them looking backwards."

These stories of my Pilgrim Mother Entrepreneurs tell of hope and inspiration – of the everyday epic.

The world needs heart and soul-centred – authentic – entrepreneurs: people living from their passion; behaving ethically; enjoying balanced lives; building communities; leaving legacies; and feeling fulfilled.

These women entrepreneurs are doing just that.

They have all answered their calling.

Have you answered yours?

If yes, may these stories have inspired you further along your journey.

If not yet, or you are unsure but you feel that inner yearning, read and reread these chapters, reflect on the stories you're most drawn to and listen to your inner guidance.

The world is changing.

It's time to change our lives for the better — not just for ourselves but for *everyone*.

Can we have it all?

Yes, we can!

"It is our time. There is a great shift happening in the world. We are all part of it. We can grab the opportunity to be all we can be …
or we can hide away and live lesser, more contained lives.
There is no right or wrong. It is *our* choice. I believe the time has come for every one of us to step up, to stand out and to shine …
by doing what we love, what sparks our passion and what brings us joy."

JANE NOBLE KNIGHT

Acknowledgements

So many to thank…

To my fabulous daughters, no greater gift can a mother receive!

To my ex-husband, Chris, who shared over thirty years of my journey with me.

To my sister, Wendy, and brother-in-law, Ian Connor, for sharing your home with me and my dogs, Sammy and Bran, during one of the foggy stages of my personal journey. For anyone wanting a heart-centred solicitor and accountant (yes, they do exist) you can find them in the Oldham/ Bury area. My four-legged companion, Bran, would like to thank his mate, Domino, for the fun and frolics every time they meet (as well as the treats and chews he leaves lying around). Sammy, my doggy soulmate, still walks with me in spirit every day. God bless all my four-legged companions who have added such richness to my life.

To my parents, Bob and Eunice Noble… Dad for passing on your appetite for learning and Mum for sharing your love of stories.

To Jo, my 'adopted' daughter, for reminding me of the magic one experiences when one first taps into the mysteries.

To Nina Carrère, my French friend of over 25 years, with whom I have shared so much in our parallel lives – separated by geography, united by mutual interests. We first 'met' when Nina wrote a letter to Cosmopolitan asking for a British pen pal and I responded. I was thrilled that out of well over a hundred applicants, I was one of three women she chose, all of whom she is still in touch with.

To the people of Burrington near Ludlow where I lived for 14 years, especially Alan and Rosemary Laurie and Ray Wilkins, for your generous work in the community; to talented artist Tania Pearson for our friendship and joint meditations; and to Jenny Walder for my pamper treats.

To the super-talented Jane Williams of Fandango Media for our shared journey discovering more about the Pilgrims and for your generosity in sharing your expertise in all sorts of ways too numerous to do justice and for becoming a valued friend; and to Karen Kiely, who introduced me to social media. (We giggled together as she filmed me interviewing exhibitors at the Motorhome Show in Malvern.)

To my support team … Wendy Millgate of Wendy & Words for your gentle editing through 'becoming me' so we are now forever linked in friendship; Simon Davies of Access Success for giving generously of your time, talents and copywriting word-wizardry; Shari Thompson of Green Jelly Marketing for transforming my book chapters into bite-sized social media tweets and blogs; Siân-Elin Flint-Freel for your multi-faceted work behind the scenes – you were at first my daughter's friend but soon joined the family tribe for Olympic trips, theatre breaks and so on. [My first introduction to Siân-Elin will be forever etched on my heart as she made us all outfits from old flowery curtains for Sing-a-Long-a Sound of Music at Ludlow Assembly Rooms – one of those nights that leaves you hoarse and aching all over from singing, laughing and applauding]; trombone-player extraordinaire Martin Nicholson for doing the website techie bits … words fail me when I describe technology; Julia Power for your accurate and timely transcriptions of my conversations [Thank you Elance! How else would I find a brilliant ex-English teacher living in Turkey?]; Isabel Gainford for the branding 'tingle' you drew out of me; Stephanie Hale for helping me to view books differently; Peggy McColl for showing me how to launch a bestseller; Julia McCutchen, for your guidance through publishing over the years; Tanya Back for book cover design and typesetting; Marie Laywine for your stunning painting on the cover; Sara Moseley for capturing me on film; John Fisher of getmesomepublicity for press releases and interesting chats in Waitrose Newport's coffee shop; Katharine Dever for midwifing The Pilgrim Mother; and finally Anita Noyes-Smith of Virgin Astrology whose accuracy as regards my path in life has stunned and supported me over the years.

To Marianne Williamson whose iconic words beginning *'Our deepest fear is not that we are inadequate, our deepest fear is that we are powerful beyond measure'* inspire me and countless others. [These words are so often misattributed to Nelson Mandela. I'm on a quest to set the record straight! You see, I am a Marianne groupie!] Not only, Marianne, are you a brilliant wordsmith but an eloquent, spontaneous speaker too. [I regularly attend her UK workshops where she blows my mind with her wisdom, her passion and her humility. At the end of each event I chat with her and have my photo taken alongside her. I am thrilled that she always recognises me and tells me it's good to see me. She is endlessly kind and gracious. I love Marianne.]

To Katherine Woodward Thomas and Claire Zammit whose first Feminine Power telecourse in June 2010 changed my life. I suddenly understood why I had felt so unfulfilled in the corporate world. I was measuring myself by masculine and not feminine values and I needed to redress the balance … and so I did. Thank you. I went on to study Katherine's equally profound *Calling in "The One"* and *Conscious Uncoupling*.

To the global sisterhood I met via Feminine Power – too numerous to mention everyone – but I especially thank Barbara Junceau, Anne Risaria Langley, Nancy Frankel, Catharina Van Leeuwen and Vicky Van Praag.

To the British sisterhood, who I met in Luxor, Egypt – Mirriam, Pauline, Sonia, Janet, Maya Vati, Laura – what magical, mystical and mind-blowing times we shared both in Egypt and the UK, often in and around my home near Ludlow. Thank you for the seasons we shared. And the two young men I also met in Egypt – Neil Christie for your gentle soul and David Anthony for the loudest, most exuberant laugh I have ever heard.

To Nick Williams, the Inspired Entrepreneur, whose wonderful books I discovered in 2004. After underlining and making notes on virtually every page of your books with my 'aha' moments, I bought copious quantities to have pristine copies to give as gifts to friends.

To my work colleagues over the years with whom I experienced the cutting edge of corporate life and from whom I learned about my own strengths and capabilities: the incredibly talented actor Margaret McEwan who uses her skills to support and challenge people in business and the rest of the lively team I first worked with at LV in 1999 – Barbara Thorn, Damaris Lockwood, Paul Jamieson and Gregg Harris; one of the best coaches I know, Geraldine Kelly; the lovely, insightful Malcolm Park who knew how to draw a great team round him; Graham Hedley for my first freelance training contract in 1999; Tony Jackson and Peter Butler who in the 1990s taught me the value of open and honest communications and provided the learning ground to develop my own skills in the minefield of business relationships; the best sales director ever, Dennis Ryan; my first sales manager, Eric Lea; my very special training team members in the order in which I recruited them – Helen Barlow, Jan Mangan, Sam Banks, Bev Mealyer, Tilly Pride. It was such a pleasure to see you fly; and my colleague Suki Kaur-Cosier with whom I shared confidences, challenges and laughter. I am happy to say I am still in touch with so many of you.

To Peter Thomson and his 'family' – Sharon Thomson, Rachel Groves, Steve Harrison, Beverley Parkin, Marilyn Chapman, Martin Nicholson (again) and the brilliantly supportive mentoring group of 2010: especially Shelley Bridgman, Simon Davies (another mention), Cathy Rowan, Emma Ziff, Van Henry, Vanessa McLean, Peter Lewis, Dave Griffin, Jeff Pettitt, Helen Murdoch, Desiree Fraser, Bert Jukes and Paul Harris. Our journey together moved me to laughter and tears in equal measure.

To the business networking groups to which I belong, which continue to stimulate me and provide me with such supportive company, especially my local Women in Rural Enterprise (WiRE) group in Newport, Shropshire.

To my educators and influencers over the years ... the very wise Kevin Core who continues to influence us from 'the other side' and his wife Christine whose powerful workshops I enjoyed in both the UK and Egypt; Lea Cowin for my first experience of guided meditations and Bob Wooler for introducing me to The Quest; Lisa Stewart of The Awareness Shop in Shropshire and now in New York, for my Usui Reiki Master attunements and for initiating me into the magic of crystals, as well as providing me with the foundation stones of my extensive library and esoteric resources; the beautiful Laura Sakara Marshall for showing me The Way of the Shuvani (the Romany wise women) and introducing me to shamanic work and vision quests; Roz Crampton, Ant Sauchella and Juan Gabriel Gutiérrez, magicians whose sound baths stirred me with primal memories; Sandy Stevenson whose two workshops in Shrewsbury moved me deeply; James Twyman for your concerts and *The Art of Spiritual Peacemaking,* which remains one of my favourite books; the very talented Sarah Phoenix for teaching me the skills of hypnotherapy and past life regression; Moira Bush, for opening my eyes to the language of colour and training me in Colour Mirrors; Edwin Courtenay for your humorous talks and very insightful personal channellings; Michelle Manders whose powerful channellings held me spellbound; the legendary Diana Cooper, whose books enlightened me about angels and feathers; Lucinda Drayton, the voice of an angel, whose music I listen to most days, and whose live concerts are the most beautiful experiences you could imagine; and Craig Hamilton's Global Meditations on the last Sunday of each month ... not much is said but much is felt.

To Diana Dorell, the Dancing Goddess, who was the first American to interview me on your radio show under my Pilgrim Mother mantle; to Emma Ziff for being my first British radio interviewer as The Pilgrim Mother; to Graham Torrington for the priceless experience of being a guest twice on your much-missed live Late Night Love Show with over 1 million listeners; to Claudia Crawley who gave me the unusual experience of being interviewed for your book – I was surprised and honoured to be asked to swap roles on this occasion; and to the people at Lion TV involved in making the House Swap programme, especially to Pete and Mona (and the various runners behind the scenes) who filmed me in Ludlow, Newquay and London (fabulous people, memorable days, thank you), producer Cassie Braban for your gentle and professional presence on the Deal Day, negotiator Sunita Shroff for your warmth and encouragement, and the late Kristian Digby, who died far too young so tragically soon afterwards, who was such fun and asked me that vital question, "What next?" which set me off on my Pilgrim Mother journey.

And of course to all the amazing women in this book. I was encouraged, supported and humbled by the generosity of spirit in each of you as you shared with me so much of your time, your wisdom and your stories. Without you I could not have birthed my initial idea into the world. My deepest gratitude to you.

I love you all.

About the Author

As long as she can remember Jane has been fascinated by people. Unsurprisingly, she studied Sociology and Psychology at Liverpool University. Jane's forty years' experience spans social work, sales, teaching, training and coaching, the last thirty of which have been in people development. In 1999 Jane became a freelance training consultant, heading up national training teams with many well-known organisations, mainly in financial services. A project in which she played a leading role was runner up in a Financial Times Arts and Business Award.

Alongside her corporate work Jane studied metaphysics and qualified in complementary therapies such as Hypnotherapy, Past Life Regression and Colour Mirrors. Jane is a lifelong learner. No 'learning junkie' who studies for study's sake, once Jane finds something of value, she applies it – she walks her talk.

In 2009 Jane took part in a BBC1 House Swap programme. A presenter's question led her to discover the story of the Pilgrim Mothers and subsequently take up the quest to learn more about them and the hidden stories of other pioneering women. Along the way she bought a motorhome and set off with her two dogs to wherever she was drawn, meeting amazing women and recording their stories.

This book is a result of Jane's journey. It is a reflection of this 'calming, kind but dynamic' woman's passion for empowering others by unearthing and sharing the gems of wisdom she has this uncanny ability to find wherever Life leads her.

You are warmly invited to find out more about Jane's adventures and how to get involved at www.thepilgrimmother.com or by emailing jane@thepilgrimmother.com.

End Notes

a New York Times, In Honor of Pilgrim Mothers (Art.), December 24 1892.

b Edward Arbor 1897, *The Story of The Pilgrim Fathers, 1606-1623 A.D.; as told by Themselves, their Friends and their Enemies*, Ward and Downey Limited, London, and Houghton, Mifflin & Co, Boston and New York.

c Marianne Williamson, *A Return to Love*, Harper Paperbacks, New York, 1996.

d Allen Carr, *The Only Way to Stop Smoking Permanently*, Penguin Health Care & Fitness, 5 Jan 1995

e Bob Wooler, Homoeopathy, Reiki Master, Matrix Reimprinting. Tel: (UK) +44 1905 455742 Email: bob@doctorbob.freeserve.co.uk

f Rachel Elnaugh's Business Alchemy http://www.rachelelnaugh.com/biography/business-alchemy

g www.powhabits.com

h Stephen Covey: *People are internally motivated by their own four needs: to live, to love, to learn, to leave a legacy.* www.stephencovey.com/blog/?tag=purpose

i www.goodreads.com

j www.amazon.com/Friend-Every-City-Networking-Century/dp/0954509374

k *New Dawn* by Nina Simone. Ultrasonic Records 1992.

l M. Williamson, *The Law of Divine Compensation: On Work, Money and Miracles,* Harper One and Harper Collins, New York, 2012

Lightning Source UK Ltd.
Milton Keynes UK
UKOW020226140513

210575UK00004B/295/P